DATE DUE

CHINA RISING

CHINA RISING

THE MEANING OF TIANANMEN

by Lee Feigon

Ivan R. Dee, Publisher

Chicago

To Leanne

Library of Congress Cataloging-in-Publication Data:
Feigon, Lee, 1945–
    China rising : the meaning of Tiananmen / by Lee Feigon
      p.   cm.
    ISBN 0-929587-30-8
    1. China—Politics and government—1976–   2. Students—China—
Political activity. 3. China—History—Tiananmen Square Incident,
1989. I. Title.
DS779.26.P4557   1990
951.05'8—dc20   89-77800
                                                CIP

CONTENTS

Maps:
China and Its Major Cities, page 29
Beijing, Showing Locations Important to the Book,
page 129
Tiananmen Square and Environs, page 197

PREFACE

On April 15, 1989, news of the death of Hu Yaobang swept through the university campuses of Beijing. Hu had been ousted as secretary general of the Chinese Communist party in early 1987 ostensibly because he appeared sympathetic to student demonstrations that year which had demanded free elections. Now the students determined to capitalize on Hu's death to seek greater democracy, more freedom of the press, and an end to official corruption.

A confused political establishment tolerated the growing unrest for more than a week. Then, on April 26, the government broadcast a warning to the students to cease their demonstrations or face severe repercussions. The next day, April 27, the protesters defied the authorities and marched anyway, pushing through police and militia lines and mobilizing the support of the people of Beijing. Stung officials seemed to back down, acknowledging many of the students' demands. Taking advantage of this changing climate, an increasingly militant Chinese press corps began to ignore restrictions on its reporting.

For a while it seemed this was as far as things would go. But on May 13 about three hundred students began a mass hunger strike in Tiananmen Square in downtown Beijing on the eve of an historic visit to China by the head of the Soviet Union, Mikhail Gorbachev. The world media, which had their cameras in the square to cover the Gorbachev visit, focused instead on the "Chinese Woodstock" that developed. The people of Beijing began to make trips to the square to view the students and show their support. Most of the lower and middle levels of the government also came over to the side of the demonstrators.

These protests accelerated a power struggle already under way within the upper levels of the Chinese Communist party. The reformist secretary general of the party, Zhao Ziyang, supported the students; hard-liners opposed them. On May 19 Zhao made an historic early-morning visit to the square to talk with the students. After that he disappeared from view and was soon ousted from office. Late the next evening, the hard-liners announced that martial law would be declared and ordered soldiers into the city.

To everyone's amazement, advancing troops were stopped by tens of thousands of civilians who blockaded the roads to the city until the military withdrew. A spontaneous people's government seemed to be forming. But the people's victory was short-lived. On June 4, 1989, tanks and troops pushed their way through the crowds, killing hundreds, possibly thousands of workers and students. The square was cleared, and over the coming weeks Chinese citizens were intimidated into acquiescence and silence. The students, who had experienced a rebirth of revolutionary idealism, ended up witnessing a militaristic regime massacre its own citizenry.

I was particularly close to these events because I saw many

of them firsthand. In the spring of 1989 I lived on the campus
of People's University in Beijing. The students whom I knew
played a key leadership role in the movement, one that few
Western observers noted. Their role demonstrated the close
connection between the leadership of the Chinese Communist
party and the student rebels.

The People's University campus has known few Westerners. The school has traditionally had a close relationship with
the highest leadership of the Chinese Communist party. It still
maintains the only Department of Chinese Communist Party
History in all of China. Like most other foreign scholars, on
my past trips to China I had always been associated with
Beijing University and had lived on that campus. In 1989,
living for the first time on the campus of People's University,
I observed close up the differences between the activists of
this school and other Beijing students.

I have written this book to bear witness to what I watched.
I have long been a student of Chinese revolutionary movements, particularly Chinese student movements. My biography of Chen Duxiu, founder of the Chinese Communist party,
seemed especially relevant to the events of 1989. In the late
1920s Chen was kicked out of the party as a "Trotskyist
deviationist and opportunist" for advocating many of the
same ideas proposed by the students in 1989. In the 1980s
some of those interested in reform looked to Chen Duxiu's
ideas to demonstrate a tradition within the party for openness
and democracy.

The former secretary general of the party, Hu Yaobang,
whose death touched off the 1989 protests, had been one of
these reformers. In 1984 Hu publicly praised my study of
Chen and suggested a meeting with me. In early 1987, when
I visited China, I was hoping to take him up on this
invitation. But on the day I entered China it was announced
that Hu had been ousted from the leadership of the party. In

1989, when I again returned to China, Hu Yaobang died, and his death touched off the massive student demonstrations that rocked China.

In writing this book I have devoted much attention to the legacy bequeathed to the student protesters of 1989 by earlier generations of Chinese student leaders such as Chen Duxiu. I hope to show that the tradition of student activism which has enveloped China for much of the last century encouraged among the students a feeling of self-importance and a belief that they could have a vital effect on politics in their country.

I also focus on the Cultural Revolution. This period created the psychological climate—both good and bad—that set the stage for the protests of 1989. To some, my views on the Cultural Revolution may seem revisionist. But Deng Xiaoping was never simply the benign dictator, victimized by the zealotry and fanaticism of the Cultural Revolution, that most Americans have pictured. Although Mao and his allies have been blamed for the terror of the period, many of the attacks on intellectuals that inaugurated these so-called "ten wasted years" and traumatized Chinese society were actually begun by some of the same people who sent troops against the students in 1989. Moreover, the Cultural Revolution was not only a time of horror but also one of extraordinary growth which saw the creation of some of the economic enterprises for which Deng Xiaoping later took credit in the 1980s. The key problem which the students confronted in the Cultural Revolution—an oppressive and corrupt bureaucracy—was one that also bedeviled students in 1989.

I think it is important to understand the Cultural Revolution, because some of the students who took part in the demonstrations of 1989 had begun to reassess its legacy. Although vividly aware of the irrationality of that period, they suspected that much of the openness and economic decentralization that had occurred in China since 1977 had been made possible because the Cultural Revolution had weakened the institutional base of the Chinese Communist party and forced the government to make reforms in order to maintain its power. They noted that Chinese students in the 1960s had managed to overturn one of the world's most powerful and entrenched bureaucracies, and they saw no reason why they could not repeat the achievement.

As I will demonstrate, many of the problems that wreaked havoc in China during the Cultural Revolution resurfaced after 1987, when growing economic and social change weakened the party to the point where the central government began to lose control over most of the basic regional decision-making processes. As in the time of the Cultural Revolution, people were confused about what the policies of the government and the party were. Between 1987 and 1989, as different factions of the government fought about policy, the central government became progressively weaker, and an increasingly frequent series of incidents and disturbances resulted. In each of these incidents, a paralyzed government hesitated so long in dealing with the situation that it developed into a major crisis.

Because of this government weakness as well as the economic problems that had helped to bring it about, significant sectors of the urban population came to support the students. But, as I seek to show, most of these people were probably uncertain allies at best. While they joined the students in agitating for democracy, had the students succeeded the workers might ultimately have opposed them, for many of them feared reforms which had already destroyed much of the security and stability in their lives.

Moreover, although the major government bodies from the Politburo on down seemed to be on the side of the students, this mattered little because neither the government nor the party had final authority in China. This was controlled by a group of elderly officials, none of whom, except for Deng Xiaoping, held any formal position with the government. And Deng was not even a member of the party's Central Committee, the lowest-level major decision-making group in the government. Students were confused about the government attitude toward their cause and unclear about where authority lay. In spite of their defiance of the government, they were willing to trust that reformist leaders could emerge from this group. Similarly, although party leaders such as Zhao Ziyang seemed to be trying to help the students, even he was not willing to act against Deng and the other party elders. For most of the actors in this drama, the state and the society were one. And for such older leaders as Zhao, Deng Xiaoping and the state were inseparable.

In rebelling, the younger generation believed they had finally broken with the authoritarian patterns of the past which implied that the party and the government were to be obeyed without questioning. Like earlier activists they sought to imitate, they saw themselves as breaking with tradition. But, in fact, like these earlier protesters, their gains were achieved partly because some of those in power had no interest in stopping them. In the end, many of the students could not totally break with the authoritarian patterns they believed they had rejected. They really did not understand democracy and human rights nearly as well as they believed they did.

Their movement ended in tragedy, a tragedy caused by a militaristic, autocratic government representing none but its own interests. But it was also a tragedy compounded by the lack of sophistication of those who opposed the government. If there is one bright spot in the entire affair, it is that the violence of the government has ended the naivety of those who opposed it. The process of educating the Chinese people about what they must do to change the system has begun.

I could not have written this book without the help of a number of people at many stages in its completion. Some, to whom I am most grateful, cannot be mentioned without being personally endangered. Among others, I would like to thank first my wife, Leanne, for tolerating me and taking time from her own schedule to offer me editorial assistance. Several of my students gave me valuable help as well, bringing books and references from the library to my office and reading the manuscript for me. In particular, I wish to thank Alex Day, whose eyewitness accounts of the student demonstrations figure prominently in this book. I am also grateful to Chris Hobart, who, like Alex, was with me at People's University and helped to check my manuscript for accuracy. Finally, I wish to thank Merrie Post and Ron Thompson, who also helped with the legwork for the book.

A number of people read the manuscript at my request. Michael Martin looked over the early chapters on the economy and the Cultural Revolution. Luk Takchuen and Lee Chiuchin offered useful criticism. I wish to thank my father-in-law, Jack Star, and my mother, Ethel Feigon, for their help at various stages in my work.

CHRONOLOGY

Major Dates in the History of Chinese Student Movements

1851–1864   Taiping Rebellion

May 2, 1895   Kang Youwei inaugurates reform movement with a petition from examination candidates to the government

June 11–
September 21, 1898   Hundred Days of Reform

1904   Establishment of a new system of education

1905   Elimination of the examination system

October 10, 1911   Beginning of the uprising that overthrows the Qing dynasty and establishes a republic

1915   Founding of *New Youth* magazine and beginning of the New Culture or May Fourth movement

May 4, 1919   May 4 Incident

July 1921	First Congress of the Chinese Communist party
May 30, 1925	May 30 Incident spurs organization of Chinese working class and increases membership in Chinese Communist party
July 1926	Beginning of the Northern Expedition
April 12, 1927	The White Terror, in which Guomindang forces turn on their Communist allies and slaughter many of them in the streets of Shanghai
December 9, 1935	Student demonstrations protest government appeasement policies and lead to the creation of a mass, anti-Japanese leftist movement
October 1, 1949	Proclamation of the People's Republic of China
1956–1957	Hundred Flowers campaign
June 1957	Beginning of the anti-rightist campaign
1958–1960	Great Leap Forward
June 1966– December 1969	Great Proletarian Cultural Revolution
1966–1976	"Official" period of the Great Proletarian Cultural Revolution
April 5, 1976	Public outpouring for Premier Zhou Enlai in Tiananmen, which leads to the removal of Deng Xiaoping
September 9, 1976	Death of Mao Zedong

1978–1979	Democracy Wall movement
1983	Spiritual Pollution campaign
December 5, 1986	Beginning of student demonstrations in Hefei demanding freer elections
January 16, 1987	Announcement of the resignation of Hu Yaobang
April 15, 1989	The death of Hu Yaobang triggers a new series of student demonstrations

CHINA RISING

A LEGACY OF STUDENT POWER

Chinese student rebellions predate not only the People's Republic of China but the rise of Western civilization. The first large-scale incident of student protest was recorded in 542 B.C.E. About 400 years later, in the first century B.C.E., thirty thousand students gathered in the capital to demonstrate against corrupt government practices. A thousand years ago, in the tenth and eleventh centuries, periodic episodes of student unrest, many of them violent, became a regular feature of Chinese life.

Student protests increased during the Song dynasty (960–1279), not long after the Chinese abolished a hereditary aristocracy and established a regularized system of civil service examinations to qualify young men for high office. The Song ushered in a phenomenon that in some ways still continues. Periodically, young men would crowd the major cities of the country hoping to be chosen for advancement and high office on the basis of merit, instead often finding corruption and favoritism. In the nineteenth century, as China was battered by new influences, the pressures on examination candidates increased, and student activism became more obvious and important.

The civil service exam ostensibly determined if the students possessed the moral character to become members of the Chinese ruling body. The system encouraged the students' sense of righteousness and feelings of self-importance. They felt a duty to remonstrate against what they considered unjust government policy, and students began to see themselves as what one scholar has referred to as unofficial "spokesmen for public opinion."

This student presumption could be explosive at times, especially during those biannual or triennial periods when the exams were held and large numbers of privileged but shiftless members of the elite were suddenly brought together in urban areas. As potential future officials, students then, like those today, were accorded high esteem by the government and the local population. But the generally wretched living conditions of these candidates who crowded the major Chinese cities for the imperial examinations in past centuries were out of step with their status. A disregard for many ordinary social and political conventions became the norm. Unscrupulous examination candidates often took advantage of their numbers and their status to rob and extort local merchants, seduce women, and generally flout the authorities. At times of political and social unrest, some students turned to unorthodox ideas.

One scholar, Chen Duxiu, has left an *Autobiography* vividly describing his experiences as an examination candidate in the waning years of the nineteenth century. At that time, he related, most of the "scholars" going to examinations in Nanjing would rent a large junk and hoist a yellow flag on the mast inscribed with the characters "By imperial decree we are traveling to the Jiangnan provincial examinations." Inside the boat they would stash contraband articles from other parts of China, normally subject to high interprovincial tariffs.

"Although the guards at the customs points realized that the students were smuggling goods," he explained, "they did not dare check their boats."

Chen further described how many of the students waiting for the exams indulged in constant whoring and pranks. A favorite student trick was to accuse a small shopkeeper of cheating. The noise of the dispute would attract other passing students, who would "rush to help," whether or not they were acquainted with the offended student. "The merchants knew that the real reason the candidates came forward was not to help in the battle but to steal as much as they could in the confusion. . . . Even if they were informed of the theft by the merchant, the officials could do nothing about the many and influential candidates."

Raucous behavior among students, emboldened by their youth and a sudden lack of parental authority, was often exacerbated when many failed an impossible examination, dashing their hopes for enrichment and success. They faced very few ladders of advancement within the crowded corridors of Chinese society—a problem that persists to the present day.

When the examination system first began during the Tang dynasty (618–907), no more than one or two of a hundred candidates passed the top-level exam which qualified them for high office. By the time of the Ming (1368–1644) and Qing (1644–1911) dynasties, only one of every three thousand examinees made the final cut. There was, of course, prestige for those who took part in the exams, probably even more than is the case for college graduates today. A ditty popular among Qing dynasty students illustrates this: "Even if I do nothing but sit and fart, by taking the exam I have done my part."

Still, many who had originally aspired to the illustrious ranks of Chinese officialdom were disappointed and disgruntled. It has become almost a cliché of Chinese history to find

a popular rebellion led by a failed examination candidate. In
modern times the most famous of these rebels was the
nineteenth-century Hakka revolutionary Hong Xiuquan. In
the 1840s Hong tested first in his village and district in the
qualifying heats of the imperial examination. But he failed
the first level of the national competition held in the port city
of Canton. Distraught, he returned to his village and prostrat-
ed himself in front of his family, declaring that he had
disappointed them. Then, like many other unsuccessful candidates, he collapsed into delirium.

But a few months later Hong recovered his self-esteem.
Having become acquainted with the rudiments of Christian
doctrine while taking his exam in Canton, Hong now proclaimed
that he was the younger brother of Jesus Christ, determined
to create a reformist Christian kingdom in China. He capital-
ized on the discontent of the region's peasants and began
what became known as the Taiping Rebellion (1851–1864).

Hong's rebellion convulsed south China for more than a
decade and may have resulted in more than thirty million
deaths. It almost succeeded in overthrowing the dynasty.
Chinese historians still maintain that it was only because the
Western powers eventually intervened on the side of the Qing
dynasty that the rebellion was suppressed.

After the failure of the Taipings, student rebellions grew
more frequent and became qualitatively different from earlier
varieties. Hong Xiuquan was the first student leader to be
inspired by a foreign model, however superficially, in his
revolt against political authority, but by the twentieth century
virtually all student-led rebellions were accompanied by calls
for some form of Western-style democracy and political and
economic change. Democracy was rarely seen as a goal in its
own right; rather, it was almost always viewed as a way of
achieving the economic and military power of the West. The
distinction between individual rights and state power is still
not totally understood today.

It was during the 1897 exams in Nanjing, attended by Chen Duxiu, that large numbers of Chinese students first began to make the democratic argument. The issue that galvanized the students was China's recent loss to Japan in the Sino-Japanese War of 1894–1895. During the 1895 examinations immediately following the war, many candidates had signed petitions protesting the government's acquiescence in a peace treaty and demanding reform of the Chinese political system. When many of these same candidates renewed their protest at the 1897 exam, they found an even more sympathetic audience. One reason for this was the deteriorating Chinese economy. Throughout the twentieth century, townspeople have joined student demonstrations when galloping inflation and severe monetary dislocations have disenchanted them with the existing government. This was the case in 1897 in Nanjing. Examination candidates found agreement with their complaints from residents who suffered from a rampant inflation said to have been caused by China's onerous indemnity to Japan following its military defeat.

Protests led by Kang Youwei and his disciple Liang Qichao, proposing democracy and accelerated social and economic change, excited those who gathered for their tests in Nanjing in the same way that radical political and social notions had agitated Chinese youth for generations. Even to modern eyes, Kang's advocacy of total sexual equality seems startling. To avoid discrimination, men and women were to dress alike, enjoy equal opportunities for education and office, and command similar powers to sign and terminate short-term marriage contracts. Kang even suggested such contracts for homosexuals who wished to set up housekeeping together. It is true that these ideas were written at a time of despair and were not part of Kang's official proposals. Still, given the audacity of some of Kang's notions, it is amazing that he attracted the extent of support that he did. This occurred not just because of the attractiveness of his ideas to student rebels but because they suddenly began to receive high-level government support.

Throughout this century, for all their activism, Chinese students have rarely enjoyed much success without official encouragement. They have been a formidable force, but they have also been a dependent one, often used for their own purposes by one or another government faction. In 1898, a year after the Jiangnan exam at Nanjing, a new emperor adopted the platform of the student radicals and gave their movement an important boost.

In early June 1898 the young Emperor Guangxu broke with old supporters who had controlled the government, urging his subjects to learn useful foreign information—a radical proposal for the time. A few days later the emperor held an interview with Kang Youwei. In the days that followed, the government adopted many of Kang's proposals, issuing edicts that promised a new educational and political system throughout the country. A central feature of this movement, like that which occurred almost a century later, was a reformation of the legal system and an attack on corruption. Suggestions for these kinds of changes had previously attracted attention, but no one had dared try to enact them until the emperor intervened. Now the movement exploded. Students throughout the country formed study groups to discuss and implement Kang's ideas. Gentry and local officials were pressed to carry out the emperor's reforms.

The 1898 reforms continued for a hundred days, ending when conservative forces moved troops into the city of Beijing and overthrew the emperor, who lived out the rest of his short life under virtual house arrest. Kang Youwei and Liang Qichao managed to flee the country, but six other student reformers, including Kang's younger brother, were caught and executed by government forces as a lesson to their countrymen. Eventually, most of the edicts enacted during this period, few of which had been put into practice by the bureaucracy, were reversed.

Government actions in suppressing this 1898 movement, however, marked the start of the radicalization of the Chinese student population. It soon became clear to almost all young Chinese intellectuals that an education in traditional social dogmas was inadequate for their needs or for those of society. Government attempts to continue the study of the Confucian classics and to retain the traditional examination system failed. New-style schools arose to teach Chinese students to compete with the economic and military might of the West. As students congregated at these new academies, they developed a revolutionary youth culture that brought them into increasing conflict with surroundings and families.

Those students, like today's, studied doctrines at odds with the values of their own society. Tensions between the students and the outside world, always great in any student group, grew. Students felt increasingly frustrated by the world around them, which failed to operate as it should according to the new ideas they absorbed. Since the Western learning of these students often worked to undermine the traditional elite's sources of prestige and power, student anger was often reciprocated by political authorities who had no stomach for self-righteous youngsters. So the Western-educated had difficulty finding employment, and this helped turn their alienation into rage.

The inadequacies of the educational system further heightened the frustrations of most Chinese youth. Few in China understood the new materials which the students demanded to be taught. An American in China in the early 1900s reported that a candidate for the position of "Professor of English" at a provincial school in Guangdong, upon being asked how much English he knew, replied: "Numbers, one to ten; a hundred words beginning with 'A', and ten words rhyming with sing.'' Because there were no other candidates, the man was accepted for the position.

Guo Moruo, a future writer and Chinese Communist cultural functionary, told how in the highly regarded middle school he attended, ''The geography teacher placed Korea in the south of China; the biology teacher described the mouth of the octopus as its rectum... an English teacher spent half a year to teach us the basic phonetics.''

Displeased with their lot and educated in a milieu that separated them from their traditional society, students often had no choice but to maintain an uprooted existence. Even at the age of thirty or forty many found it impossible to do anything but continue their studies. As a consequence, students began to constitute a large, extremely volatile segment of the population.

One solution for students faced with growing government restrictions over their activity, and anxious to learn what their teachers clearly were unequipped to teach them, was to go abroad. In the early 1900s the location of choice was Tokyo, one of the few places that seemed receptive and affordable for Chinese students. A second choice was the foreign-controlled treaty port city of Shanghai, which occupied a position in the early part of this century similar to that now maintained by Hong Kong.

A radical Chinese student culture, one which is still a model for Chinese students today, thus began to form in Shanghai and in Tokyo. In 1902 students in Tokyo created the Determination Society. At first this was simply an organization which gave lonely Chinese a chance to socialize, but within a short period a radical faction of the group emerged, insisting that the Chinese political system was incapable of peaceful political change. Revolutionary organizations began to proliferate among the students, and many became involved in confrontations with Qing authorities resident in Japan.

In April 1903 Russian encroachments in Manchuria aroused

many of these students. Infuriated by the failure of Chinese authorities to take a firm stand against the Russians, students began to return to China where they attempted to infiltrate the military and form provincial revolutionary societies to overthrow the dynasty. Then, as now, the authority of the central government was weaker in the provinces than in the capital. Merchant and gentry groups, worried about interference in their economic affairs by agents of the Qing, often protected the student revolutionaries and welcomed their ideas about self-determination and democracy.

Yet while they sometimes sheltered them, many of the gentry were horrified by the behavior of the radical students. Often the rebels lived in communally shared lofts or small houses. They edited underground newspapers, ran schools, and organized illicit political activities. Many thought of themselves as poets and writers. The men frequented bars and the company of dance-hall girls, often overindulging in wine, food, and sex. Attacks on the traditional family, especially on sexual inequality, became one of the hallmarks of this new political movement. Women, too, joined the bohemian culture that grew up in Shanghai and elsewhere.

More often than not, Chinese students, like their peers throughout the world, initially vented their anger and frustration not at the Qing government but at the authority closest to them—the school. Almost all institutions of higher learning became the focus of demonstrations. Some appeared to originate in minor rows, like those between merchants and examination candidates described above by Chen Duxiu. But their content now became much more political. The future educator, Jiang Menglin, for instance, described how at the Provincial College of Zhejiang, which he attended, a minor fracas between a student and a sedan bearer of the imperial governor set off a demonstration. ''All of the students went on strike in consequence and left the college in a body. Many incidents of like nature occurred in other schools with eventual disruption

of a number of institutions of new learning. It spread throughout the country." At Jiang's school, he and his fellow
students organized their own institution called the "School of
Reform and Progress," which, however, lasted less than half
a year.

But the students were not all flash. Many grew so frustrated that they turned to assassination as a means to bring down
the Chinese government. Anarchist groups plotted to kill
Qing officials using bombs or bullets. The most famous of
these efforts was that undertaken by the beautiful young
heroine Qiu Jin, who was later executed for her role in a
planned assassination and uprising in Zhejiang province in
1907.

Rapid social and economic change had diminished the
government's grip over the country, and these assassinations,
coupled with a growing string of radical-inspired military
uprisings, began to worry Qing officials. On October 10,
1911, an insurrection in the central Chinese city of Wuhan
frightened the Manchu governor-general. He fled in terror.
Without opposition, the poorly organized rebels were able to
take over the local garrison and arsenal.

The revolutionaries were inexperienced youths astonished
by their own success. Suddenly they found themselves in
control of one of the largest cities in China. The national
leader of the revolutionary movement, Sun Yat-sen, read
about their success in a Denver newspaper, assumed it to be
momentary, and continued on his overseas tour. Sun's second-
in-command, Huang Xing, had been informed of plans for
the Wuhan rebellion; he thought it unlikely to succeed and
did not bother to come to central China to offer help.

As the young rebels searched for a figure of power and
authority to lead them, they found it in General Li Yuanhong,
the local brigade commander. In ensuing days, events in
Wuhan inspired similar actions in towns and provinces through-

out south and central China. By the close of 1911 the central government had collapsed, replaced by a republic.

In most of the provinces the gentry simply declared their independence from the central government. Because there was no structure to take the place of the old regime, the country soon divided into a series of military satrapies. Many former student rebels now became leading political and military operatives, but most proved to be little better than the Qing officials they had replaced. The Chinese found it impossible to establish a democratic political order or even to create a stable central government.

The only leader with sufficient prestige and credibility to maintain authority in Beijing under these circumstances was a former Qing military official, Yuan Shikai. Yuan had been dismissed by the Qing government shortly before 1911. This made him acceptable to the revolutionaries, even though he had commanded the troops that had entered Beijing to end the Hundred Days of Reform in 1898. The revolutionaries wanted someone who had exercised inside political power, and they turned to him. Their trust in Yuan proved misguided. After taking power, Yuan soon dissolved the new parliament. An attempt by progressive forces to overthrow him failed in 1913. Many student leaders again had to flee abroad, and within a short time Yuan moved to have himself declared emperor.

It was this situation that in 1915 inspired Chen Duxiu, the future founder of the Chinese Communist party, to begin the journal that was to become *New Youth*. He began his publication in hopes of inspiring a new generation of students to pick up the mantle for change. A former student revolutionary himself, Chen after 1911 served briefly as a high-level official in Anhui province. In 1913 he quit his job in disgust but retained his political ties. In starting a magazine dedicated to acquainting his young readership with the values of "science and democracy," Chen, who in 1915 was still a great admirer of the West, hoped to reinvigorate the Chinese political process by turning to the group which had supplied the impetus for change before 1911.

The journal had little influence in its first few years. After Yuan Shikai's death in 1917, some of Chen's political cronies brought him to Beijing to serve as dean of the School of Arts and Letters at the prestigious government-sponsored Beijing University. Chen was now a governmental insider with a pulpit for his ideas. His popularity soared.

Chen Duxiu's publication of *New Youth* is usually referred to as the start of the New Culture movement, more often called the May Fourth movement after the protest of May 4, 1919, which it fostered. In the decade after 1915 the intellectual atmosphere in China was much like it was to be in the country in the 1980s. Both times represented periods in Chinese history of new ideas and experimentation.

During the May Fourth era an old-fashioned, politically repressive bureaucracy remained in place in Beijing, yet for a time after Yuan Shikai's death it seemed that a more progressive central government might emerge in China. In late 1916 Li Yuanhong, the Qing dynasty official pressed into service as the leader of the republican revolution, became the head of government after the death of Yuan Shikai. He appointed as the chancellor of Beijing University the liberal educator Cai Yuanpei. A series of military-backed leaders controlled the provinces. Although these various leaders are now usually considered collectively to have been oppressive warlords, some, like the Guangdong socialist Chen Qiongming, were actually quite progressive. In certain areas of the country, there was economic progress and a relative freedom to express new ideas. Everyone resented the division of China, but for some there was hope that China's problems might soon be solved.

Progressive students influenced by Chen Duxiu and some of his colleagues on the magazine—such as Hu Shi, the

American-educated student of John Dewey, or the famous writer Lu Xun—looked to the West for inspiration. New journals modeled after *New Youth* appeared almost daily, advocating every new fad that came from the West. Some of the best-known of these in 1919 were *Reconstruction, Weekly Critic, Effort,* and *The Guide.* Almost all of them saw science and democracy as solutions to China's problems.

While May Fourth leaders embraced the West, they attacked China's traditions. Lu Xun suggested more than once that the history of China was that of a tribe of cannibals. The mild-mannered Hu Shi repeatedly denounced the falsity and pretensions of China's ancient literary traditions, widely regarded as the greatest of China's accomplishments. Chen Duxiu argued that the only way to preserve and develop China was to eliminate the ideas of the past. As he put it, "I believe that the provisions of a democratic constitution and the Confucian *dao* are by nature mutually contradictory. . . . "

Three major onslaughts on tradition were the anti-Confucian campaign begun in the pages of *New Youth,* attacks on family structure carried out by writers for that journal, and attempts by members of the *New Youth* editorial board to inaugurate the use of the vernacular in Chinese writing. These three campaigns were correctly seen by political leaders as an attack on the authority of the old elites. In showing the bankruptcy of the ideas of the old regime, *New Youth* writers undermined its legitimacy and soon attracted a massive student following.

Although the May Fourth movement was chiefly cultural, gradually a student political organization began to coalesce around Chen Duxiu, the Beijing University librarian Li Dazhao, and other members of the *New Youth* editorial board who were seen to be allied with reformist factions within the government. As study societies proliferated on campuses throughout the country, students formed close ties and friendships which later served them well in political activities.

The importance of these small groups was officially recognized at the fourth annual conference of the National Federation of Education Associations held in 1918, when the establishment of clubs for young men was urged. One observer has claimed that this virtually gave "any so-called 'student club' or 'young men's club' the right to run the local school system. It was both a recognition of a condition and a stimulus to its development."

Of many groups formed at this time, one was the small gang of "physical culturists" in Changsha, headed by the future Communist leader Mao Zedong and the Communist martyr Cai Hesen. Many of its members were later to become famous names in Chinese communism and in the history of the Chinese Revolution. Mao felt so warmly about his activities during this period that in the autobiography he related to the American writer Edgar Snow, he devoted more words to his experiences in Changsha than to any other part of his life. It is perhaps not surprising that he soon developed a theory of revolutionary organization based on small friendly units apparently modeled after this student organization in Hunan province.

Other influential leaders similarly cherished the friendships and values formed during this period and likewise saw them as important to the later development of the Chinese Revolution. The well-known historian Gu Jiegang, for example, remembered a youth group devoted to strolls in the countryside and revolutionary agitation in the Suzhou region, though he participated in its activities only briefly. The future Chinese Communist Premier Zhou Enlai was so attached to the friendships he formed at the boarding school he attended in Tianjin that even in the darkest days of the party's history, when arrest and execution constantly threatened, each time he traveled incognito to Tianjin he telephoned Principal Zhang to offer greetings. Zhou repeatedly risked calls to old friends, confident they would not betray him to Chiang Kai-shek's police.

The importance of the clubs became clear after the events of May 4, 1919. The personal ties formed in these little groups gave students the organizational basis from which to coordinate their actions and demonstrations.

But it is unlikely that the students would have been able to take to the streets at all if, before 1919, as earlier in 1898, a period of reform and optimism had not begun to wane. China during the years of World War I experienced a great spurt of industrialization which began to fade as soon as the war ended. One reason this early industrialization failed to take root was that in the last years of the war, Japanese financial support for the northern warlords bought them many influential government leaders, who then allowed the Japanese sway over influential segments of the Chinese economy. When the war ended, the Japanese blocked the start-up efforts of independent Chinese merchants, who in turn later aided the student demonstrations. These government failures encouraged intellectuals to criticize the political system.

As the attack by Chinese students and intellectuals on Japanese interests intensified, the government responded by attempting to limit the proponents of new ideas and to censor their thoughts. In the spring of 1919, before demonstrations began, traditional conservatives forced Chen Duxiu to resign his deanship. Chen and his fellow reformers felt betrayed and disappointed. The democracy that a few years earlier had seemed just around the corner was still a dream. In particular, members of the May Fourth movement had expressed faith in the proposals of President Woodrow Wilson for the self-determination of all nations in the aftermath of World War I. The betrayal of Western promises at the Versailles peace conference, which drew up the treaty officially ending the war, discouraged Chinese students and intellectuals. They were outraged when word reached them in late April that the

conference had voted to transfer the former German concessions on China's Shandong peninsula to Japan.

In the days that followed, students convened a number of
meetings condemning the government for acquiescing in this
decision and demanding that China not sign the treaty. On
May 3 the government warned the students not to continue
plans for a demonstration. Meanwhile, political authorities
made plans for a crackdown. But the failure of the government to enforce its threats encouraged the student movement.

On May 4, in defiance of the government, more than three
thousand students from thirteen colleges throughout Beijing
took to the streets in protest. Although the march began
peacefully with little interference from the police, a small
group of demonstrators had planned more militant action.
They burned the house of the minister of communications
and assaulted China's minister to Japan, both pro-Japanese
officials.

The police intervened. Thirty-two students were arrested.
One student died a few days later as a result of police
beatings and became a martyr to the cause. In the weeks that
followed, demonstrations spread throughout the country. In
many cities, workers and merchants joined the students,
striking Japanese factories and boycotting Japanese goods.
The numbers of publications soared as China experienced a
brief renaissance of press freedom. Ultimately the government capitulated, though the victory was a rather superficial
one. Arrested students were freed, the cabinet resigned, and
China refused to sign the peace treaty with Japan. But the
new cabinet was drawn from the same pro-Japanese group,
and the new government was controlled by the same military
clique. Soon many prominent intellectual and political leaders had fled Beijing to avoid arrest.

In retrospect, one of the reasons for the seeming victory of
the 1919 student movement was that, like Kang Youwei
before them, the students won acquiescence from at least

some elements of government. Although the students enjoyed the sympathy of the masses—who probably felt there was little danger in joining the struggle when the police were allowing unpopular ministers to be roughed up by students— more important was the fact that government troops peacefully stood by during most of their protests, only intervening after damage had been done. This may have been a mistake on the part of inexperienced security forces, or it may have been due to the purposeful inaction of officials sympathetic to the students. There is no doubt that students were aided by the actions of southern warlords and politicians who saw the student movement as a way to increase their own power. As a result, the apparent victory of the students was in some ways a repetition of what had happened in 1898 and again in 1911. Student activists succeeded only as long as government authorities, working for their own ends, supported them.

The May 4 incident, however, was to exert enormous influence over China for much of the next twenty years. A new generation of students had now been politicized, picking up where the pre-1911 generation had left off. Newspapers and magazines proliferated. Libraries and reading societies were formed to promote radical ideas. Student behavior was radicalized, and many students denounced what they considered to be Confucian or even bourgeois notions of marriage and sexual inequality. Others angrily split with their families. Women bobbed their hair and began to live with their boyfriends. Some experimented with novel Western clothing like suits and ties, and with romantic writing and art forms. Every aspect of student life became daring and new. More important, myriad new political organizations took shape.

Many moderates, now embittered at the political establishment, became extremists. It was the former democratic leader Chen Duxiu, now disillusioned with the West, who formed the Communist party at this moment because he saw it as a way of providing the kind of political leadership China needed. Others turned to military action or even terror.

One of the key themes of the period may be seen in the writings of the anarchist novelist Ba Jin, who came of age during the May Fourth movement and whose novel *Jia*, or *The Family*, became the student bible of the time. Reasserting Chen Duxiu's criticisms, Ba Jin concentrated on the failure of traditional family leadership in China. In the novel, which is so closely interwoven with Ba Jin's own personal biography as to be virtually indistinguishable from it, the grandfather, the head of the family and a pillar of the Confucian Morals Society, is portrayed as a brutal, dictatorial old man who despoils young girls and hangs out with male prostitutes. He and the other old men of the Confucian Morals Society go so far as to publish a list of the best male prostitutes. But although Ba Jin implies (with a sentiment later imitated by many writers) that the Confucian generation of his grandfather is composed of nothing but perverted old hypocrites who destroy their own young, he acknowledges that the older generation does, at least, possess strength. In the novel it is the grandfather's presence that holds the family together. When he dies, the family disintegrates.

The next generation, represented in the book by the weak, pathetic uncles of the hero, are powerless. They cannot enforce their own rules and ideas. When the hero revolts against them, promising to revenge the abuse of the women of the house, they can do nothing. In the end, the hero runs off to Shanghai to join the revolution, taking his place among friends and comrades who can give him the kind of support he cannot find in his family. The message seems quite at home in the People's Republic today, where parents who have endured autocracy and suffering all their lives have found that they cannot dissuade their children from rebellion against the culture they helped to create.

In *Jia* it is implied that the hero who runs off to Shanghai will join an anarchist group. In fact, anarchism was only one of many ideas that competed at the time with the Communist party. In the tolerant and heady atmosphere that existed among student groups in China immediately after the May 4 incident, anarchists, democrats, and others were members of the initial cells of the Chinese Communist party, which then functioned more as a study group than a Leninist organization.

The May Fourth movement created a new community and culture in China, one which dwarfed earlier student movements both in intensity and size. For a while, though not for long, even ideological disagreements could be put aside by members of this culture in their dealings with one another. This culture became the inspiration for the Chinese Revolution and a focal point for future generations of students and intellectuals.

The simple sociological explanation for this burst of Chinese student activism is that the May Fourth generation marked the first group in Chinese history to be crowded together in small dormitories, living the kind of cramped communal existence that was, and still is, ideal for building a tightly knit political organization. Their average age was twenty-three, which was then young for political activists by Chinese standards. The May Fourth generation was born in the waning years of the Qing dynasty and received a traditional childhood education; but they learned from parents who were already disillusioned with the ideals and practices of the past, and after they grew into their teens they studied a set of radical new ideas. They were taught not to be restrained in their search for truth and felt few restrictions in trying to implement new ideas. As a result, the courage and sense of experimentation shown by May Fourth activists became a model with which later Chinese have compared themselves, and one which successive governments have learned to regard with awe.

The May Fourth generation began a groundswell that

inaugurated a period of unprecedented student activism in China. From 1919 until 1949, college, middle-school, and even elementary-school students have periodically surged into the streets to protest unpopular government policies and to demand action against imperialist insults.

At first, few students were pro-communist. Although students organized the Chinese Communist party and served as cadres to agitate workers, merchants, and eventually peasants to join their campaigns, most students in the 1920s and 1930s were not interested in an oppressive Leninist organization. What excited Chinese students was what they deemed a just cause. Unfortunately, the political climate of the times gave them repeated opportunities to find this, and Chinese students became martyrs to successive Chinese governments.

After 1919, the next major confrontation was the so-called May 30 incident. On May 30, 1925, student demonstrators protesting the death of a Chinese textile worker at the hands of a Japanese foreman met the bullets of the British-controlled Shanghai police force. Thirteen students died that day, and their deaths spurred the organization of the city's working classes. The membership of the Chinese Communist party mushroomed, and for the first time it became a major independent force in China.

Incident followed incident. More students died on June 23, 1925, in demonstrations that followed the May 30 episode. Two hundred Beijing student demonstrators were killed in 1926 when the forces of the warlord Duan Qirui opened fire on one of their demonstrations. Each time, death deterred only a few and propelled most into further protests.

The outrage against these student deaths—in a society which still revered the moral purpose and supposed rectitude of its educated and attached a special status to its students—helped doom the warlord cliques that then ruled Beijing. The May 30 incident and its aftermath paved the way for the Northern Expedition of the following year, in which the

Chinese Nationalists, or Guomindang, headed by Chiang Kai-shek began a military movement to unify China. The expedition began in the south China city of Canton, where the Guomindang was headquartered, and moved north. The heart of the Nationalist army was a small cadre of students who had been given military training by Soviet and Chinese Communist leaders with whom the Nationalists were then allied. As Nationalist forces moved northward, student activists in city after city of central China worked to mobilize workers and peasants against the existing government. Faced with this internal and external pressure, the now discredited warlord armies began to capitulate. Probably few Chinese, students included, bothered to distinguish the Chinese Nationalists from their Chinese Communist allies during this period. So when the Nationalists turned on the Communists and purged them from the party in April 1927, in a brutal White Terror, most students continued to attend Nationalist schools and to remain loyal to the Guomindang.

But just as student activists, enchanted with their own power and purpose and disgusted by the corruption and ineffectiveness they saw around them, had earlier helped to destroy first the Qing and then the warlord-controlled government of the Chinese republic, so now they attacked the Guomindang. The Nationalists appealed to the students' patriotic values, but by the late 1920s the students grew disheartened by the failure of the Guomindang government to stand up to growing Japanese encroachments on Chinese soil.

In response, the government, for whom the May Fourth movement was not a distant memory, urged the students to stay out of politics, a tack which only made the students more sympathetic to the Chinese Communists. Few students had any real experience with a communist government. The Communists appeared to them only as another political power, even if a sometimes distant one, which could provide them with friendly support and direction for their demonstra-

tions. As students demanded more changes in China's domestic and international policies, the Guomindang became
more repressive. Instead of dampening student radicalism,
government policies drove the students toward the Communists. By the 1930s, students disillusioned with the Guomindang
had begun to desert their cause in large numbers, depriving
the government of badly needed legitimacy and of some of its
ablest supporters.

In 1911 it was the military leader Yuan Shikai who
succeeded in picking up the pieces after the Qing fractured
from the blows of student activists. In 1919 warlords inherited
a Chinese central government battered by student protests. In
1927 Chiang Kai-shek became the beneficiary of the May 30
protests and their aftermath. In the 1940s it was a newly
muscular Chinese Communist party, one which had long
since abandoned the tolerant spirit of May 4 in which it had
been born, that profited from student protests against the
Guomindang.

By 1949, when Chinese Communists established the People's Republic, the student legacy in China was a mixed one.
On the one hand, students had conclusively demonstrated that
they enjoyed sufficient power and prestige to help overthrow
a series of Chinese governments. But their protests had also
demonstrated a hollowness. It was not just that few students
grasped the subtlety of democratic ideals they claimed to
espouse, but also that they rarely seemed able to act without
first gaining legitimacy from institutions that were anathema
to their ideals. It was the emperor who gave Kang Youwei
and his followers their initial strength. It was the gentry who
protected the anti-Qing activists of the early 1900s. It was
warlord-supported politicians and educators who provided
support for May Fourth actions. Even the student demonstrations during the May 30 incident would have come to little
had there not been an independent Guomindang government
with its own army in Canton which had followers throughout

the country. Similarly, student-led demonstrations in the 1930s would have been meaningless and probably much smaller had they not been exploited and often organized by Communist agitators who had their own army and base in the countryside.

Over the years, the students' reliance on existing political power to support an independent political movement has not worked. Chinese students have toppled governments and created a legendary lore about themselves, but their actions have almost always proved counterproductive. The students have been admired—by themselves as much as by others—for their courage, their daring, and for the excitement they have engendered in a society that still loves the spectacle of public executions. But each of their protest movements has created a new organization just as inimical to student ideas as the one they helped to destroy.

2

THE CULTURAL REVOLUTION: A CLOUDED HISTORY

On the evening of April 27, 1989, I stood with thousands of Chinese on the broad, tree-lined avenue outside the gate to People's University. Student demonstrators had left the University at 9 a.m. to march to Tiananmen in the center of the city. It was now midnight as we waited for them to return. A vanguard of a few students passed by on bicycles, some pedaling and others riding on handlebars and back racks. They flashed victory signals or waved banners. The crowds on the streets cheered wildly.

"Long live the students! Long live the students!"

Rowdy young workers began to flag down passing cars and trucks, ordering them to turn around and pick up the marchers, rumored to be still four or five miles from the campus. Even by the most direct route, the walk from the school to downtown Beijing takes several hours. But the students had traveled a convoluted path to Tiananmen in order to intersect with most of the other colleges and universities and recruit more followers into their demonstration. By midnight they had already walked at least fifteen hours, fighting their way through lines of police along the way. They had to be exhausted.

After some persuasion, a group of trucks and buses was dispatched to pick up the marchers. As we watched, the students of nearby Beijing University and Qinghua University streamed by in the newly recruited vehicles, waving out the windows as the crowd shouted.

But still there were no students from People's University, the group which had led the parade throughout the day. Then word came through the crowd.

"They refuse to split up."

"The students from People's University are marching back together, just as they marched out in the morning."

Everyone was moved.

It was after 1:30 in the morning when we first saw them, arms still linked, flags and banners waving in front of them, their faces a mixture of joy, determination, and exhaustion. Someone set off fireworks by the University gate. The roar of the crowd was deafening.

"Long live People's University! We have won! We have won!" They shouted over and over.

In back of me stood an old man. He was crying.

"Imagine," he said to his son, choking on his words, "what they could do if the school was close to Tiananmen and they did not have to waste so much of their energy walking?"

The distance of the school from the center of the town, I thought, was no accident. It represented the distance and the increasing ambivalence of the relationship between student activists and the Chinese Communists throughout the history of the party. Party leaders have been quick to use the students when they needed their help, but they have also been quick to send them off, out of the way, once their usefulness ended.

As early as 1939, as the Chinese Communist Revolution

began to gather momentum, Mao Zedong summed up his party's cautious attitude toward the role of students in the Chinese struggle. "The whole of the Chinese revolutionary movement," he acknowledged, "found its origins in the action of young students and intellectuals." But, he warned, "if the young people wish to achieve results they must also establish friendly relations with adults." A few months later, as young people deserted the Guomindang in droves and flooded into Chinese Communist party headquarters offering their services, Mao became even more restrained in his attitude toward student activists. It was nice, he suggested, to have "new blood and enthusiasm," but "lack of experience is the natural failing of our young comrades."

After the Communists came to power in 1949, the anniversaries of student uprisings such as May 4 and December 9 became national holidays or occasions for annual celebration and discussion. Educational improvement became an important goal of the new government. Among the first construction projects undertaken by the new regime in the capital in the early 1950s was the building of spacious new university facilities for students.

The government located these new student quarters on the outskirts of the city, far from the center of government. This location may have been a matter of space requirements, but many have speculated that officials also moved China's best schools to remote new locations to make it difficult for the students of these institutions to demonstrate against the new government as they had done with past regimes, when they were located closer to the center of town.

The Chinese Communists began as part of a student revolution. They knew about the powerful attacks that Chinese students have mounted against various governments throughout this century. They were determined to avoid falling prey to student zeal. But they too failed.

A few years after seizing power, Mao Zedong grew disgruntled with the slow pace of change under the cumbersome bureaucracy his own regime had created. He again turned to the students to help speed the pace of development. In 1956 he asserted, "Youth is one of the most active and vital forces in society." Rather than insist that the young learn from the old, he now claimed: "Old people and adults are relatively conservative in their thinking. They often retard the progressive activities of the young. Only after young people make a success of something are their elders willing to concede."

That same year Mao began the Hundred Flowers campaign. The movement drew its name from the description of a famous period in Chinese classical history when "a hundred flowers bloomed and a hundred schools of thought contended." The campaign attempted to grant greater freedom of thought and speech to intellectuals. It was spurred in part by Khrushchev's denunciation of Stalin in the Soviet Union, which made clear the dangers of excessively authoritarian rule. But it was also an attempt to win over intellectuals and gain their support in economic development and in eliminating corruption and bureaucratism.

Students and professors were urged to speak freely about Communist policy. They responded hesitantly at first, but by late spring 1957 critiques were being leveled at almost every aspect of Chinese life. At Beijing University hundreds of posters appeared at a spot known as the "Democratic Wall." In posters and speeches the students denounced the government's educational policy, questioned the lack of progress in raising China's living standards since 1949, and attacked the suppression of freedom of speech and publication.

As they had done in 1898 and again in 1919, Beijing students fanned out across the country, bringing word of the movement to friends and colleagues. Students stirred throughout China. On June 12 and 13, 1957, student riots broke out in the north China town of Hanyang in Hubei province.

Students in the provinces, removed from close proximity to

government power, jumped into the action too late. By the time the Hanyang demonstrations occurred the government had already signaled that dissent had gone too far. The dissenters were seen as rightist opponents of revolution. In early July an anti-rightist campaign was launched to "cut off the heads of the poisonous weeds" that had sprouted amidst the flowers of revolutionary debate. Many students and prominent intellectuals were criticized; some were arrested. In Hanyang, in an ominous portent, the leaders of the student riots were executed.

A friend of mine who was a minor party official during this period told me one day how the campaign worked. Each work unit was given a quota of names to be reported to the government as "rightists." My friend was told to send the authorities three names. After searching the ranks, he reported that he could find only two people who could be labeled rightists. Fine, came the response, then you will serve as number three. My friend was imprisoned for three years.

Who was responsible for carrying out this campaign to search out counterrevolutionaries, later to be imitated during the Cultural Revolution and once more in practice today? It was Deng Xiaoping, a man whom moderates had earlier regarded as one of the proponents of the Hundred Flowers movement.

The horrendous end of the Hundred Flowers movement was followed by the disasters of the Great Leap Forward. Deng can be blamed for the excesses of the anti-rightist campaign, but it is Mao who was responsible for the Great Leap.

The Great Leap Forward was a continuation of Mao's attack on bureaucracy and elitism which had been curtailed by the start of the anti-rightist campaign. Now agricultural and political decisions were decentralized. The country was organized into large-scale, self-sufficient communes where distinctions between experts and laborers were said to have

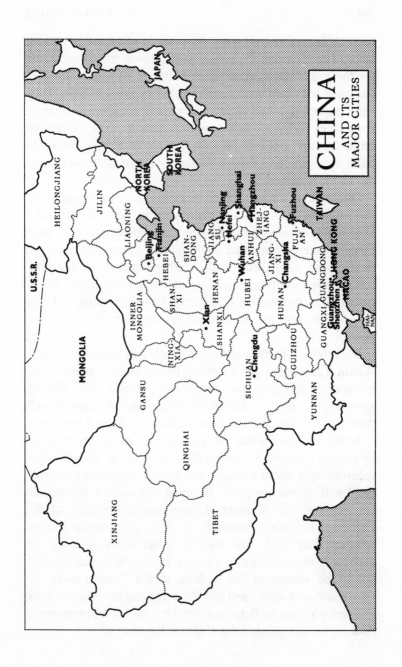

CHINA
AND ITS
MAJOR CITIES

been abolished and all were expected to take part in manual labor. The idea that China's vast manpower could substitute for the machines used in other countries was epitomized in the small backyard steel furnaces built in every village. They were expected to eliminate the need for expensive, large-scale steel factories. Everyone was sent to work, including professors and students, who in the city of Beijing helped to build some of the massive monuments that still tower over the nation's capital.

Overzealous cadres forced peasants to melt down badly needed farm implements to make steel in backyard furnaces. Disgruntled peasants faced with the appropriation of their property often slaughtered their animals. Communally owned fields were neglected. Bad weather from 1959 to 1961 compounded the problems. One of the worst famines in the country's history resulted. Millions starved to death, and tens of millions suffered from malnutrition over the next few years.

By 1960 the party was forced to relax its ideological zeal. Within a few years the economy began to hum again. Soon bureaucracy and corruption flourished once more. Mao Zedong grew angry about "pleasure-seeking" cadres ready to sell their soul for "good food, good clothing, and good housing."

In the mid-1960s Mao decided to take advantage of pent-up student activism to combat the dissipation of revolutionary spirit brought about because bureaucrats supposedly ignored the "will of the people." Defining the will of the people became a matter of much dispute among members of the Chinese Communist hierarchy as well as pedantic foreign scholars. But Mao, who had few other allies on whom to depend at this juncture in Chinese history, believed that the youth and vitality of the students would "sweep away the freaks and monsters" and put the party and the country back in line with what he determined to be "the mass movement." And so he inaugurated the Cultural Revolution.

Today the Cultural Revolution is officially considered a period of totalitarian excess in which decent, talented people were cruelly tortured by vicious and often sadistic groups of officially sponsored vigilantes. It is viewed as "ten years of waste," a time when cultural relics were destroyed and much of the economy of China ground to a halt. These descriptions are basically correct: it *was* a time of official and anarchistic intemperance. But it is also true that many students who responded to Mao's call during this period acted, like their peers throughout this century, because they hoped to end the harsh, arbitrary rule of corrupt bureaucrats. Unfortunately, they were once again manipulated by those in power, including Mao Zedong and Deng Xiaoping.

In the China which Deng Xiaoping leads today, the Maoists have been blamed for all the destruction and violence of the Cultural Revolution, a characterization questioned by groups of student scholars who met informally in China in early 1989. As the students later discovered, the same party propagandists who wrote the history of the Cultural Revolution also claimed that the Chinese army, which carried out a ruthless massacre of its citizens in Beijing on June 4, 1989, were actually victims of "counterrevolutionary violence."

There is another similarity between the two periods. In the spring of 1966, as in the spring of 1989, an intense power struggle was under way within the upper reaches of the Chinese government. In both cases, one side sought support by claiming it wished to open up economic and political decision-making.

In March 1966 the Maoists tried to advance their cause by talking of the lesson of the Paris Commune. They called for the need for the masses to control the government. Those who did control the state apparatus were thought by Mao to be infected with "bourgeois ideology"; their organizational commitments had submerged their ideals.

Mao's first target was the Beijing party apparatus, which

in the past had sheltered many writers who had publicly satirized Mao and led the resistance to his attempts to launch a Cultural Revolution. In May one of the chief obstacles to this mass movement was removed. Peng Zhen, the mayor of Beijing and head of the Beijing party apparatus, was purged from office.

On May 25, 1966, a few days after Peng's dismissal, a woman philosophy teacher named Nie Yuanzi gathered together six of her friends and mounted a wall poster on the campus of Beijing University. She denounced school officials for curtailing the discussion of a play which satirized the character and revolutionary virtues of Mao Zedong. Peng's failure to deal adequately with the author of this play, the vice-mayor of Beijing, Wu Han, had been one of the ostensible reasons for his dismissal. In the poster, Nie detailed the relationship between Peng and Beijing University President Lu Ping. She revealed that factional ties existed between the three top men in Beijing's political-academic power structure— Peng Zhen, Wu Han, and Lu Ping—implying that the party organization which these men dominated was in the wrong. To combat this power structure, she urged "revolutionary intellectuals" to "go into battle." The school authorities promptly tore down her poster. They could not, however, prevent its contents from leaking to the school community.

At the time, Nie's poster was hailed as a spontaneous revolutionary gesture. It now appears that members of the cultural revolutionary group supporting Mao Zedong contacted Nie during a visit to Beijing University shortly before her poster appeared. They may have encouraged her to take this action.

A few days later Mao publicly praised the poster. The party elite grew terrified. Party business in China, especially a purge, was supposed to take place behind closed doors. Nie had violated this rule and revealed events behind the scenes. She had made a public case against a high party official.

Politics had been brought out into the open, and Nie, the instigator, was not only a local party secretary but one supported by the chairman of the Chinese Communist party. Everyone understood that the ground rules had changed. Soon, similar wall posters appeared on campuses throughout the country. Some were even placed on public buildings, including one on the Beijing Municipal Office attacking the head of the citywide party organization. Student rebel groups formed on campuses throughout China to fight the school authorities. Within a short while, party officials such as Chinese President Liu Shaoqi and his assistant Deng Xiaoping realized that their power and position were now under attack. Their response traumatized China for years to come.

Deng and Liu believed that party discipline was essential to preserving order in China. In early June 1966 they moved to protect the party. Party work teams led by high-level enemies of Mao moved into the schools, doing what bureaucrats in similar positions always do. They assured the students that their struggle was well motivated but suggested that their grievances could be better handled by the authorities. The students were told that "a distinction should be made between inside and outside the party": "wall posters should not be put up in the streets," and "meetings should be held only on campus."

Disciplinarians such as Liu and Deng expected that their arrival on campus would produce student acquiescence. When students proved unruly, they acted harshly, separating people on the basis of their class background and attempting to isolate the troublemakers. Their heavy-handedness was exacerbated by team members from peasant backgrounds who were unused to dealing with intellectuals.

The work teams quickly ran into problems. Student groups spurred on by Mao and his supporters had tasted victory, and they were not easily put off. Students were not shy about expressing their criticisms of Deng Xiaoping, Liu Shaoqi, and other leaders. They put up wall posters denouncing the work teams, and surrounded and humiliated members of some of these teams. When one work team attempted to limit the damage by making University President Lu Ping the scapegoat for the school's problems, the students turned the planned criticism session against Lu into an attack on the work teams themselves.

Liu Shaoqi, Deng Xiaoping, and their cohorts responded by singling out for criticism a group of writers and professors. The Cultural Revolution had begun as a result of Mao's outrage at stories which satirized him, written by such authors as Wu Han. So those on the defensive attempted to muddy the waters by attacking all intellectuals as well as anything smacking of the old culture. The work teams demanded that students criticize their professors; those who refused were themselves subject to attack. Senior professors humiliated by the work teams were required to wear dunce caps. Even after Gao Yiheng, the president of the Beijing Steel Institute, was driven to commit suicide, the work teams did not relax. Many similar deaths followed, including those of some of China's most talented artists. In factories and offices throughout China, party secretaries anxious to show that they too were part of the campaign reported so-called rightists in their own units. Often these denunciations were made by people with personal grudges, and often with little or no evidence. Millions were slandered and libeled. Countless others were beaten, abused, and driven to early deaths.

Deng and Liu needed people whom they could trust to help them enforce this kind of terror. In time-honored Chinese fashion, they called on their relatives. Liu Shaoqi's wife and daughter joined the work team at Beijing University. Soon the children of other high-level party officials also jumped into the fray. These teenagers, spurred on by Maoist calls for student activism, organized the first Red Guard groups. As their parents watched, they brutalized the weak and the helpless.

In 1966 the most strident and activist of these Red Guards formed in the middle schools, not in the universities. University students, older and more mature, were content to beat and humiliate their professors, forcing these distinguished elderly men and women to empty out latrines and to stand for hours enduring insults. Compared with what their younger brothers and sisters were doing elsewhere, their violence was minimal. The real zealots were impressionable teenagers. They shouted, "Long live Chairman Mao," but cocksure of their own position they also recited the following couplet: "If the father is a hero, the son will be a brave man; if the father is a reactionary, the son will be a scoundrel."

At first these young offspring of officials and soldiers, considered to be of good revolutionary lineage, merely vandalized street nameplates and store signs, closed barber shops, sealed off the offices of democratic parties, and destroyed religious temples and historical relics. Eventually they began to single out large numbers of teachers, branding them "monsters and demons." Particularly vulnerable were older teachers and teachers of capitalist, rich peasant, land-lord, or other so-called "bad class origin," almost none of whom were able to escape. Teachers were locked in small rooms or cowsheds where they were beaten and tortured. Neighborhood houses were systematically searched for counterrevolutionary material, but this was often little more than an excuse for young ruffians to steal valuable jewels and other art objects.

A friend once told me how as a boy of ten he listened through the wall of his room all one night to the agonizing screams of a young mother, a schoolteacher, slowly being tortured to death in front of her small children. In some households even the children were taken out and killed. A saying from the time which referred to those whose families had once been capitalists, landlords, rich peasants, so-called counterrevolutionaries, and bad elements or rightists, went: "To kill one of these damned five black categories simply means good riddance. It would be better to have all of them killed; then the dictatorship by the proletariat would be further consolidated."

The worst incidents occurred after Liu and Deng had already lost power. But party officials such as these men, who were fighting for their political lives, certainly encouraged excesses in support of their position. They helped to create the system which later grew out of hand. When the young bullies sometimes gave them more than they had bargained for, they did not complain until they themselves were victimized—and then it was too late.

At first, Mao too did not seem upset by the violence. He may have thought that "counterrevolutionaries" were expendable. But it was eventually Mao, not Liu or Deng, who in late July ordered the withdrawal of the work teams from the campuses and condemned the "fifty days of White Terror." He also demanded the destruction of the dossiers compiled against so-called rightists by supporters of Deng and Liu, so that the slanders by party authorities against innocent people could not be used in the future.

Mao's action made the old party authorities vulnerable and isolated those Red Guards who were composed of the children of high-level cadres. Without the work teams on the campus to inhibit them, students could organize more freely against the party. New student groups multiplied after August 5, when Mao mounted his own wall poster urging students to "bombard the headquarters." This was a call to attack the Chinese Communist party, which Mao referred to as a "bourgeois dictatorship."

The Red Guards from "good families" had claimed that as the children of party officials they were pure. But the party itself was now under attack. They had been discredited.

"Revolutionary Red Guards" now began to oppose the original Red Guard groups. Their members included students who had been sneered at, including some from landlord and merchant backgrounds who, in the complicated politics of post-1949 China, had become the most disparaged elements within the society. Encouraged by Mao, they marched on party headquarters throughout the country, raiding secret files and forcing party leaders from their offices. They posted secret speeches and documents on the walls of buildings. Security forces complained to Mao that state secrets were being published, but he appeared unconcerned. Restraints on the Revolutionary Red Guards were lifted further, and their actions became more frenetic and disorganized.

The Red Guards formed exclusively by the children of high-level cadres counterattacked. To protect their parents they attempted to prevent the Revolutionary Red Guards from entering party buildings. By the fall of 1966 the power struggle began to involve more senior officials of the party. The student groups met in scenes reminiscent of New York street gang fights. Among the victims was one of Deng Xiaoping's sons. Escaping from his tormentors, he fell or was pushed from an upper-story window. He survived, crippled from the waist down. The object of much sympathy in the West whenever the story of Deng Xiaoping has been related, in 1989 he was accused by student demonstrators in Tiananmen of utilizing his father's name and position to engage in corruption.

In August 1966, Liu Shaoqi had been officially labeled "the leading person in authority taking the capitalist road," and Deng Xiaoping had been called the "second leading person in authority taking the capitalist road." By late that year the two had disappeared from public view. Liu died in 1969 while being transferred out of Beijing. Deng spent seven years in the countryside.

Now the official avenues of communication between top

and bottom were gone, and society broke down. Maoist leaders attempted to contact the various Red Guard groups, hoping to give them personal instruction. But it proved impossible for the central government to control day-to-day affairs. New rebel factions formed daily. The situation grew more chaotic when Revolutionary Red Guards attempted to seize power in factories, sometimes struggling with workers.

While chaos and brutality reigned in the streets, in some factories the authorities had been stripped of their power. Workers were able to take advantage of this vacuum to gain benefits for themselves. One author, himself a former Red Guard, has suggested that in December 1966, "For the first time the broad ranks of workers were able to give their superiors a piece of their mind without fear of being beaten down as anti-party, anti-socialist elements." Frustrations were aired as the "rank and file took the cadres to task." They reprimanded them over "the unreasonable treatment they had been subject to over the years. Petitioners began to pour into Beijing, making clear their complaints about items ranging from the 'insufficiency of labor insurance' to the lack of employment for high school graduates." In some places, as conservative party managers tried to restrain the leftists by rewarding workers with goods and money, "factories disbursed long-overdue overtime pay, raised the limits of compensation on certain items of medical insurance, and expanded the coverage."

Such "liberation" does not outweigh the horrors of the Cultural Revolution. But the vacuum left by the elimination of effective central power did permit a series of unprecedented initiatives from the masses. In some places workers joined with students to push for a new, more representative form of government. Several times they came close to creating an independent political organization. The best-known of these events occurred in January 1967 in Shanghai, where a mass movement overthrew the municipal authorities and a horrified

Mao Zedong, fearing that the masses were trying to abolish all "chiefs," proclaimed that events had gone too far. He hastily dispatched loyalist troops to the scene to take charge of affairs and quash the demonstrations. On January 23, 1967, Mao ordered Lin Biao, commander of the People's Liberation Army, to intervene in political struggles to support the "revolutionary left" and maintain order. Over the next few months the Chinese army intervened repeatedly in Chinese politics, as it has done throughout the history of the People's Republic and as Chinese armies have done for centuries.

That Chinese soldiers would be willing to brutalize their fellow citizens should come as no surprise. Describing the Chinese army, a well-known traditional saying proclaims, "Just as good iron is not beaten into nails, so a good man does not become a soldier." During much of the past two hundred years, after central power collapsed and China divided into a number of rapacious military satrapies, the army plundered Chinese citizens. This was the background against which the communist People's Liberation Army, later known as the People's Army, operated.

There were some differences. Although many soldiers and even the commanders of this army were former warlord forces, from the start a discipline unusual to China was enforced. Troops ordinarily paid for food and lodging, and tried not to brutalize those on whom they depended for support. They sometimes helped the people with construction projects and at harvest time. But from the start they killed other Chinese. They were, after all, formed during a civil war, and their purpose was to eliminate "counterrevolutionaries," sometimes loosely defined to include former allies. After the Chinese Communist victory in 1949, the army became a prized career among peasant youths. But this did not stop the military from occasional meddling in Chinese politics.

China is an immense country with an exceedingly cumbersome chain of command. New policies can be implemented only slowly. When policy changes at the center, as it did in 1967, the government cannot bring the country instantly into line. As late as April of that year, in only four provinces were there revolutionary committees with which the central government felt comfortable.

At first the army seemed to help the Revolutionary Red Guards in their struggle against the party. But often the army supported the old conservative party organization or, on more than a few occasions, Red Guard factions composed exclusively of the children of military commanders. In some places, by late spring, leftist Maoist groups which had welcomed the army as an ally now began to struggle against it.

Massacres resulted in many parts of the country. The worst incident is said to have taken place in distant Qinghai province. On February 23 the deputy commander of the military district, Zhao Yongfu, ordered his troops to machine-gun unarmed civilians. More than three hundred people died, many of them teenagers. Similar incidents occurred in other parts of the country in what has been referred to as the "February crackdown."

As different army units supported different groups around the country, talk of civil war grew. In the central Chinese city of Wuhan in early July 1967, the army unit which had seized control of the city supported the old party organization and refused to turn power over to the radicals. Members of the central government rushed to the scene to resolve the problem and were themselves arrested. Lin Biao was forced to call in other military units to surround Wuhan. Outnumbered and outgunned, the local military forces backed down.

In the following months, fighting between different Red Guard units increased. "Conservatives" attacked and killed many of the radicals. At the end of July, Mao's wife, Jiang Qing, told the Revolutionary Red Guards to "defend yourselves with weapons." The struggle against the old party organization intensified. Pitched battles raged in many cities. But within the government at large, the power struggle had been won. In September Mao called for an end to the turmoil. He again ordered the army to intervene, and this time he forbade people to interfere with its functions.

Students who had helped Mao to begin the Cultural Revolution had once again become expendable. They were ordered "to go to the countryside to be reeducated by poor and lower-middle peasants." Isolated on farms and reduced to manual labor, the students' revolutionary ardor cooled. In 1970 the government reopened the universities, closed since 1966, on a limited basis.

There was to be one more major victim of this period. During the Cultural Revolution army commander Lin Biao was designated Mao's heir apparent. Lin's support ensured Mao's victory over the party organization of Liu Shaoqi and Deng Xiaoping. But as the country returned to civilian rule, the relationship between Lin and Mao weakened. Even now the details of what happened are still cloudy, though most believe that in 1971 Lin Biao was killed in a plane crash as he attempted to flee the country after an unsuccessful coup attempt against Mao.

Mao Zedong died in 1976. The next year the so-called Gang of Four, a group of Maoist supporters who had come to power during the Cultural Revolution, were overthrown in a successful coup which put Deng Xiaoping back into power. The struggle and chaos of the Cultural Revolution had lasted from 1966 to 1969; but after Deng returned to power the entire decade until 1976 was referred to as the era of the Cultural Revolution, and was considered China's "ten wasted years." In fact, however, by 1971 the government, then under the control of Mao Zedong and the Gang of Four, implemented many of the positive policies for which Deng has since taken credit. The Cultural Revolution, for example,

is said to have crippled China's industrial growth, but throughout the period from 1966 to 1976 China had almost no
inflation and an industrial growth rate of between 8 and 10
percent, respectable by any standards and one to which
China's current regime would be happy to return.

Nor should Deng Xiaoping be allowed to take credit for
China's supposed "opening to the West." Members of the
Gang of Four did oppose China's dependence on foreign
trade, but the initial diplomatic accord between China and the
United States, which ended the country's twenty-year period
of isolation, occurred in the early 1970s when the Gang was
in power and with the sanction of Mao. In the short period
from 1972 to 1974, foreign trade jumped from approximately
$4.5 billion (in constant 1963 prices) in 1972 to $6.1 billion
in 1974, an increase of 30 percent.

After 1977 Deng worked hard to develop the economy,
making expansion of China's relationship with the West one
of his main policies, often in spite of overt opposition from
such rehabilitated party stalwarts as Peng Zhen, the former
mayor of Beijing and the first person whom Mao had purged
during the Cultural Revolution. In the 1980s Deng also
allowed radical new experiments with private ownership and
joint ventures with foreign corporations (though similar arrangements had been made with Soviet firms in the 1950s).
But these accomplishments would have been impossible if the
basis for them had not been laid in the early 1970s.

Deng did oversee the transformation of Chinese agriculture. The redivision of the land into private plots championed
by the recently deposed secretary general of the Chinese
Communist party, Zhao Ziyang, allowed a boom in agricultural productivity during the 1980s. But the gains would not
have occurred without the infrastructure built from 1966 to
1976. For instance, a good part of the increased productivity
of Chinese agriculture was the result of an expanded use of
fertilizer that became available in the early 1980s from

chemical plants that had been purchased from the Japanese *before* 1976. The failure of Deng Xiaoping's government to expand fertilizer output has been one reason for the decline in agricultural growth that marked the late 1980s.

Before the 1989 massacre in Tiananmen Square, many would have argued that Deng's greatest legacy was the new openness he had encouraged among the Chinese population. The relative toleration of diverse ideas in the 1980s has often been contrasted to the narrowminded zealotry of the Cultural Revolution. Not only is this "openness" now questionable as a result of events in the spring of 1989, but it can now be seen that much of the zealotry and violence of the Cultural Revolution were attributable to Deng and his allies.

It may in fact be argued that the ideas underlying the student movement of the late 1980s first emerged in China at the close of the Cultural Revolution, as student leaders became discouraged with the self-serving actions of Deng Xiaoping, Liu Shaoqi, and all the Chinese leadership, including—though it was not stated—Mao Zedong. In the summer of 1967 a Revolutionary Red Guard organization was created in Hunan province known as Sheng Wu Lian or the "Hunan Provincial Proletarian Revolutionaries' Great Alliance Committee." Picking up on Mao's criticism of Chinese officialdom, this group suggested that the relationship between leaders and followers in China had become that of "exploiters and exploited." As a middle-school student named Yang Xiguang wrote, "At present over 90 percent of our high-ranking officials have actually formed into a unique class—the 'red' capitalist class." The Cultural Revolution had concentrated on personalities, he argued, and had never penetrated to the power basis of this group—the undemocratic bureaucratic system that created it. Nor had the Cultural Revolution touched the chief group which kept the bureaucracy in power—the military. The Sheng Wu Lian believed that 90 percent of all cadres could be eliminated, in which case the society would likely become more, not less, productive.

Other students formed similar conclusions. The Cultural Revolution attacks on the party organization and the vicious response of the party to these criticisms destroyed its legitimacy for many people. During the Cultural Revolution, many Chinese began to act according to their own interests and inclinations. By breaking down organizational control and forcing people to criticize almost everything they had been told to take for granted, especially the Chinese Communist organization, the Cultural Revolution encouraged among a limited few a spirit of independent judgment and self-reliance. China scarcely became a pluralist society, but people learned to organize small action groups with others of similar interests and backgrounds. Many began to doubt authority.

In the wake of the Cultural Revolution the government was forced to tread carefully. In 1989 many of the Chinese students who camped out in Tiananmen Square believed that the far-reaching economic and political reforms of the 1980s would have been impossible without a Cultural Revolution. As a result of the Cultural Revolution, it was said, Chinese authorities in the 1980s had a weakened institutional base and thus were forced to listen to the needs and wants of the people to an unprecedented degree in seeking to revive the economy.

Chinese students of the 1980s looked back to the Cultural Revolution with a well-trained eye. Like the Revolutionary Red Guards, they questioned those in power. They saw that students in the 1960s had overturned one of the world's most powerful and entrenched bureaucracies, and they felt they could do the same. Moreover, they shared some of the same goals. The idea of eliminating bureaucracy and corruption—a central focus of the Cultural Revolution—was also a major focus for Chinese students in the 1980s.

Shortly before the Cultural Revolution began, Chairman

Mao complained that one could buy any party leader in the country with a pack of foreign cigarettes. With the inflation of the 1980s, Chinese students feared that one could buy any Chinese leader with a Mercedes. Students were incensed by the sight of their leaders driving around in foreign-built limousines.

But students in the 1980s were led astray by the whims of a vain old man, just as were the students of the Cultural Revolution. For there were two important lessons that students of the 1980s failed to absorb from the history of the Cultural Revolution. The first of these is that in order to effect real change, students cannot depend on those already in power. Like most earlier Chinese student movements in this century, this one had no independent base of its own. In the last stages of the Cultural Revolution, many student groups did strive for independence, sometimes in alliance with workers and other urban groups; but ultimately they behaved like puppets, responding to the manipulations of political and military powers of all stripes.

The second unlearned lesson of the Cultural Revolution is that the party organization responds viciously when its power is threatened. In the wake of the Tiananmen massacre, Chinese propaganda has already confused the facts of the event. Many students did not realize how much they had absorbed official propaganda which since 1977 had portrayed Deng Xiaoping as a decent, humane man victimized by the Cultural Revolution. After all, it was said, Deng once studied in France, the country that gave the world the ''rights of man.'' Amidst their hopes for the future, many Chinese forgot that not only Mao Zedong but also Deng Xiaoping and his associates were capable of violence and brutality.

3

THE RISE OF DEMOCRATIC MOVEMENTS

In January 1987 I stood in the living room of a house in Beijing, talking with the son of friends. A few days earlier Deng Xiaoping had forced Hu Yaobang to resign as secretary general of the Chinese Communist party and accept responsibility for the student demonstrations of the winter of 1986–1987.

The protests had begun in December on the campus of the University of Science and Technology in the small town of Hefei in the central Chinese province of Anhui, an unlikely setting for a school which in fact caters to the elite. The demonstrations started a chain reaction that spread throughout China.

The young man I spoke with was a freshman who had taken part in the protests. He had been an admirer of Deng Xiaoping, but now he was disillusioned. In demonstrating, he had thought he was helping Deng to achieve democratic goals. Now he was coming to conclude that Deng was a phony democrat, one who, like Mao before him, raised people's hopes only when he wished to use popular protests to discredit political opponents.

This young man's analysis shocked his parents. Both senior members of the Communist party, they had spent time abroad. Believing China had a glorious future, they wanted their son to be educated at home. They thought the University of Science and Technology an ideal place. Considered to be one of the finest scientific institutions in China, the school was located in Beijing before the Cultural Revolution. During the turmoil of those times, the University was moved to Hefei. After Mao's death it elected to remain in its provincial location rather than contest the new occupants of its old campus.

The school in many ways symbolized the mythology of Deng Xiaoping's China. Deng had asked the elite to make compromises in their living standards and to be understanding about the backward nature of Chinese society. If they did, he promised, China would soon be a prosperous modern nation, a leading member of the family of nations.

The people whose home I was visiting had bought this mythology. Although they realized that their son would have to endure some physical discomforts in a small city such as Hefei, they saw the school's provincial location as an advantage. Students and teachers in Hefei faced none of the enticements and dangers of their big-city colleagues. When their son, a bookish young man with a head for equations and chemical formulas, was accepted for study at the University of Science and Technology, they relaxed. His future was secure. There would be nothing in Hefei to distract him from the library and laboratory they were sure would help transform backwaters like Hefei into the Chinese equivalents of Silicon Valley. Now, like so many of his predecessors throughout this century, the awkward youth they had sent off to "techie" paradise had returned a defiant rebel shocked at the treatment the Chinese government had meted out to him and his friends.

They shouldn't have been so surprised. Since 1976 Chinese students had been regularly used and then abandoned by Deng Xiaoping when they no longer advanced his political agenda. And students had suffered a similar fate throughout this century. Whether it was southern warlords in 1919, Chiang Kai-shek in the 1920s, the Communists in the 1930s, or Mao and Deng during the Cultural Revolution, political powers have manipulated the interest in democracy, however loosely defined, that has characterized Chinese student movements since at least the time of Kang Youwei at the turn of the century.

"All we wanted," my friends' son repeated over and over again to me in disbelief, "was democratic elections.

"They misstated the numbers!" he continued angrily. "The Chinese papers lied. They said that only a couple of thousand people marched in Hefei. It was really more than twenty thousand."

The accuracy of his count was important because of the absence of a free press in China. Without this freedom, the government, which also controls the security apparatus that can stop most protests, decides what most people learn about protests. When large-scale demonstrations occur and become known, it is largely because certain powerful forces wish to limit or destroy the targets of these demonstrations. Before 1986 Deng Xiaoping had done this so skillfully, largely through his manipulation of newspaper, television, and other information channels in China, that most believed he would encourage any just democratic cause. When those, like the student with whom I spoke, suddenly discovered that Deng's government distorted their protests, and then promulgated petty rules to ban them, they were shocked.

My friends' son, for instance, was livid that the authorities branded the student demonstrations as illegal because they had no permit to march, even though they were "peaceful" and "didn't hurt or disrupt anything."

"Tell him," his father interrupted, looking at me. "Don't you need a permit to march in the streets in the United States too? People can't just demonstrate at will, interrupting the normal functioning of a city."

"That's true," I admitted, reluctant to have become a part of this debate. "Even in America you are supposed to have a police permit before you can march."

"But we tried!" the boy shouted. "We went to the police station to get the proper permits, but no one would give them to us."

He and his friends had expected government cooperation in their protests. This was not only because of his faith in Deng Xiaoping. It was also because in 1986 members of the "liberal coalition" within the government had deserted Deng for the first time and supported the students.

Encouragement came, most notably, from Fang Lizhi, a well-known astrophysicist then serving as vice president of the University of Science and Technology. When demonstrations at his school began, Fang Lizhi responded that the students had every right to protest. In the wake of his statement, larger protests erupted in Shanghai and Beijing. Fang's statement gave the protesters momentum—although he was primarily a scholar, he spoke in an official capacity. Students inferred that their goals and actions were in accord with government policy, something Western journalists who spoke with Fang at the time also tended to believe.

In a way, Fang did speak for the government—but only that part of the government represented by Fang and his allies, none of whom had much authority. The fact that in 1986 low-level officials such as Fang could play this game was evidence of the central government's distintegrating powers. But it nonetheless confused the students.

It also put Deng Xiaoping on the spot. Always before,

when he turned on the students, Deng had been able to pretend that he was being forced to do so by government hard-liners. The actions of Fang Lizhi and the students in 1987 forced Deng out of the closet. He made it clear that he wanted the students to help him when he needed help, but he would not permit them to aid others. Although most observers in China and abroad had not understood it, this had always been Deng's game.

In 1973, after the Cultural Revolution, Premier Zhou Enlai recalled Deng Xiaoping to high office. Late the following year Zhou announced his "Four Modernizations" program in which Deng was given a major role. The program promised to improve living standards which had changed little in the previous decade. It awakened hope in many Chinese, particularly intellectuals, whom Deng promised to enlist in the campaign.

Then in January 1976 Zhou Enlai died. On March 25 an article appeared in a Shanghai newspaper accusing Zhou of having been a "capitalist roader." Because Zhou was already dead, it quickly became apparent that the article was really an attack on Deng. The people responded in support of the regime—not in Shanghai where Maoist authorities were still quite strong, but in the nearby city of Nanjing. Late March is the time of the traditional tomb-sweeping ceremonies, when the people of China commemorate their dead ancestors. The day the article denouncing Zhou Enlai was published, wreaths remembering him began to appear all over Nanjing. People in other cities soon followed suit. On March 30 wreaths went up in Tiananmen Square in Beijing.

As in the early days of the Cultural Revolution, students, particularly middle-school students, were at the forefront of the action. They covered Nanjing University with posters, many condemning the Shanghai article and others suggesting that a "Khrushchev-type individual"—a terrible insult in those days—sought to usurp power. Democratic sentiments awakened. With Zhou dead, Mao dying, and the government split between several contending groups, Deng's supporters within the government encouraged these sentiments. So did provincial authorities who feared that a strong new central government such as that advocated by Deng's enemies, the so-called Gang of Four—Zhang Chunqiao, Wang Hongwen, Jiang Qing, and Yao Wenyuan—would limit their powers.

Initially, few of the people who carried wreaths for Zhou Enlai thought or cared much about Deng. But day by day, as mourners came to Tiananmen Square, word filtered out that he backed them. Sympathy for Deng grew. Meanwhile, Deng portrayed himself as a past victim of cruel government policy, one ready to divide up the economic pie and right old wrongs. He became the people's choice, embodying the demands of the masses as they marched into Tiananmen.

As the demonstrations in Tiananmen grew larger and larger, the government seemed paralyzed. For five days growing numbers of mourners occupied the square. Hundreds of thousands came to speak, sing songs, and write poetry. Then, on the evening of April 4, police abruptly emptied the square.

Angry crowds returned the next day. At 9:35 that evening, as one observer reports, "all the lights in the square were switched on, making it almost as bright as day, and loudspeakers blared a military song. Thousands of men with Workers Militia armbands and staves marched out of the Imperial City. . . . They began to clear the square, surrounding one section of the crowd at a time." Some estimates have claimed that as many as a hundred were killed and thousands arrested that night, though the real numbers were probably considerably less.

Government propagandists refused to say that the police had suppressed a popular demonstration. Instead, on April 17, 1976, the *People's Daily* ran an editorial claiming that "the heroic people of the capital crushed with one stroke the counterrevolutionary incident at Tiananmen Square planned deliberately over a long time. . . . The whole nation warmly supports the two resolutions of the Central Committee vehemently denouncing the counterrevolutionary activities of a handful of class enemies, and indignantly criticizes the crimes of [a certain comrade] in attempting to subvert the dictatorship of the proletariat and restore capitalism.'' In 1976 the certain comrade denounced was Deng Xiaoping. The words were almost the same as those Deng himself used thirteen years later to condemn the students of 1989.

In 1976 Deng was rumored to have been under house arrest even before the government attacked the demonstrators in Tiananmen. On April 7, 1976, two days after the demonstrations ended, the government stripped him of all his offices and criticized him as "an unrepentant capitalist roader." A chill spread over the political climate. In the next few months, thousands, perhaps tens of thousands, were arrested. Deng was spared this indignity because sympathetic members of the army protected him.

Soon the military helped Deng seek his revenge. In September 1976 Mao Zedong died at the age of eighty-two. With Mao dead, Deng played on a field against weaker competition, and this time he won. His dismissal after the Tiananmen demonstrations had greatly boosted his popularity. His past record was forgotten. He became the people's choice, and the military moved to support him. A month after Mao's death, military officers helped arrange a coup which toppled the Gang of Four and returned Deng to power.

Deng had used popular protest to undermine the Chinese government and return to power. But his authority within the new government was initially limited. Deng shared power with some who had ascended during the Cultural Revolution, most notably Hua Guofeng. After Zhou Enlai died, Hua had become premier, personally approved for the job by Mao Zedong. In late 1976 Hua assumed Mao's old job as the head of the Chinese Communist party. Like Deng, Hua had been an enemy of the Gang of Four. He supported their overthrow. But he was not a Dengist. To overcome the influence of Hua and his allies, Deng appealed to all those moderate groups later to be the spearhead of the democratic movement.

The first of these were the intellectuals. They had been hurt during the 1957 anti-rightist campaign and then in the Cultural Revolution, in no small way as a result of Deng's actions. Now Deng portrayed himself as the champion of the intellectuals, promising them new status and autonomy.

People have short memories. In 1976 the events of the Cultural Revolution were still confused. Many believed Deng when he said he would end the injustices of the Cultural Revolution. He pointed to the fact that he was successor to Zhou Enlai and had himself been twice purged during the Cultural Revolution. Everyone knew Deng had spent seven years in the countryside. For the seventeen million former Red Guards still banished to remote areas of the countryside, Deng offered hope. "Millions of ordinary citizens who had suffered political condemnations and physical and psycholog- ical abuses looked to Deng to bring about a 'reversal of unjust verdicts,' " Maurice Meisner wrote. The student pro- testers of the late 1980s were children then, but they formed an image of Deng as a liberal reformer.

So did others. For the next several years Deng played on pent-up democratic aspirations in much the same way that Gorbachev has more recently in the Soviet Union. Deng rehabilitated at least a hundred thousand former political prisoners. He reversed the verdict on the April 5, 1976, Tiananmen incident. He saw to it that those jailed for their activities in the square were now labeled heroes who had engaged in a "revolutionary event," and that officials who had suppressed the demonstrations were swept from office.

During the first few years of his return to power, Deng, like Gorbachev today and like Mao Zedong in the 1960s, encouraged a nascent democratic movement. During the Cultural Revolution some Red Guard members, particularly former Conservative Red Guards such as members of the Sheng Wu Lian alliance in Hunan, grew disillusioned by the way they had been manipulated by government officials and began to see the entire Chinese bureaucracy as an enemy that suppressed democratic rights. Many of these people worked in urban factories where they had formed workers' alliances. In the late 1970s, with Deng's encouragement, they criticized the government, undermining Deng's enemies within the bureaucracy.

At the time Western papers spoke of Deng's reforms with almost as much enthusiasm as they now speak of Gorbachev's. By 1978 a Democracy Wall had been established in downtown Beijing as well as in most other major and several smaller cities in China. The wall began with the government's encouragement after the party rehabilitated those who had participated in the April 5 Tiananmen incident. It received a bigger boost after Deng told American columnist Robert Novak that he considered the wall a good thing. "The Chinese people want freedom!" Deng proclaimed. "We have no right to prohibit the people from putting up big-character posters!"

The people soon used these posters to air all sorts of grievances as well as to analyze political and social policies. In 1978 I spotted a poster in downtown Hefei in which workers complained that they were not allowed to play basketball during lunch break. Most posters were more serious. A growing number of young workers and former Red Guards demanded a "fifth modernization"—democracy. Few if any of the writers had a clear idea of what human rights entailed, but that did not stop them from embracing them. Posters advocated a multi-party system, demanded the punishment of corrupt officials, called for the rehabilitation of political victims, and even asked for more sexual freedom.

Not everyone thought about broad-ranging liberties. People came to Beijing and other cities to ask the government to remedy their individual cases of injustice. Some petitioners traveled thousands of miles, camping out in the streets hoping to be heard. While they waited for the government to redress their wrongs, they studied the young people's democracy posters and often put up their own. One poster that made fun of both the government and the students warned: "Go fuck yourself with your 'socialism' and 'communism' in a society where people don't have enough to eat or clothe themselves decently."

By early 1979 these democracy walls became scenes of heated discussion and argumentation. Bolder protest groups printed unofficial magazines and newspapers. New underground organizations formed to advocate these ideas. Western newspeople were often called to the wall to see certain posters.

The publicity pressured the Chinese government and helped Deng achieve a stunning victory over Hua Guofeng during the famous third plenum of the party's Eleventh Central Committee which met December 18–22, 1978. The group known as the "whatever" faction—because of their support for whatever Mao Zedong had said—lost power. The following month Deng made a triumphant tour of the United States.

American writers in the late 1970s were generally sympathetic to Deng, because he seemed to encourage those who espoused democratic ideals. But many in China recognized that Deng had adopted Mao's Cultural Revolution tactics to best his foes. He used a mass movement to pressure the government and overturn opponents within the party. Writing in 1980, one young supporter of the movement admitted, "Cooperation between the reform faction within the party and the democratic youth factions proved so successful that the Whatever faction and Western critics suspect that this was the result of Mao Zedong–style collusion." But the writer confidently asserted that students would not be used by the government as they had been during the Cultural Revolution because "youths understand how to bring their own interests and courage to bear upon influencing the nation's affairs."

At heart, Deng was still a "disciplinarian" attached to "ideological orthodoxy." Having regained control of the party, once he returned from the United States he clamped down on the democracy movement. In March 1980 a speech began to circulate in which Deng claimed he was being forced to close down the democracy walls because of pressure from hard-liners within the party. Many took the hint. Others, like the well-known dissident Wei Jingsheng, spoke out, claiming that Deng had "laid aside the mask of the protector of democracy."

On March 28 the government issued a new regulation prohibiting "slogans, posters, magazines, photographs, and other materials which oppose socialism." The next day the police jailed Wei Jingsheng. Wei received the longest sentence of any of the arrested dissidents as a vengeful Deng showed that he would silence anyone who questioned his authority. Other arrests followed as the movement for democracy attempted to reassert itself throughout the next year. Free elections which the government had promised were greatly restricted, and those who resisted these limitations found themselves punished.

I lived in China from 1980 to 1981 as the government crushed the remnants of this democracy movement. Once, a friend riding home with us in a taxi was pulled from our car and searched. Another time, an acquaintance who handed my wife a birthday present in public was dragged into a police station for questioning. Western books and literature were still relatively rare. Chinese could not visit foreigners without registering their names and addresses with ubiquitous doorkeepers. Every day, when the cleaning people in our building came to empty our trash, they carefully separated all scraps of paper with writing on them into a big pile which they removed for inspection.

In spite of these actions, Deng retained his mantle as a liberal reformer. He still controlled the media. Few understood very well what had happened to Wei Jingsheng. Those who did tended to believe that Deng was forced to act because of the continued presence of dark forces within the government. They remembered the chaos of the Cultural Revolution and feared its return. They were grateful to Deng for improvements in their lives and believed he would continue to make things better.

He did. In the next few years the scope of new freedoms broadened and life improved. It became easier for me to meet with Chinese friends, and visits to their homes became more generally accepted. New literature appeared on the streets. Foreign books and periodicals were sold in greater numbers. Deng and his allies, it was said, wished to establish legal procedures to avoid the arbitrary arrests and accusations of the Cultural Revolution.

Periodically, however, the government would employ a frightening crackdown, such as the 1983 campaign against "spiritual pollution." This effort began, it was rumored, after Deng Xiaoping's car was waylaid by a group of orphans from the earthquake-damaged town of Tangshan. Angered, he ordered an assault on criminals which turned into an attack on all "deviations" of foreign influence. The government jailed new dissidents, criticized intellectuals, and renewed arrests. Western books and records were temporarily removed from shelves. People wearing Western-style clothes and make-up were sometimes harassed. For scholars, access to libraries became more difficult. Periodicals, once open to everyone, were classified. Some historians who had attempted to re-evaluate the Stalinist-dominated policies of the Chinese Communist party in the 1920s were criticized. But the campaign against spiritual pollution lasted only a short while. On a trip to Japan, Communist party chief Hu Yaobang mocked the whole concept of it. When he returned to China, Deng Liqun, the reputed hard-liner behind the campaign, was pushed aside.

By the spring of 1984, when I was again living in China, the campaign had become a memory. The economy grew freer. Private ventures were encouraged, and joint ventures with foreign companies became frequent. Black-market money changers appeared on the streets. Most of my friends managed to buy color TVs and cassette players. Some spruced up the blackened walls of their apartments. The well-to-do in Beijing employed maids, selecting sturdy peasant girls from Anhui province. Many foreigners were so enchanted by the tall new buildings and Western-style hotels being constructed in urban areas that they believed China was on the verge of becoming a Western-style democracy.

Meanwhile, Deng Xiaoping was working to reestablish a core group of Communist party managers tied to him by friendship and family. A variant of the nomenklatura system used in the Soviet Union, they were an elite group centralized in the Chinese Communist party who reviewed all important administrative and financial appointments. Control of wealth and power remained concentrated in this small body of men (in the top echelons of government, few women were allowed).

In 1985 Deng retired from front-line management of the party. Two years earlier he had complained that the "old ones occupy the toilets without taking shits. They have to go." Now he decided to serve as an example and relinquish his position as vice premier, the only formal state administrative title he held. In fact, Deng retained his chairmanship of the Central Military Commission, and in that capacity he maintained veto power over almost all important government decisions. Similar subterfuges were developed for other senior figures who retired at the same time but continued to maneuver behind the scenes.

This situation naturally created tension for the two highest officials of the Chinese Communist party, Hu Yaobang, secretary general, and Zhao Ziyang, premier. Zhao was more concerned with the day-to-day operation of the economy and so was subject to less interference than Hu. Hu Yaobang chafed at the way his leadership was constantly undermined by Deng Xiaoping and other senior cadres.

Deng's actions unintentionally served to weaken the power of the party he had worked so hard to protect. Now there were two centers of power, the official one headed by Hu Yaobang and the unofficial one headed by Deng. The party had always at least pretended that it controlled the army, but now the head of the Military Affairs Commission was not a formal party official. The party seemed like a shell.

Economic and political reforms had already weakened the party's position and authority. Its power stemmed in large part from its ability to make economic decisions—assigning jobs and apartments, setting production quotas and prices, and allocating scarce goods. But economic changes in the 1980s decentralized the economy and diminished the power of the central government, causing a de facto political liberalization. Even the party's theoretical journal *Red Flag* noted that "ideals are far away, politics are meaningless, but cash is real." The first Secretary of the Beijing Communist party, Li Ximing, complained that many party members believed "no money, no work" and "work according to the amount of money." In some urban areas, high school drop-outs with their own small businesses exercised more power and authority than party members. Disturbed conservatives, not realizing how much their own actions had contributed to the problem, began to talk of reinvigorating the party by returning the country to the old values. They questioned the economic reforms.

Prominent intellectuals sponsored by Hu Yaobang responded, suggesting that the party give in to the inevitable, open itself up to free elections, and even allow competing political parties. Hu himself cited Western democratic theorists, particularly Montesquieu, and praised Western freedom. All this threatened to take the selection of the nomenklatura out of the hands of the party elders and give it to the people. It was too much for Deng, who had always stressed the role of the Chinese Communist party in bringing change to the country.

Deng reverted to the duplicitous style that had served him well in the past. In August 1980, after he had quashed the democratic movement, Deng had spoken forthrightly about political problems in the party and had called for reform. He had repeated this message in 1983 on the eve of the spiritual pollution campaign, and he had tried it again in early 1986. His intent, however, had clearly been to keep this reform under the control of party leadership. In the summer of 1986, alarmed by some of the radical suggestions he now heard, Deng put the brakes on his party secretary. He made it clear that any reform would be directed by the party. In September the party issued an important document on "building socialist spiritual civilization." While appearing to endorse reform, it actually rebuked Hu Yaobang's calls for more democracy by upholding "the leadership of the party and the people's democratic dictatorship."

Tired of interference, Hu Yaobang had already begun to wonder out loud when Deng would complete his retirement. During a visit to the United States Hu was asked by a Chinese journalist why he had to wait until Deng died to become the head of the Central Military Commission, the organization through which Deng controlled the army and exercised effective power over the government. Hu answered with a pregnant silence. In response to a further question from a *Washington Post* correspondent, Hu suggested that the issue would be resolved at the upcoming Thirteenth Congress.

Hu now began to campaign for Deng's retirement in earnest. Rumors spread that Deng was no longer capable of performing his job. In late December Deng's daughter had to deny a rumor to Hong Kong papers that her father was in bad health. Gossip about Deng's family proliferated. His son, it was said, used his position to extort money. His daughter, an artist, was said to dress lavishly and to have taken advantage of the family name to sell paintings in Hong Kong for hundreds of thousands of dollars each. Some observers suggest that hard-liners spread these rumors, trying to blackmail Deng. Others say it was Hu Yaobang and his supporters. In any event, the struggle became highly personal. In the summer of 1986 the issue of Deng's retirement had been debated in party meetings but not decided. In the fall it burst into the open with contending articles in several regional Chinese papers.

By November Hu's efforts had boomeranged. Word spread that Hu, not Deng, would be replaced at the party congress. When Mao was on the losing side of a power struggle in the 1960s, he turned to the masses. Nor had Deng been afraid to embrace the protesters who surged into Tiananmen in 1976. In both cases, the losing side allowed student protesters to attempt to alter the situation. It is a trick everyone in China likes to play, and now it was to be Hu's turn.

A year earlier, in September 1985, on the fifty-fourth anniversary of the Japanese occupation of Manchuria, hard-liners had tried to enlist student allies. At the time China was swept by a series of demonstrations against the country's growing economic relationship with Japan. The protests seemed aimed at closing down China's "opening to the outside." The reformist faction within the party put an instant stop to these demonstrations, but not before they had enlisted a number of students generally disgruntled with the government. Students in China can always be found to join any anti-government demonstration; in this case not all of them agreed with the hard-liners.

By late 1986 other students with connections within the

nomenklatura began to defy the hard-liners. Pro-democracy demonstrations began in Hefei at the University of Science and Technology, a school attended almost exclusively by the children of the elite, almost 90 percent of whom are said to have the opportunity for foreign study. Why should these students begin the demonstrations? As the children of intellectuals and members of the science bureaucracy, they represented the segment of the party most loyal to Hu Yaobang. Fang Lizhi, then the vice president of the school, had spoken of giving a leading democratic role in the country to the intellectuals. By taking to the streets, students put pressure on the Chinese government to follow through on this promise.

On December 1 a wall poster appeared on the campus suggesting that the scheduled elections of the provincial people's congress, the basic level of the major representative body in China, were a fraud. The poster complained that the people were not "puppets" or "dummies." They did not want a "rubber stamp" congress. It demanded real elections, not only for the congress but also for mayor and district head. The proposal set off a spirited debate on campus.

On December 5 several thousand students peacefully protested the vetting of candidates for the elections to the provincial congress. Four days later, on the anniversary of the 1935 student demonstrations which inaugurated the "Resist Japan" movement and undermined the credibility of the Guomindang, students from the University of Science and Technology, this time joined by students from other schools in the Hefei, marched again. Another demonstration began that day in the central Chinese city of Wuhan, where the provincial authorities tore down a poster written by a student who declared himself a candidate for the election.

The student demands were ones that had been repeated time and again throughout the twentieth century. As students in Hefei paraded through the streets, they shouted, "No democracy, no modernization," "We want democracy," and other slogans reminiscent of the 1978–1979 Democracy Wall protests and other student movements dating back to the May Fourth era.

The students in Hefei also repeated the time-honored methods followed by their predecessors in 1898, 1919, 1957, and 1966, spreading the word to friends throughout the country, hoping to influence others to follow their example. In Beijing two posters appeared on the campus of Beijing University. One, signed by a group called "Warriors of Democracy" of the University of Science and Technology in Hefei, called on the government to serve all the people, not just a small group, and demanded that people fight for democracy. Other students from Hefei showed up in Shanghai to foment protests by students there.

The first response from the authorities encouraged the students. Acting on behalf of the University, Fang Lizhi postponed for three weeks the university elections scheduled for December 8, promising to allow the students to nominate their own candidates. "The students' requests were very correct," he stated. He also insisted that the students "have the right to demonstrate and put forward their views, which have been taken into consideration." Not long afterwards, an official of the state education commission declared that "Chinese citizens have the right to hold demonstrations," though he objected to the use of wall posters. The treatment contrasted quite dramatically to the harsh response of the government to the anti-Japanese demonstrations of the year before.

Like everyone else in China, students are used to reading between the lines of official pronouncements. When the authorities responded so timidly and, in the case of Fang Lizhi, with such encouragement, students assumed that political circles were endorsing their demands. Few understood at the time that they were a small group of intellectuals set against a weakened and reticent party apparatus.

A few days later the protest spread to Shanghai. On December 18 about a thousand students of Tongji University defied school administrators and broke through the gates of the school, carrying banners for "Freedom," "Democracy," and "Human Rights." On December 19 at least ten thousand students from most of Shanghai's major universities marched to the Shanghai municipal building in the center of town shouting, "We want freedom," and "Down with bad government."

Shanghai Mayor Jiang Zemin agreed that the protests were legal, but in answer to student demands for an end to censorship of the press he argued that he could not tell the media what to report. "They have the freedom to select the news stories they want to publish," he maintained. Jiang asked the students to keep their protests within the bounds set by the Chinese Communist party. After he spoke, some students staged an all-night sit-in in front of his office. The police removed them early the next morning. There were reports of beatings and arrests. The next day many more students returned, some now bearing banners complaining about police brutality. By the third day the demonstrations had grown to an estimated fifty thousand to seventy thousand people. Workers joined the student protesters, filling Shanghai's vast People's Park in the center of the city.

As demonstrators shut down the center of Shanghai, commerce in China's largest city ground to a halt. Young toughs overturned vehicles and burned cars. Some carried signs calling for the ouster of Deng Xiaoping, the first time this had happened in China. Other students asked not just for freer elections but also for better food in the dining halls, less crowded dormitory conditions, and measures to regulate the academic quality of university staff.

The participation of workers is said to have particularly worried the government, which grew concerned that a Polish-style Solidarity movement was beginning in China. After early arrests, workers were kept in custody while students were released.

Meanwhile, new fractures in the government appeared which prevented conservatives from responding firmly. Voices of support for the students were widespread. The pro-Communist Hong Kong newspaper *Da Gong Bao* went so far as to say that the four basic demands of the demonstrators—democratic reform, freedom of the press, recognition of the legality of parades, and no arrests—"sound fair enough and have been accepted by the authorities."

Unable to win the battle in the streets, the conservatives mobilized within the top reaches of the party. When they began to counterattack in the media, they resorted to old tricks. They cited incidents of violence and the extremism of some demands. On December 22 local Shanghai media denounced disruptions caused by "a small number of criminals and people with ulterior motives." New regulations were announced, requiring that protesters obtain an official permit from the government. The media warned that anyone taking part in banned activities would be "severely punished." That day about ten thousand students marched nonetheless—mostly younger students who, according to some reports, were organized by older colleagues.

Still the demonstrations continued. By the end of December 1986, demonstrations had been reported in at least fifteen cities, including Shenzhen, Xian, Nanjing, Tianjin, Suzhou, and Guangzhou. On December 23 they reached Beijing, where a small number of students staged a march to Tiananmen. Wall posters highly critical of the Chinese Communist party began to appear on the walls of Beijing universities. On December 29 the first large protest in that city occurred, though it was smaller than the ones in Shanghai. Coincidentally, this was the last day that Hu Yaobang appeared in public.

The government still controlled the media, and it now

began to use it against the students. Referring to the specter of the Cultural Revolution, a number of articles made ominous comparisons between the student demonstrators and the Red Guards. Government propagandists explained that the "great democracy" which the students wanted was not real democracy but anarchy. Television reporters interviewed workers discussing how disruptive and unpopular the demonstrations were. Professors warned students about the need to go slow. Parents wrote letters, printed by the newspapers, asking for government action and imploring their children to stop their demonstrations.

As television showed pictures of arrested workers looking downcast and beaten, broadcasters referred to their criminal intent. Taiwanese spies were said to have stirred up the demonstrators. A foreign radio station, the Voice of America, was chastised for instigating the demonstrations by broadcasting lies about them.

On December 30 Deng Xiaoping invited Hu Yaobang, Zhao Ziyang, and other party leaders to his home. There in a speech, later issued to party members, he suggested that the student demonstrations be dealt with severely. Deng called Fang Lizhi "outrageous" and advocated his expulsion from the party.

"We cannot," he insisted, "let those slanderers confounding right and wrong, black and white, get away with it." For the first time Deng openly bragged about his role in shutting down the democracy wall movement seven years earlier and imprisoning those responsible for it. "Didn't we arrest Wei Jingsheng?" he asked, insisting that an ordered and disciplined China was what foreigners like best. "Did that hurt China's image? China's image has not been hurt because we arrested and detained him. Instead, our reputation is getting better day by day."

But if Deng cared about China's image abroad, that is not to say that he wanted China to adopt foreign values. China,

Deng indicated, could not adopt "bourgeois democracy." It was a sham. "American capitalists use their three branches of government as a trick to handle foreigners." Once China achieved "an annual gross national income of $4,000 per capita," it would show the "superiority of socialism over capitalism." To ensure this victory, more arrests would be necessary, though hopefully without bloodshed. The Chinese government, said Deng, should imitate the example of Polish leaders who acted properly when they suppressed Solidarity.

Once again Deng had demonstrated his deep faith in party order and discipline. For the first time he alluded to his role in the 1957 anti-rightist campaign, when thousands of intellectuals who had been encouraged to speak up during the Hundred Flowers campaign were jailed and purged. Admitting that some people were treated unfairly at this time, he also suggested that "we have not declared the movement a complete mistake. Likewise, anti-bourgeois liberalization is necessary."

By this time the students in Hefei who had begun the 1986 protest had ceased their activities. But the demonstrations continued a few days longer in Beijing, with street marches and a public burning of copies of the *Beijing Daily*.

It did no good. Fang Lizhi and other liberal intellectuals began to lose their posts. In early January the government removed Fang Lizhi, as well as the president of the University of Science and Technology, Guan Weiyuan, from office and drummed them out of the Communist party. Two other prominent intellectuals, the investigative journalist Liu Binyan and the writer Wang Ruowang, were also expelled from the party. Some student leaders were dealt with more harshly: the government waited until they left their university campuses, then arrested them.

On January 16 Hu Yaobang's resignation was announced. The tide had turned. Although the government response was slow, central authority had not been severely undermined.

Protests were stopped without much violence before they had gone too far.

But in acting as they did, government leaders continued to weaken the party they were supposedly trying to protect. Hard-liners showed little concern for the legal niceties they had demanded of the students. According to procedure, the decision on Hu's resignation should have been by a meeting of the Politburo. But when the eighteen Politburo members failed to take the action favored by Deng and the other elders, they were joined by seventeen members of the Central Advisory Commission—a board established for older, semi-retired officials—as well as other important comrades. As Mao Zedong had packed earlier meetings, the hard-liners now violated rules and procedures, repeating the events of the Cultural Revolution which they claimed had so revolted them.

The party elders now suggested that Hu Yaobang had not been sufficiently zealous in enforcing "leftist" policies. The party charged that in 1984 Hu had opposed the campaign against spiritual pollution and anti-bourgeois liberalization. By putting an end to this campaign, Hu created "the tide of bourgeois liberalization that flooded the fields of ideology and culture in the nation. . . . These developments prepared the way for the nation-wide student disturbances that took place in the winter of 1986." A party circular also charged that Hu opposed "unified thinking." He tolerated too much freedom of thought and attempted to "rectify the party to boost the economy." He was also accused of overstimulating the economy by "putting consumption before production," which caused economic dislocations. The men who packed the Politburo meeting felt that too often Hu disregarded party stipulations, made unauthorized statements to foreigners, and ignored party resolutions.

Deng and the other party elders worried that China might begin to resemble the bourgeois economies of Hong Kong,

Taiwan, and the United States. In criticizing Hu they suggested (probably correctly) that bourgeois liberalization was something the United States wished to encourage in communist countries.

Throughout much of the preceding decade, Deng had appeared to be on the side of the moderates. But in 1987, when push came to shove, Deng responded like every other Chinese leader in this century. He needed the students to gain power, but like his predecessors he was not willing to allow their insolence to threaten his position after he secured it. He understood how a popular movement could delegitimize the most well-entrenched elite.

This did not mean he cared to discard all the gains that had been achieved by his regime. He realized the need for reform if China was to preserve its economic progress. By the end of January 1987, an attempt was made to limit the scope of the anti-reform movement so that it would not interfere with technical and economic work. Still, the campaign that ended the student demonstrations and brought down Hu Yaobang did not end. Selected speeches and writings of leading dissidents such as Fang Lizhi were circulated to party members to show the heresies which these people had spread and to identify those who had published their works. A blacklist was made of intellectual and political figures who had seemed to support the idea of reforming the party in the months before the student protests.

For a short time, then, things relaxed. Just as the former secretary general of the party Hua Guofeng was not immediately expelled from the Politburo after his fall from power, neither was Hu Yaobang. Foreign observers breathed a sigh of relief when the moderate Zhao Ziyang was named secretary general, even though Li Peng, who replaced him as premier, was a hard-liner.

In 1987, as life appeared to return to normal, most China observers should have recognized how ominous the situation

was. Just when reform in China had been brought to a point
of no return, the hard-liners had blinked and pulled back. Not
many months earlier, in the summer of 1986, when the party
still debated the liberalization proposals put forward by Hu
Yaobang and his allies, Premier Zhao Ziyang mentioned to a
Yugoslav reporter that China was "bound to undergo far-
reaching changes as a result of economic reform." Confronted
with these changes to their accustomed methods of operation
and their patronage network, the old cadres hesitated. They
reacted again as they had during the 1957 Hundred Flowers
movement. Students and intellectuals, whose help was essential if the government was not to stagnate, were encouraged
to speak, but when the government realized what they were
saying, they decided they did not want to hear it after all.
Once again, Deng Xiaoping led the crackdown.

Until 1987 Deng had been able to play both ends of the
Chinese political scale. In the 1950s he was seen as a Maoist.
In 1957 he was viewed by some as a supporter of the
intellectuals and by others as the man who began the anti-
rightist campaign against them. During the Great Leap Forward he was one of the great proponents of Mao's radical
economic visions. In the 1960s he emerged as an economic
pragmatist. He attacked intellectuals during the Cultural Revolution, yet in the 1970s intellectuals supported his ascendancy
to high office. Throughout the late 1970s and early 1980s
both sides believed him to be secretly in their camp.

Even as he repressed the democratic movement of 1979–1980,
he still managed to make most Chinese—though not the
dissident Wei Jingsheng—believe that he was forced by hard-
liners within the government to take this action, that he was
secretly on the side of the reformers. Until 1987 then, Deng
was truly the Teflon chairman.

In 1987, however, Deng Xiaoping unmistakably showed
his hand. After the suppression of the 1987 student movement, many Chinese intellectuals concluded—as they had

after the Cultural Revolution—that China's chief problem was its new class of bureaucrats. The person who had benefited most from the crackdown, they noted, was the new premier, Li Peng, rumored to be the adopted son of Zhou Enlai and his wife. In selecting him for the job, some of the older cadres were said to have remarked that they felt more comfortable if the children of high-level cadres were in charge. Thus the politics and style of the past still poisoned the future. Like Chiang Kai-shek before him, Deng had decided that the ruling class must be preserved at all costs.

This was not just a question of personal power; it was also a matter of intellectual and political commitment. For Deng it was inconceivable that change could occur in China if it was not under the centralized and bureaucratized leadership of the Chinese Communist party.

Although most Western scholars missed it, the ramifications of the purge of Hu Yaobang became clear to many of my friends. During my visit to the home of the family mentioned at the beginning of this chapter, whose son participated in the Hefei demonstrations, the father took me aside and suggested that conditions would be bad in China for at least the next five years. At the time I was stunned. I had heard this man vehemently defend China in bitter arguments with his family. Now he suggested to me, a foreigner, that things looked bad. I knew he was an informed insider, a man so quick on his feet that even during the Cultural Revolution he was not criticized or exiled to the countryside. "For now," he suggested, "we have to look after ourselves." Then he asked if I could help get his son into a good college in the United States. Soon after the son went off to America, the father and mother also found excuses to leave China.

The man was not alone. In the next two years, when most foreign observers thought China was becoming freer and more relaxed, many of those who knew better used this breathing spell to get themselves and their families out of the country. The demonstrations had tested the waters, and the hard-liners had come up winners, reversing the outcome of every power struggle in China since 1977. Those who were quick on their feet knew that the students would challenge Deng again, and they were fairly certain how he would react. They also knew that the party was deteriorating rapidly. This time the government had been able to put down the students without much bloodshed; next time, if the normal channels of the party failed, the old men might have to resort to a bloody crackdown using the military, one of the few institutions they still controlled.

No longer was Deng seeking to manipulate democratic forces against the government. Now he would use the government to harness the students.

4

THE DILEMMA OF
ECONOMIC REFORM

While living in China in 1980–1981, my wife and I hired a nanny for our children. A portly woman with a hacking cough, Ayi (Auntie) grew up in a peasant family on the outskirts of Beijing. When the expanding metropolitan area stretched past her door, she became an urban worker. Before marrying she toiled for a while in a noodle factory, and she could still roll out by hand the best noodles I ever tasted.

Ayi's husband repaired and installed refrigeration units for a division of the Friendship Hotel, where we lived during this period. Her husband's connections and her demonstrated party loyalty brought Ayi the approval to work for—and, no doubt, report on—foreigners. She and her husband were better off than most urban workers. Still, through Ayi and her extended family we got a sense of working-class life in Beijing and were able to observe some of the effects of the new economic policies on Chinese workers.

Watching Ayi's family, we came to realize just how ambivalent many Chinese workers were toward the economic reforms carried out during the 1980s. They enjoyed the benefits that came from these reforms, but they feared the insecurities. Raised to believe in a society in which equality was a paramount socialist value, they resented the few with good connections and a comfortable background who prospered—often as a result of graft—from the economic changes. They sympathized with protesters, but often for the wrong reasons. Confused about what was happening, they often seemed more sympathetic toward halting the reforms than continuing them. When economic problems struck China late in the 1980s, many became bitter.

Ayi and her family lived in the Friendship Hotel complex. These buildings were originally constructed for the benefit of Russian technicians who poured into China in the 1950s. When the Russians moved out, Chinese workers assigned to the Friendship Hotel unit quickly occupied some of their old apartments. In the early 1960s Ayi and her family took possession of a flat that remains the envy of most ordinary Chinese. Most of our other higher-status friends crowded into two- or three-room cold-water dumps. Ayi had her own kitchen, bathroom, several bedrooms, and running hot water. Because of her husband's job, the family had long had a refrigerator, something quite rare in China before the 1980s.

Like most workers, Ayi welcomed the improvements in Chinese living standards under Deng Xiaoping. In the early 1980s her family acquired a color TV, a stereo, and a washing machine. Many times she contrasted life in the 1980s to that of the early 1960s, just after the Great Leap Forward, when food rations in the city were reduced and everyone was on the brink of starvation.

Her children also had good jobs. Her two oldest sons were drivers, one daughter worked in a shirt factory, and another was a maid in the hotel.

By Chinese standards, Ayi had it so good that she attracted the jealousy of her neighbors. The intense rivalries and hostilities left over from the various political campaigns that have rocked China over the last forty years became vivid for me in the fall of 1980 when an American friend pulled me aside one day to warn that her nanny was concerned for our children.

"Why?" I gasped.

"She claims your Ayi has tuberculosis and has tried to conceal it from the officials so she can keep working. She didn't want to rat to me, but she's worried that your one-year-old might be infected, and she says it is deadly for someone that young."

This confirmed my worst fear. Ayi had a deep persistent cough which had long troubled me. I knew TB was widespread in north China. My nature was often to worry that Ayi might be passing something horrible to our children. Now I had been told this was so.

I ran home to confront Ayi.

"Was it that other Ayi who told you this?" she asked, unflustered. "The one who works for those friends of yours in the corner apartment?"

"How did you know?" I was taken aback. I hadn't said anything about the source of the rumor.

"She's been my enemy for a long time. In the Cultural Revolution she denounced me as the daughter of a landlord. Every time I go to work for a new family, she tells them I have tuberculosis."

In the end, Ayi volunteered to go to the doctor for an x-ray, actually a fluoroscopy. X-ray machines are too expensive, so patients in China stand behind a machine, being zapped with radiation, while a team of doctors peers at something that resembles a television screen to determine if there are any irregularities.

Ayi received a clean bill of health. Her cough, the doctors assured us, was caused by chronic bronchitis, probably a result of sensitivity to Beijing's ever-present dust. We insisted they give her a certificate testifying to this condition so that she would not have the same problem with her next family. We had received a good lesson in the way resentments could upset Chinese life. Our family had been paralyzed for two days while we waited for Ayi's x-ray. Multiplied by a billion people, such incidents could destroy the productivity of an entire society. This happened in the 1960s. It began to occur again in the 1980s.

Ayi did not have the vicious streak her enemy had displayed, but she too was filled with envy and resentment. As early as 1981 she talked about how much money her husband could make if only he could retire from his state job and work in the new private sector. She heard stories of others with his same skills bringing home ten and twenty times as much money as he did. She thought it unfair that the work unit to which he was assigned would not let him retire, even though he was well past what was supposed to be the mandatory retirement age, because they said they needed his skills.

About the same time, Ayi's younger daughter decided to try to attend college. She had studied French in school, and a family friend was a French teacher who translated for French workers at the hotel. He offered to tutor her. While the daughter hunched over her books night and day, Ayi rushed around searching for presents for the tutor in return for the favor he was doing for her family. But it was in vain. The daughter had begun her studies too late. Even with all her cramming, she couldn't pass her college entrance exams and so remained a hotel maid. Ayi said nothing, but I could tell she resented the ease with which the children of well-educated intellectuals and middle-class bureaucrats passed these same tests and moved up in the world.

In the 1980s China once again rewarded the privileged. Those like Ayi and her husband who had pulled themselves up by dint of hard labor and good luck now worried they might fall back again. Ayi grew more concerned when her youngest son graduated from high school and could not find a job. Unemployment was rampant in the cities, and jobs were scarce, even for a graduate of one of the best middle schools in the country. He ended up working as an apprentice chef in a private restaurant. Ayi put a brave face on it, talking about how much money he would make if the restaurant did well.

"He's doing here just what you said I could do if you brought me to America and set me up in a Chinese noodle restaurant," she joked.

But she worried.

By the mid-1980s when I would visit, the family looked materially much better off, but like many others in China at this time they complained that goods were growing expensive. They could barely afford food now and couldn't even think of other purchases anymore. They were hemmed in by bosses who arbitrarily assigned jobs and rooms. Her husband was well into his seventies and still working. Her oldest son had given up his job as a bus driver because he worried about the difficulties of navigating through the awful pedestrian and bicycle traffic. If he hit someone, he would be fired; so now he worked as a mechanic. Three of the children still lived at Ayi's home with their respective spouses. A granddaughter by a son who lived on the other side of town had also moved in with the family, because her parents' apartment was too small. These kinds of problems, which almost all Chinese workers experienced then, helped fuel the student protests. They also made the insecurities caused by the reform movement more difficult to bear.

These insecurities became apparent to me one day when Ayi's daughter took me aside and complained at length that people were being fired at the Friendship Hotel because they had bad attitudes towards their jobs. The examples she cited were of people who had stolen items or been involved in fights. She acknowledged that they deserved to be punished, yet she did not like what had happened to them.

"They say that from now on," she continued, almost shaking with apprehension, "they're only going to give bonuses to those who work hard. It's not fair. Some people need the money, and now they may not get it. Who's going to feed their children?"

I was surprised. The daughter, like the other members of her family, was a diligent worker. She stood to profit from this new system, yet it made her uneasy. I wondered about the resentments of less talented workers.

Members of the family told me one day of an incident in 1983 at the Friendship Hotel. Some African students got into a fight with hotel employees who had refused to serve them beer during a hotel dance. On the campuses the foreign students all talked of the racist treatment doled out to blacks by the Chinese. The Friendship Hotel was near Beijing University, and students often came to the hotel for a drink. Black students complained that they had trouble being waited on. Ayi's family saw it differently.

"The hotel employees were only doing their jobs," the daughter informed me. "They stopped a couple of the black students from entering the disco dance because they didn't have their IDs. The Africans didn't like that, so they began to act crazy. I'm sure they were drunk again. A few of them punched one of the workers. They were experts in martial arts. The boy who worked at the desk was afraid. What else could he do? He and his friends beat the Africans with boards and bottles. How else could they subdue them? Maybe they should have stopped before they sent one of them to the hospital, but it's not so easy to judge things in the middle of a fight.

"The Africans all stuck together. Their friends from Tianjin and even Shanghai came to Beijing. There were thirty thousand of them. They marched on the Friendship Hotel, planning to burn it down.''

I had heard it was a peaceful demonstration. In any event, I knew that there were nowhere near thirty thousand African students in all of China. Ayi's family saw foreigners, including Chinese, every day. If they believed these kinds of rumors, what must others think?

The daughter's reaction to her government's handling of this incident also indicated how ordinary Chinese felt that the government no longer sided with its workers. She thought that officials capitulated too quickly, discriminating against Chinese for the sake of foreigners. "They were so afraid of the Africans," she claimed. "They brought the case to trial in only three days. That's much faster than it should have been.''

She reported that the leader in charge of the hotel that day, who participated in the beating, was sentenced to three years in jail. She admitted that he was a proud, arrogant person who deprived others of their monthly bonuses if they were guilty of even the slightest infraction; but now she felt sorry for him. She was more outraged that the other workers were dismissed from their jobs.

"That's even worse than being sent to jail!" she cried. "The boss man who was sent to jail can return to his old job when he gets out. But the workers who have been dismissed are young. Now they'll have no way to support themselves. Their lives have been ruined!''

In fact, in the Beijing of the 1980s they probably had a good chance to become private entrepreneurs. But Ayi and her family, like most other urban workers, had not adjusted to the new system. They were insecure. Changes came too fast. They could not appreciate the benefits they received. They worried about what they had not gotten, castigating the government for the reforms it had made as much as for those it had not made. They liked the products of free enterprise, but they did not really want more of it.

The same was true of their attitude toward foreigners. Although they liked foreigners—in fact they derived their living from them—they blamed outsiders for their problems. Ayi once told me that the cockroaches that swarmed over the Friendship Hotel had come to China from Pakistan, brought by dark-skinned Indian types, whom she disliked almost as much as Africans.

Urban workers such as Ayi and her family worried that China's new economic reforms tampered with the "iron ricebowl" that had given everyone in China job security. They did not like being on their own. They did not understand a world in which salaries could vary. They feared they might one day be on their own altogether, and they would not know how to get along.

However much workers may have resented the old system, they appreciated the extent to which it took care of them. Their apprehension in dealing with the outside world on their own, unprotected by a work unit, became continually apparent to my wife and me when we discussed travel plans with friends. Almost every weekend we hopped on a train with our children in tow and rode to a new and distant point in the country, hoping to experience the variety of locales which China had to offer. This horrified our Chinese friends.

"Who's going to meet you when you get off the train?" they always asked.

"No one. We'll find a cab and take it to the nearest hotel."

"But what if there are no cabs? How will you know where the hotel is? How do you know there will be rooms?"

Our Chinese friends had an endless series of questions like these. Even when we purchased tickets in advance and made arrangements ahead of time, it was inconceivable to them that someone would travel without a work unit on the other end to assume responsibility for them. They had been looked after for more than thirty years, and they feared going out on their own.

Conscious of the downside created by the reforms, they saw how the new economic policies were often applied inconsistently and unfairly. One year, when one of Ayi's daughters needed money to get married, a fire broke out at the Friendship Hotel because some careless electricians had installed faulty wiring. The hotel lost money, and all its workers were deprived of their bonuses for the entire year. The family was more annoyed with the policy than with the electricians whose sloppy workmanship caused the disaster.

Many who like Ayi and her family had prospered under the old system were reluctant to change, even though life was now even better for them. They formed a constituency, even if a reluctant one, for those conservatives within the government who sought to halt the reforms so that their power base would not be threatened. At times the needs of the two groups meshed. Ayi and her family knew how to operate with older bureaucrats.

When one of her daughters planned to marry another worker in the hotel, she had a problem because her prospective husband had not worked in the complex long enough to have his own apartment. The problem was solved by Ayi's husband, who went to the leaders and explained that the boy lived far away and would not be able to get to work if the rule were not waived. It was, and the couple was married, the father's influence and connections no doubt counting for more than his logic.

When people knew they could rely on these connections, they felt more secure. After hard-liners in the government began to exercise more power in late 1988, Ayi's family relaxed. I saw them in 1989 just after the student demonstrations began. They still carried some resentments against the government; they were aloof but sympathetic to the student movement. But this time they acknowledged that life had improved for all of them. They were getting what they wanted.

The son who had gone to work as a mechanic was a driver again, this time of a much better vehicle. The youngest child, who had previously worked as a chef in a private restaurant, now was also employed as a driver, one of the most prized jobs in modern China. He was engaged. The daughter who was a maid had married, had a child, and moved to a new apartment. All had secure government positions.

Few workers in China have done as well as Ayi and her family, but her story is one which in other respects has been repeated thousands of times during the last few years. The dissatisfactions felt by Ayi were felt by many others. Ironically, many of the workers who joined the student demonstrators in the streets, first in Shanghai in 1986–1987 and later in Beijing in 1989, did so because they had been unsettled by economic reforms, not because they wished them to go further. The changes wrought in China over the last decade improved life for millions, but, as often happens during a period of rising expectations, they also made many of these same millions feel dissatisfied, resentful, and insecure.

Workers, even those such as Ayi and her family who did well, were not politically sophisticated. They sometimes supported student anti-government demonstrators because they disliked the disruption and chaos that confronted them every day, and they blamed the government for this. They liked the idea of being rid of the bosses who inflicted misery on them, but they did not wish to lose the security that the bosses also brought. They would have been upset to learn that some of the reforms proposed by those who supported the students would have made their lives less secure.

The government ignored the disgruntlement of its citizens when the economic situation was improving, as it was throughout the early 1980s. People gave the government leeway when they saw life get better from one day to the next. This was particularly true for the peasants, whose efforts powered the Chinese economic miracle of the 1980s. Peasants worked harder because for the first time in almost thirty years they could get something extra for themselves by doing so. The new responsibility system put land back under the control of individual proprietors. Peasants once again were the masters of their own fate. Once they sold their quota of grain to the government, they could sell the rest of their crops for whatever price they could get on the open market. Agricultural output increased year after year though yields soon leveled off.

In 1984 China experienced a bumper harvest. Ayi's country cousins were ecstatic. We saw many of them coming into the city on visits, piling goods onto their backs as they left. When I saw them on the streets, their weathered faces looking frightened and lost, they seemed more out of place in China than I did.

They had come to the big city to spend their money and live it up. What few realized then, however, was that the good times were almost over. The country's stock of grain soared, peasants made money hand over foot, and the resulting increased circulation of currency fueled the economic expansion. Urban workers like Ayi and her family did well during this period, but many peasants did comparatively much better. Lev Deliusin notes that "The annual income of peasants grew from 133.5 yuan in 1978 to 463 yuan in 1987. In 1980 the maximum annual income of more than 60 percent of the rural population was 200 yuan. In 1987 the number of peasants with such an income had declined to 8.2 percent." With more currency on hand, people bought more. Since there was plenty of grain in storage, commodity prices stabilized, and the excess money poured into consumer goods, inflating their cost.

Even before inflation hit, all these improvements scarcely meant that China was growing rich. At today's exchange rate the figures above show that average peasant income improved from about $30 a year to about $115, still a pitifully small sum. To put it in perspective, the average Chinese peasant earned less in a year than many American children spend on new games for their Nintendo sets. Peasant life improved, but these changes failed to bring the earnings of peasants into line with those of their urban counterparts, who themselves lived rather poorly on about double the average salary of the peasantry. The economy of China remained exceedingly fragile. By 1986 it began to experience problems which it could ill afford.

As consumer goods became expensive, peasants had few incentives to continue increasing production. The little extra money they would receive for an ever greater effort necessary to expand their crop yields could no longer be used to purchase anything worthwhile. Bad weather made this situation worse, and grain production dropped in 1985. By early 1986 peasant income was falling, and the amount of currency in circulation in peasant households dropped. The poor were once again getting poorer.

At the same time the government promoted new industries and expanded the money supply with cheap loans to supply these businesses. Prices of new shoes, dresses, and other consumer goods climbed. The dual nature of the economy made matters worse. As the supply of cotton and other raw goods dwindled, more and more necessities were bought by those with political connections and diverted for a profit to the private sector, where they were marked up. The rich and powerful grew more so. Prices soared. The result was a slowing in the growth rate which Chinese economists classified as a recession.

Government planners were especially concerned that the development of consumer goods far surpassed that of producer goods. Ayi and her family fretted that although they might live well today, they no longer had any security for the future. Others did the same. Economists also grew concerned. During the 1970s, in the decade before the reforms began, China invested almost exclusively in basic industries which did little to meet people's daily needs but gave the country a solid economic underpinning. In the 1980s standards of living improved, but long-term basic industries lagged.

Government spending for agriculture fell dramatically, from 11 percent of total capital investment in the 1970s to 6 percent in the early 1980s and 3 percent in the late 1980s—a drop of almost 400 percent. The increase in agricultural productivity in the 1980s had been derived from the benefits of fertilizer plants purchased in the 1970s and as a consequence of greater incentives given individual peasant households. But now few new fertilizer factories were built, and no new irrigation and water projects were undertaken. Without better machinery and fertilizer, peasants would have to work late into the night to continue to improve productivity. Even with the proper incentives, it is unlikely that many would have done this for long. China needed more investment in agriculture.

It also needed to put more resources into other basic industries. The growth rates for construction of energy plants and communication facilities, and for production of raw and semi-finished goods, slowed at the same time. Only the production of such items as cigarettes, bicycles, sewing machines, and shoes grew rapidly. When we lived on the campus of Beijing University in 1984 we experienced an average of two electrical blackouts a week, often for hours at a time. Our Chinese friends regarded this as better than average. The problem was more severe in other parts of the city and far worse in less developed areas in China. Some factories stopped operating on certain days to accommodate the power grid. Something had to be done if China's economic expansion were to continue. China's economic growth could not be maintained with cigarette smoke, not even from China's famous "Long Life" brand cigarettes.

But the system was difficult to change. During the reform era, in most factories the authority of the local Communist party secretary was supplanted by that of a professional manager. In theory this was designed to bring the factory under efficient management. But because the party secretary remained in the factory watching the manager, the manager's authority was circumscribed. In a Western factory the manager is the boss. He represents the interests of the owners or stockholders and works to develop their investment. The Chinese manager has no such power. His only base of support comes from the workers. Like Ayi, most Chinese workers are scared and suspicious of the changes occurring around them. As a consequence, Chinese factory managers have been unable to invest very heavily in productive enterprises. To cultivate their employees they must place much of their funds into such items as workers' housing and bonuses. This has given the managers a base independent of the central party organization which, operating on behalf of the central government, has tried to restrain consumer spending in order to dampen inflation and save to build the economy. Managers have made themselves popular at the expense of the party secretary. But the system has not produced the kinds of economic decisions that augur well for the economy.

The factory situation parallels that in agriculture. Peasants once again till individual plots for which they have sole responsibility, but the government retains the leases for the land. The government also insists that peasants grow at least a certain percentage of grain to be sold to the state at a low fixed price. Under these circumstances, few peasants have been willing to make long-term investments which might increase future land productivity—better irrigation, larger plots, trees, shrubs, and the like. Instead they have worked hard to produce crops that will provide immediate rewards and have sloughed off when, as at present, the rewards appear less immediate.

The government is doing no long-term investing, and neither are individuals. The China of the 1980s has been very much a live-for-today kind of society, as much as that is possible in a country where the average salary is rarely more than $200 a year.

There are two solutions to this problem. One, favored by old-line Chinese economists, calls for a return to the Stalinist system of the 1950s. Controls would be placed on the production of consumer goods, and resources would be diverted to the development of heavy industry under the direct control of the central government. In agriculture, the government would build the dikes, irrigation facilities, and fertilizer plants that the peasants need. To enable people to use them more efficiently, it might be necessary to recollectivize in certain areas. China would revert to the past.

The second solution calls for further decontrolling of the economy, allowing price to control demand. The government would discontinue fixing grain prices. Peasants would be encouraged to increase production. As peasant life became more secure and further removed from government control, farmers would invest more in their land. In the cities, managers would be totally divorced from party control, so they would have truly independent power to expand their plants and industries. Instead of simply working to satisfy their workers, they would try to develop the kind of producer industries China so desperately needs.

Ironically, these decontrols are not necessarily in the interests of workers, at least not in the short term. The more total the manager's control, the less willing he will be to cater to the interests of his employees. Instead he will be interested in expanding the plant. Money will go into new equipment, not housing or bonuses. Job security will be threatened. Housing will no longer be subsidized, and rents will gradually rise to the point where they pay for the maintenance of the buildings, something not now the case in China. Workers will probably be worse off for a long while.

In 1986, proposals by Hu Yaobang and his followers for greater party democracy would have loosened government controls over the economy. When most Chinese intellectuals discussed democracy, they seemed to have envisioned that it would be people like them, not less well-educated party people, who would be elected to office. Little thought was given to the possibility that workers and peasants might have their own candidates in mind. Fang Lizhi, for instance, discussed intellectuals as "a driving force for society." The technocrats who supported increased democratization also favored rising food prices, higher rents, and dismantling of the job security system, proposals that in no way would have been supported by most workers. These were precisely the kinds of policies that would have horrified people such as Ayi and her family, who have not been happy with the idea of having plant managers and other technocrats free to grow and expand their plants without providing for immediate worker welfare. Those allied with Hu Yaobang seem to have been more concerned with using democracy to eliminate the power of hard-line party bureaucrats rather than considering where this kind of democracy would take China.

No wonder party officials were horrified. Hu's party democracy was intended not only to give people a say in the government. It was also a way to drive the party bosses from office. From their point of view, these reforms were a return to the Cultural Revolution. As during the Cultural Revolution, they feared they would once again be on the losing end of a power struggle which called for the masses to throw them into the streets. Those within the central government worried that in the 1980s, as in the 1960s, China would dismantle the huge patronage networks built under the leadership of Deng Xiaoping. Party leaders would no longer have jobs to dole out to loyal followers and their relatives.

Nor would the jobs provided by the party be as desirable after democratic reform. The dual system whereby some goods are bought at low prices by the state and others are sold at higher prices on the free market has given many party members a means of accumulating undreamed-of wealth. Under the present system it has often been easier and more lucrative to use connections to purchase scarce state goods and resell them through the private sector than to begin new factories to compete with the state. While crippling the growth of Chinese industry, the system has provided cadres with a remunerative source of graft. Local party officials did not wish to see it threatened. They opposed more democratization, but many also resisted a return to the old Stalinist system.

While inflation is a serious problem, so is unemployment. In the late 1980s an estimated 100 to 150 million excess peasant laborers not only put pressure on the hard-pressed rural economy but periodically burst into the cities, straining services and increasing the ranks of those looking for jobs. A few months before the 1989 Tiananmen demonstrations, more than a million rural workers seeking employment suddenly flooded the streets of the south China city of Guangzhou, as they have done around the New Year for the past several years, causing panic and mayhem. The situation is not intolerable, but in order for agriculture to improve, these people cannot be permitted to remain as peasants.

The average peasant now cultivates a plot of less than six acres. Experts have estimated that farms of twenty acres per person would be more efficient. The answer is to develop more rural industry and commerce. This creates problems of pollution and waste, and many rural industries are insufficiently funded and inadequately staffed. Most of all, this solution poses a fundamental threat to party authority. These rural businesses, especially the marginal ones, can function only if they can freely buy commodities. This would mean the elimination of the dual economy in which party cadres become conduits for graft from peasants anxious to have goods counted towards quotas. Greater accountability and electability for local officials would eliminate some of this corruption, but it also would fill party ranks with new members who have no loyalty to existing patronage channels. Party officials do not want this. They also see no great benefit in a return to the Maoist system in which the party attempted to control local businesses. But they are aware that the situation is almost out of control.

Their way of reacting has been to stifle change, for which Chinese students have become the lightning rod. This is what happened in mid-1986 when old-line party bureaucrats derailed Hu Yaobang's reform efforts and threatened to send him to the sidelines. In early 1987, after student protests failed and Hu was removed, those seeking to reverse the economic reforms seemed to have the upper hand. The leasing of land in the countryside was said to be leading to the return of the "landlord system." In urban areas, the creation of small enterprises was said to allow "capitalists" to get rich from "hired labor." There was once again talk of the socialist ideal of total egalitarianism—though in practice this had led to increased bureaucratic power for the select few.

But powerful voices within the society spoke up for the continuation of reforms. Few could fail to see the concrete signs of progress which the changes had produced. Intellectuals particularly supported the reforms. Perhaps most important, many provincial and local areas benefited from the reforms and enjoyed increased autonomy from the central government. Officials who feared that a further loosening of the system would challenge their graft networks had no desire to see the dual price system that had greatly increased their own prosperity eliminated, even if the party they represented gained more power as a result. In many areas, local businesses had already established a close working relationship with the authorities, and they too wanted no interference in their situation.

In effect, the economy had created its own internal stasis. A new network of mutually supportive political and economic interests had developed. Further reform threatened these interests, but a reversal of reform also threatened them. All of China had become Ayi and her family.

The forces opposing the so-called hard-liners were far from the most progressive elements within the society. In the last few years local and provincial interests supported the construction of factories that made no sense in terms of the national economy. At a time when the government attempted to conserve capital for badly needed industries, local authorities demanded their own factories to manufacture bicycles and electronics—items already in oversupply nationwide. The newly constructed local factories produced radios and blankets inferior to those made in Shanghai and other urban centers. To ensure the competitiveness of their region, local officials sometimes prohibited the import of "outside goods."

Over time China may have been able to work itself out of this situation. But time was one thing China did not have. Only a major cataclysm could transform economic policy and push China decisively in a new direction.

In 1987 the reformers could not win in the streets. When the student demonstrations ended, the hard-liners seemed to have the upper hand. But they could not prevail in government councils. Hu Yaobang was retained in the Politburo, and a few months later high officials again discussed the need for political reform. The Thirteenth Party Congress held from October 25 to November 1, 1987, reversed the events of January and seemed to be a victory for the reformers. Zhao Ziyang, a reformer, was confirmed as secretary general of the party, replacing Hu Yaobang. Old hard-liners, including Deng

Xiaoping, retired—gracefully, it seemed, though their back-stage power was not yet discerned. Newcomers flooded into the Central Committee and other organs of power. Zhao Ziyang was so carried away by his apparent victory that as the announcement of the changes was made, reporters observed him clasping his hands together over his shoulder in a victory gesture.

Speeches and reports to the congress seemed to confirm this assessment. The right of small rural businesses and other enterprises to develop was ratified. Zhao himself called for the increased use of markets—not only for commodities but for labor, real estate, technology, and information. He also demanded further separation between party and state. There was even discussion of a wider distribution of ownership which would provide for greater use of stocks and bonds. Power was to continue to be decentralized and disbursed.

But this continuation of reform proved ephemeral. The person picked to succeed Zhao as premier, when he moved up to his new job, was the plodding Li Peng, a Soviet-trained technician who was the clear favorite of the old party bosses. The army held fewer positions within the new government, but eighty-four-year-old Yang Shangkun, a Russian-trained former secret police operative, was confirmed as permanent secretary general of the party's Military Affairs Commission, making him the second most important military official in the country. His standing was further enhanced when he was named president, formerly a ceremonial position.

In the months that followed, the economy moved somewhat. New stock and bond markets were created. More private businesses were established. Joint ventures with foreign companies flourished. China entered the takeover game, buying foreign companies in Australia and the United States. By 1989 industrial output was said to have climbed 21 percent over the preceding year.

But structural problems had not been touched. Party bosses

remained more firmly entrenched than ever in rural areas. Nor was much effort made to root them out of urban factories. Most of the economic growth continued to be in housing and consumer items. Inflation raged. Agricultural production continued slow; China had to turn to foreign markets for grain and cotton. Foreign television sets and cameras poured into the country. Foreign exchange dried up.

Under Mao China had prided itself on its refusal to borrow money from foreign countries. This changed during the Deng years, but most foreign bankers believed that the Chinese government kept a careful eye on the country's debt situation. By the late 1980s this was no longer the case. Between 1984 and 1986 China's foreign debt increased an average of 32 percent each year. The increase then slowed but remained high. By 1988 the country was almost $40 billion in debt to foreign bankers. Debt service costs rose. By the late 1980s both the World Bank and the International Monetary Fund began to warn China that its debt problems were beginning to resemble those of Third World problem nations. By 1989 China had moved to bring its debt under control, substituting many of its short-term loans for longer-term issues. But there was also talk of delayed payments by some Chinese borrowers. Foreign joint-venture operators complained of the liquidity crunch that squeezed their operations. Efforts were made to solve these problems, but no viable solutions seemed forthcoming.

As the economy went from bad to worse, another debate took place within the reaches of the central government. In the summer of 1988 party chairman Zhao Ziyang, who a year later was ousted for his support of the student demonstrators, argued that China had to go past the point of no return and dismantle more state economic controls. Although Zhao admitted that a short-term increase in inflationary pressure might follow, he and his supporters were said to have felt that once a free supply of goods was allowed onto the market, inflationary forces would slow. He allowed new money to pour into the economy. The old guard, however, resisted losing their controls and perks. They attempted to cool the economy as they had in the past, by cutting back on imports and controlling domestic production.

The result was that one part of the economy careened wildly out of control, consuming raw materials in a frenzy, while the other part of the economy wallowed in price controls. Perhaps they had not planned it this way, but party officials prospered more than ever before, as deals were made left and right to shift goods from the controlled sector of the economy to the uncontrolled. Those who were clever and had connections took advantage of the situation. Ayi's family secured their jobs at this time.

Others cried. In September 1988 I received a delirious phone call from one of my best Chinese friends. "Leave for China today," he urged. "As a scholar you have to see what is happening. It's crazy. The country is on the verge of falling apart."

I had met this man and his family in Beijing in 1980. In the spring of the following year he left China to attend graduate school in the United States. He availed himself of my contacts to bring his family over to visit. They remained. Another child was born. Green cards in hand and looking very Americanized, they returned to China for a visit for the first time in almost a decade in the summer of 1988.

He was shocked. This was not the China he had left. Unlike foreign tourists, he did not notice the fancy new hotels and shiny Japanese cars. He saw a society out of control. Prices shot up daily. Strangers fought in the streets over money. Once comfortable academics on fixed salaries now could barely afford the food to sustain themselves.

"When I visited Shanghai," he told me, "my brother went to the market to buy crabs for a banquet in my honor. He asked the price at one booth. He thought it was too high and started to cross over to another stall on the other side of the market. The man in the first stall jumped on his back, knocked him to the ground, and starting hitting him over the head with a stone. If I hadn't intervened, he would have been killed.

"But then you know what happened?" my friend continued. "I insisted we report the incident to the market authorities. When we did they screamed at my brother. They told him he had better buy his crabs from the owner of the first booth and not try to haggle. It's crazy. China can't exist like this. Go now, so you can see what it's like before the country falls completely apart."

The country did not fall apart, but in the coming months the chaos did not subside either. The hard-liners who retained control of the state apparatus continued to believe they could use the heavy-handed methods of the past to cool the economy. The success of their efforts, however, was confined largely to the lumbering state enterprises still under central government control. Provincial authorities and many new private enterprises ignored the government decrees. Corruption and inflation worsened. The production of consumer goods grew as did imports. Only the development of heavy industry slowed. The government clamped down harder, but still the inflow of luxury items continued, draining foreign currency reserves while government-regulated necessities dried up.

One of the most important casualties of this policy was phosphate fertilizer, the manufacture of which suffered from China's growing energy shortages at the same time its import was restricted by the government. In April 1989 I visited a small village near Tianjin. The leaders of the local agricultural cooperative took me to a warehouse where they normally stored bags of fertilizer. It was empty.

"Tell your friends we will send them whatever they want,"

they implored, "if they can find a way to ship us some fertilizer."

There was no way. In order to export items a Chinese company needs "export power." The government had not granted "export power" or "import power" to this little company. They could sell the pond-raised frozen shrimp they produced for sale abroad only to another Chinese company in south China, which in turn exported it. They had no power to export shrimp themselves. And they had to depend on this same company for their supplies of fertilizer, which were not forthcoming.

They turned to me.

"Perhaps you can get us export power?"

"How can I, a foreigner, get you export power, if you can't get it from your own government?" I asked.

They thought all foreigners were friends with Deng Xiaoping, and that I could use my influence to help them. It was a sign of how desperate and out of touch they were.

With currency resources scarce, government officials in many parts of the country forced the peasants to accept special certificates in lieu of cash for their crops. The peasants suffered even more as the hard-pressed government proved unable or unwilling to redeem these special certificates. Lacking both incentive and fertilizer, peasants again cut back on efforts to increase such crops as grain and cotton, and held back sales of grain to the state.

Even in this area in which the Chinese economy had performed best—agriculture—government ineptitude was terrifying. People feared a return to the situation that existed in China from the time of the Communist victory in 1949 until 1976, when, with the exception of only one year, 1957, per capita food consumption in the erstwhile Middle Kingdom failed to reach even the meager levels that had existed in the country before World War II.

Faced with this crisis, the hard-liners reacted. In late 1988 they took over economic policy from Zhao Ziyang. In early 1989 a pullback began. In March 1989, on the eve of the outbreak of student demonstrations, Li Peng announced new austerity measures. Speaking to the meeting of the National People's Congress, he called for sacrifice and greater controls over the economy. China had tried to change too fast. Income distribution was far out of line. In order to remedy this situation, consumption was to be cut. Central planning would again take precedence. Some reforms needed to be rolled back. Only defense, agriculture, and education would receive more money.

This should have served as a warning to observers. Agriculture and education were falling apart; they needed the money. But why defense? In 1985 the government had decided that the People's Liberation Army would go hungry while the civilian sector developed. Since that time the military budget had been cut 25 percent. China faced no outside threat. Reversing policy and increasing the military budget at a time when the country was starving for capital indicated that the army's influence was growing just when China could ill afford it.

In the next few days the government announced that it would begin to close some of the small private businesses that used scarce raw materials or seemed inefficient. There was also talk of new taxes on those businesses that remained. State construction projects were delayed. Thus fertilizer and steel production continued to decline, as did badly needed coal. Growth in the old Shanghai factories and in the nation's interior slowed, but coastal areas ignored the new policy and continued to burgeon. More, not less, inequality ensued.

With the dual system of management still in place in the factories, the government could not cut wages. Bonuses continued to be handed out to urban workers. Demand remained high even as real income fell. Only the supplies of badly needed producer industries had been cut. But the state no longer controlled vast portions of the country. During the 1980s the state-owned share of total industrial output had dropped from 80 percent to 64 percent. Growth did not ease, and inflation continued. When state banks halted loans, new coastal businesses turned to private sources.

This growing contradiction between public and private sectors led to even more opportunities for graft for party officials. Understandably, they aimed to preserve the new order. As reformers within the upper levels of the government pulled one way, hard-liners at the top pulled the other. As always, workers and peasants, such as Ayi and her family, were caught in the middle.

5

THE CRUMBLING OF THE OLD ORDER

Before I arrived in China early in 1989, I had been told that moderates and hard-liners were enmeshed in a struggle that had paralyzed the highest levels of the regime. As each side reached out for support, popular movements were alternately encouraged and then discouraged. Those in the middle waited to see which faction would win and refused to act. This political deadlock was leading to chaos in the streets. "Soon," one of my Chinese friends argued, "there will be either a popular rebellion or a military crackdown."

When I disembarked in Beijing, things appeared calmer than I had been led to believe. People looked comfortable. I saw only one street fight during my first week in town. At first glance it seemed that nothing was going on. I knew that the economy had problems, but perhaps the government was dealing with them.

On closer inspection, the calm proved deceptive. Outside the University gates and in other upscale areas of the city, merchants from China's distant Turkish province, Xinjiang,

hawked hashish and marijuana. Taxi drivers refused passen-
gers unless they agreed to pay in foreign currency notes,
which were convertible to many times their official value on
the black market. A group of illicit money changers, who
operated out of an alley near the embassy, had hired guards
with walkie-talkies to stand on the corners and warn them of
impending police patrols. Pornographic books were being
sold openly on the streets. Coming back from a short trip to
the nearby city of Tianjin, I shared a cab from the train
station with two expensively attired prostitutes on their way
to a gig at a foreign hotel near the school. When they got out
of the cab, they paid from a wad of cash thicker than my fist
and then demanded a receipt from the driver so they could
show it to their pimp. For someone who had first seen China
during the mid-1970s, when Chairman Mao was still alive,
all this seemed quite strange, but I had seen a lot worse in
other Third World countries, not to mention nearby Taiwan
and Hong Kong or even New York.

I had a real inkling of trouble when I noticed how volatile
students and minority groups had become. Over the past
century, these groups have had much to be discontented
about. They have also been especially sensitive to such issues
as national rights and democracy. The slightest sign of
government weakness has often brought them into the streets.

A number of small incidents between late 1987 and the
spring of 1989 involved students. The biggest was in June
1988. A Beijing University student had been killed in a brawl
with thugs at a restaurant near the campus. In response, his
classmates marched into Tiananmen Square demanding that
the assailants be brought to justice and better security be
provided on the campuses. The protests quickly escalated.
Student posters demanded democracy, a free press, an end to
government corruption, more funding for education, and an
improved legal system. Government leaders, including Li
Peng, Zhao Ziyang, and even Deng Xiaoping, were criticized.

Crowds of demonstrators surging into Tiananmen brought to mind the demonstrations that Deng, in 1976, had used to undermine the Gang of Four. Caught off balance at first, the government soon moved quickly to prevent matters from escalating. When students planned a new march, worried officials hurriedly cordoned off the square. Squads of policemen turned away the few students who dared enter the area. Faced with this pressure, the protests fizzled, but in the coming months grievances against the authorities broke out around the country. The situation seemed more explosive than at any time since the Cultural Revolution.

Hard-liners in the government yearned to deal with the crisis by returning to time-tested methods. Concerned students talked about their fears of the Brezhnevization of Chinese society, a revival of a rigid, highly centralized political structure accompanied by a stagnant economy. It was a fear that had plagued them since 1986. Now they saw it as an imminent reality. For evidence they pointed out that the previous autumn, top party members had met to talk about strengthening party discipline and enhancing the authority of the central government. This was part of the economic retrenchment discussed earlier, under which Zhao Ziyang began to lose power. At the time officials took pains to explain the difference between the purges of corrupt officials which they planned and those carried out during the Cultural Revolution—an ominous sign for those used to reading between the lines.

The plans scared foreign businessmen. They worried that a recentralization of the government would ruin deals they had arranged with many newly independent provincial enterprises and create more red tape for the little business that remained. Chinese authorities assured them there would be little change in economic policy, but there were occasional slips. Vice Premier Wu Xueqian told a group of Japanese corporate executives that foreign investors would face problems in 1989 as the government tried to cut back industrial growth.

The Japanese took the hint. Their investments in China dropped. Urged on by advisers such as Henry Kissinger and former Secretary of State Alexander Haig, American businessmen forged ahead. U.S. investment in China grew to new heights as Americans seemed oblivious of China's mounting political and economic problems. They believed Deng Xiaoping, believed that the reforms were the wave of the future and could not be reversed.

They should have been more sensitive to Chinese history. The repressive May Fourth movement followed several years of rapid economic development and change, as did the Cultural Revolution. Old ways die hard in China. Change leads to pressure from many different directions, both inside and outside the country.

They might also have paid more attention to what was happening in Tibet. Areas on the fringes of any society are often the most sensitive to new currents, providing a barometer for the entire country. In the Soviet Union, the Estonians, Latvians, Lithuanians, Armenians, and Azerbaijanis reacted first to Gorbachev's reforms. In China it was the Tibetans. In 1989 what happened in Tibet foreshadowed what was later to occur in Beijing.

Before the 1980s the Tibetans, like many other Chinese minorities, had suffered onerously under Chinese rule. Their language had been suppressed, their temples destroyed, and their agriculture ruined. During the Cultural Revolution, Red Guards systematically smashed hundreds of precious Tibetan relics and closed all the country's monasteries. The Chinese government allowed few native Tibetans into the new government. It settled hundreds of thousands of ethnic Chinese in the Tibetan capital of Lhasa, where they often occupied former Tibetan homes and businesses. The Tibetans who reacted most strongly to this discrimination were not the oppressed underlings of Tibetan society but the traditional ruling class of the area—the monks and nuns whose monasteries maintained a feudal hold over the region before the Chinese began to integrate Tibet into China in 1959.

In the 1980s the Chinese attempted a new, softer policy toward minorities, especially towards Tibetans. Under this self-proclaimed "enlightened" program, temples were rebuilt, native dress and customs encouraged, millions of dollars in economic aid pumped into the area, and growing numbers of Tibetans brought into the government. Greater local rule meant increased autonomy. But the more people get, the more they want. In Tibet, just as recently in many parts of the Soviet Union, the people took advantage of their new freedom to vent the resentment and bitterness they felt towards their rulers.

In the late 1980s demonstrations erupted in Tibet against the Chinese occupation every winter. Each time, protesting monks and nuns demanded independence for the region. At least four times, fierce fighting broke out between Chinese police and Tibetan nationalists.

Emotions ran high. On one occasion a British tourist wore a T-shirt with a picture of the late American comedian Phil Silvers in the streets of Lhasa. As she strolled into a crowded shopping area, a passing soldier mistook the portrait of the man who once played Sergeant Bilko on TV for Tibet's most revered and holy figure. In a scene that the American actor would have loved, the soldier accosted her and tried to rip the shirt from her back. While this was occurring the befuddled young woman was surrounded by a chanting and screaming mob of Tibetans who excitedly pointed at her chest and cried, "Dalai Lama! Dalai Lama!" Eventually she was whisked to safety.

To the Chinese government this expression of sentiment for the return of the former ruler of the region was not funny, but they tried to accommodate it. In the 1980s the official attitude

towards the Dalai Lama and other members of the traditional
Tibetan ruling class became more tolerant. The Chinese
regime allowed members of the Dalai Lama's entourage to
tour Tibet, and they put out feelers for his return. They
restored monasteries and permitted the training of new monks,
hoping to work with these indigenous authorities to develop
this vast region. But these mixed signals confused local
officials who became unsure about the policy of the central
government towards pro-independence demonstrators. Newly
installed native Tibetan officials, who understandably did not
wish to use force against their own people, may also have
contributed to the problem.

The situation in Tibet mirrored that in China itself. Liberalization placed more power in local hands, especially local
elites. In Tibet, as everywhere else, the Chinese government
found itself at the point of no return. Tibetans did not want
partial control over their own lives, they wanted full control.
They distrusted the representatives of a regime which over
twenty years had taken every possible opportunity to obliter-
ate Tibetan culture and mercilessly persecute the Tibetan
people. Given the opportunity to assemble and speak their
minds, they demanded further self-rule.

The solution would have been the creation of a semi-
autonomous region ruled by Tibetans and linked only tenuously
to Beijing. Such a government would have established a
precedent not only for minority areas such as Tibet but also
for places such as Hong Kong and Taiwan. Although Chinese
officials continue to float the possibility of just such an
arrangement for Taiwan and have promised it in 1997 for
Hong Kong, in the late 1980s hard-liners were not ready to
abandon control over Tibet. Instead the government proclaimed
a new policy of toleration in the region. Tibetans remained
skeptical. Several hundred thousand soldiers continued to be
garrisoned there. Ethnic Chinese, who constituted only 3

percent of the population, filled more than 40 percent of official posts and managed most of the factories and businesses.

Tibetan protests intensified in late December 1988, not long after news of another visit by the Dalai Lama's brother to Beijing failed to arrange for the holy leader to return home. Fighting again erupted. On December 10 about thirty Tibetans marched into the center of Lhasa to confront the authorities. Government spokesmen claimed that the police fired warning shots into the air to frighten the crowd, and a melee broke out. Foreigners who witnessed the incident stated that the Chinese police fired directly into a crowd of peaceful protesters. One person died and thirteen were injured, including a woman from the Netherlands. In an apparent attempt to justify the injury of a foreigner in this incident, the Chinese labeled her an agent of the Dalai Lama.

Throughout the twentieth century, when faced with threats to its power from groups which it had encouraged in order to effect change, the Chinese government has been divided between a policy of toleration and one of decisive action. Confronted by new outbreaks of violence in Tibet, many in the government were reluctant to jeopardize the new, more tolerant policy towards the region. As late as March 1989, moderate government spokesmen had argued that more autonomy was necessary for the region. These officials sought to make the region an example for all those groups pushing for more independence from the central government. They worried about what a crackdown might do to the tourist industry in the area. Before the year was over, a tough new Chinese official, Hu Jintao, was brought in to take charge of the Communist party in Tibet. But with conflicting orders from the central government he proved just as indecisive as his predecessors.

Demonstrations continued into 1989 and grew more serious in late February and early March. As March 10 approached—the thirtieth anniversary of the failed Tibetan uprising and the subsequent flight of the Dalai Lama—monks and their supporters became increasingly militant.

On March 5 about forty people began a peaceful demonstration around the Jokhang Temple in the center of the Tibetan quarter of Lhasa. Chinese police, watching the parade from the roof, pelted the demonstrators with empty beer bottles. A few angry protesters threw stones back at them. Without warning, the police then drew their guns and fired into the crowd, killing three people. When word of what had happened got back to Tibet University about an hour later, a mob of angry students rushed into the city and drove the police out of the Tibetan quarter. Over the next few days the demonstrations escalated. At least three times, soldiers poured into the city shooting wildly into the crowds, but when the Tibetans pelted them with stones from the rooftops of neighboring buildings the army retreated, giving the people a sense of victory and further inflaming their militance. For a while it seemed that the demonstrators had "liberated" whole areas of the city.

When the situation reached this crisis state, the hard-liners finally acted decisively. On March 7 Chinese Premier Li Peng imposed martial law in Lhasa. The next day more than two thousand soldiers entered the city and began arresting rioters. But whenever the soldiers withdrew from an area, protesters returned it to the "hands of the people." In frustration, troops fired randomly into mobs of assembled civilians. Thousands were dragged from their homes and put under detention. Foreigners reported hundreds of casualties. Having waited so long to act, the government now felt it could deliver its message only with brute force and violence.

In a warning of what was to come, the government denied the casualties and blamed the disturbances on a small number of conspirators whom they labeled "splitists." These splitists, it was claimed, were egged on by foreign interests. Li Peng spoke of "outrageous foreign interference" in the region.

One of my students, who had been visiting Tibet that March, was trapped in a small hotel known as the Yak in the old Tibetan part of town while the fighting raged outside his door. After the army quelled the unrest, they ordered foreigners out of the area, charging them exorbitant prices for the transportation they were forced to take to return home. When Alex protested that the government was making a profit on his expulsion, he was hauled into a local police station and accused of being one of the foreign splitists.

Few Chinese proponents of democratic rights spoke out against the suppression of the Tibetans. Two notable exceptions were the 1987 dissident leader Fang Lizhi and the writer and philosopher Wang Ruowang. Most other leading liberal intellectuals either supported the government's actions or refused to comment. On college campuses in Beijing, many of the same students later to be active in the democratic movement argued that the Tibetans had provoked the government. The only solution, one claimed, was "to wipe out the Tibetan language and culture." Native Tibetans, another suggested, "are spiritualistic. It is our duty to develop them into materialists." Even Taiwanese spokesmen supported the Chinese government's quelling of the riots.

To Chinese of all stripes, Tibet is part of China, and they did not mind seeing privileged minorities dealt with harshly. Although it would have been difficult for most outsiders to regard as privileged the generally impoverished and oppressed non-Chinese minorities, many Chinese saw it differently. They pointed to the "double standard" employed by their government in its dealings with minorities, allowing them, for instance, to be exempted from the government's "one-child, one family" birth policy and granting them clothing and food allowances not available in other parts of China. At a time when many Chinese felt themselves to be poor and underprivileged, the government's attempt to respond to some of the needs and customs of 6 percent of the population was not at all popular.

But there were other reasons for this lack of sympathy on the part of most Chinese towards the brutality with which their government had treated the Tibetans. Few knew about it. It was covered up in the Chinese media. Those who did know paid little attention. Tibet is far away. Few realized until it was too late that once they allowed the Chinese government to treat others in this imperious and brutal fashion, it might some day be hard to stop them from acting in a similar manner towards their own people.

Resentments about and insensitivity toward minorities caused other problems in China in late 1988 and early 1989. Concern that the advancement of others may be impeding one's own progress plagues all societies. These fears are particularly serious in an impoverished country such as China, where even a tiny difference in the way the pie is cut can be a matter of life and death for many. A strong central government can prevent these animosities from causing problems. But by 1989 reforms had weakened the Chinese government, and no one had a simple fix for putting it back together. As government leaders bickered with one another, volatile elements, such as minorities and students, continued to agitate.

When I lived in China in 1980–1981 I was continually amazed at the level of prejudice against blacks in Chinese society. Once I heard an otherwise sensitive and intelligent Chinese student lapse into a tirade against the savagery and stupidity of Africans, peppering his speech with the Chinese equivalents of words like "nigger" and "jungle bunny." Standing next to us throughout most of this conversation was a group of African students, long resident in China, who spoke perfect Mandarin.

I interrupted my acquaintance to ask him how he could say such things, especially in front of African students. He looked amazed at my question.

"How can they possibly understand me?" he asked. "They're not capable of learning Chinese."

Over the years this insensitivity towards Africans has led to several racist incidents on Chinese campuses in spite of attempts by the Chinese government to encourage friendly relations with African countries. In 1989, at a Christmas Day dance at Hehai University in Nanjing, two African students brought Chinese women to the party. A scuffle erupted with Chinese students and staff. According to official reports, two Africans were injured as were eleven Chinese, one seriously. Had the incident ended there, it might have been just another example of the latent racism on most Chinese campuses. But this time things got out of hand. Chinese students surrounded the African students' dormitory and pelted it with stones and bricks for most of the night. The next day the crowd returned. After breaking through the main gate, they vandalized the dormitory, beating any student they could find. For the next four days thousands of Chinese marched through the streets screaming anti-black epithets, sitting in at the Public Security Bureau to demand that the Africans be brought to justice, and terrorizing the foreign dormitories. When 135 beleaguered Africans, accompanied by a few dark-skinned Asians afraid of being mistaken for Africans, as well as some sympathetic Americans and Europeans, fled the University to the railroad station, the police gathered them into custody and sequestered them in a nearby guesthouse. A few days later the police surrounded this building. Using clubs and electric cattle prods, they beat the students, forcing some to return to their universities and detaining others. Some reporters claimed that one group of students was stripped naked, taken outside into the freezing cold, and tortured.

Although the actions of the police in this case were inexplicable and unconscionable, it should be noted that not all Chinese are racist and that the hostility which the Chinese students expressed towards their African compatriots was not necessarily a result of racial antagonism. Students were frustrated by their own deteriorating living and working conditions.

This was a long-standing student problem. During the dynastic period, distraught students with little hope of passing their examinations after years of study felt indignant when they were forced to occupy dirty, excrement-ridden lodging and examination booths as they crowded into the cities for their periodic tests. Similar problems have haunted China in more modern times. Concerns about lack of opportunity and resentment over inadequate, cramped living and working conditions also helped set off students in 1905, in the May Fourth era, and during the Cultural Revolution.

In 1989 the same problems recurred. Chinese educators had received few personal benefits from the rapid economic progress of the 1980s. By the latter part of the decade, university professors, once the most esteemed and highly paid group in China, received less than taxi drivers or some independent produce merchants. With an annual inflation rate of 20 to 30 percent, professors' salaries were barely adequate to provide food and clothing for their families. By 1987, spending on institutional frills was twice as high as all official expenditure on education. A 1988 survey found that the average college graduate earned about $9 per month less than those who had not gone to college. It also determined that intellectuals had less leisure time than other urban residents, contemplated an average life span of just fifty-eight years (ten years under the national average), and earned lower wages than common factory workers.

For students the situation was particularly bleak—worse, in many cases, than it had been for their rebellious colleagues earlier in this century. Chinese students were assigned to various university departments on the basis of standardized exams. Later these same students were often forced to accept jobs in small towns or in the countryside under dismal conditions and at poor salaries, a sorry fate for those who considered themselves among the best and brightest of their society. They were incensed that corrupt, know-nothing officials lived a life of leisure while they existed in squalor. The number of undergraduates leaving school rose 45 percent in 1988, and the number who went on to graduate school fell 75 percent.

The student plight attracted national attention early in 1989 when a college student advertised for a wife in a small paper in south central China. A young woman reader wrote to say that no one would want to marry him, but if someone did, he should try to make sure that his children did not continue on in school. "Five years of elementary school is enough; everyone nowadays uses computers," she argued. The position of intellectuals in China, the woman continued, was lower than that of beggars. "Learning is not food on the table." Although a number of readers wrote to defend the student, many also wrote to express agreement with this scathing denunciation of intellectuals.

Faced with mockery by their own countrymen, Chinese students particularly resented the disparity between their situation and that of foreign students on their own campuses. Throughout this century the Chinese have been sensitive to the way foreigners have treated them and thought about them. During the New Culture movement seventy years earlier, the same Chinese students interested in importing Western ideas and methods also took to the streets on May 4, 1919, to protest foreign slights to their country at Versailles. Lu Xun, China's most famous writer of this period, once observed that his countrymen either looked up to foreigners "as gods or down on them as wild animals."

In 1989 many Chinese felt that the difference between the way they were treated and the way African students were treated was unfair. Even at the very best universities, Chinese students lived in dormitories worse than most slums. Closet-sized rooms were shared by six to eight undergraduates, or four to six graduate students, or even two or three single teachers. Broken windowpanes and blackened and crumbling walls were the norm. Concrete stairways between floors were unlit and usually in disrepair. In the rooms there was little space to move, sit, or even store belongings. Living and studying took place on hard, ragged bunk beds. In the summer these rooms felt like furnaces; in the winter they were cold. Even in the frigid north, the heat was not turned on before November 1, and when it was, it rarely rose above the mid-fifties. There was no hot water in any of the dormitories—students had to walk to the other side of the campus for baths. Hundreds were forced to share one communal toilet. The smell and sanitary conditions in these rooms was unspeakable, and the lighting, even when it worked, was almost useless. Food was so terrible that many students could not eat it. A number of foreigners teaching in China talked of seeing their students collapse in the classroom from hunger and malnutrition.

By contrast, the conditions under which foreign students in China lived, although Spartan by most standards, seemed luxurious. Most of the dormitories for foreign students had hot water, adequate plumbing, relatively spacious rooms, and better food. It rankled Chinese that most African students, unlike most other foreigners studying in China, had been provided scholarships by the Chinese government to live and study in these comparatively comfortable surroundings. At Hehai University, where the anti-African demonstrations first erupted, for example, African students lived one to a room. At other schools two shared a room. Chinese students resented their government providing these resources to foreigners while denying them to their own people. University administrators and teachers also objected to the granting of scarce housing and teaching facilities to foreign students at a time when university resources were strapped.

These resentments do not excuse the anti-African outbursts of Chinese students. Nor do they explain why the government did not move immediately to stop them and in fact appeared to side with the Chinese students. A television broadcast showed weeping relatives of the injured Chinese worker, giving credence to the rumor that he had been killed by the Africans. It took the city newspapers four days to clarify the situation.

That the authorities allowed the Hehai incident to get so far out of hand indicates the administrative decay engulfing China by late 1988. Central authorities did nothing until early January, after the protests spread to nearby Hangzhou and Wuhan, and then to Shanghai and Beijing, where Chinese students emphasized the need for improved living conditions.

The government was now weaker and more divided than it had been during the student demonstrations of 1986–1987. Its responses to both the situation in Tibet and that of the African students appeared slow and bumbling. By the spring of 1989, moderate elements within the government, along with various democratic and dissident groups, went on the attack.

The previous summer, leading intellectuals had organized what became known as "democracy salons" on the campus of Beijing University. Held outdoors every Wednesday, these forums were usually attended by Western journalists and even embassy officials. Many of the students later to play a prominent role in the Tiananmen demonstrations met at the salons to discuss ideas about democracy. Much of the discussion was inane, but it fostered an atmosphere of dissent and daring. Prominent liberal intellectuals in China came to discuss their notions of democracy with the students. Having ended the previous summer, the salons resumed in the spring of 1989 under the leadership of Wang Dan, a Beijing University undergraduate in history and later one of China's most prominent student activists.

As students talked together about their ideas for democracy

and reform, they began to divide into small informal organizations which would later serve as a base for political action. Groups based on personal ties formed in these kinds of small, informal units had been the basis of most major political activities in China's recent history. They were to become so again.

Meanwhile, groups which had formed earlier among older intellectuals also boldly began to exploit the growing political vacuum, attempting to open up the political process. In December 1988 the prominent political theorist Su Shaozhi, formerly head of the officially sponsored Marxism-Leninism Research Institute at the Chinese Academy of Social Sciences, mounted a withering attack on Marxism at a top-level theoretical meeting. In his talk Su scolded the Chinese Communist party for its criticism and persecution of scholars and intellectuals and its outright ban of study in many fields of inquiry. Su suggested that Marxism had fallen behind the times and needed to be reassessed.

Su, who had been dismissed from his post because of his support of the 1986 student demonstrations, had made such statements before to private gatherings. The fact that he now spoke this way at a meeting called to celebrate the beginning of the reform movement was noteworthy, but it would have passed with little fanfare had his talk not been printed a few weeks later in a liberal Shanghai weekly, the *World Economic Herald*. Immediately, hard-liners called for the firing of the daring editor of the paper, seventy-one-year-old Qin Benli. The party propaganda department condemned the article, suggesting that its motive was to "rehabilitate" Su and "expose internal party matters to the public."

But Qin showed himself to be quick on his feet. While the slow-moving government debated his fate, Qin accepted an invitation from the *Wall Street Journal* to visit the United States. There he wangled a breakfast meeting with President George Bush. Qin introduced himself to Bush as the editor of the *World Economic Herald.* After that, hard-liners left Qin alone for a while.

As proponents of democracy gathered strength, tradition came under attack—as it had during earlier protest movements. During the May Fourth movement, radical intellectuals had used assaults on tradition to undermine the authority of the old regime. This cultural iconoclasm had been a precursor to political action. Now a television series provided the impetus. In the spring of 1988 the series *River Elegy* had mounted a devastating critique of China's traditional culture which outraged China's hard-liners. They complained that the series constituted a movement to "kill the fathers" (words almost exactly like those used to criticize Chen Duxiu's anti-Confucianism seventy years earlier). They managed to prohibit a repeat showing of the series in the fall.

But by the spring of 1989 intellectuals had become even more daring in their attacks on tradition. At one avant-garde display of "performance art" in February, some of the exhibitors threw coins and condoms and washed their feet in public. The most startling entry came from a young woman who walked up to her work, called "Dialogue," pulled out a pistol, and fired two bullets into it. Her act got the show closed for five days.

Throughout China that spring, books and artwork that would have been considered blatantly pornographic even in the West were published and openly displayed. New underground works about the Cultural Revolution circulated. Women demanded that the government do something about sexist job and wage discrimination. The "one child, one family" policy, many pointed out, had resulted in female babies being killed in the countryside by parents who desired boys. Highly qualified women were dismissed from jobs to make way for men. Young women graduates had an impossible time finding jobs.

Chinese intellectuals began to turn from cultural reform to

political action, preparing the way for the events of June 1989. Early that year the Peking Spring democratic movement, the group behind the democracy wall posters and leaflets banned in 1979, reorganized to campaign openly for the release of Deng Xiaoping's nemesis, the imprisoned dissident Wei Jingsheng. The campaign began with a small notice in the January issue of the leftist Hong Kong magazine *Cheng Ming*. Appealing on behalf of itself and five other organizations in Hong Kong and France, the magazine called for the release of Wei and other political prisoners.

At about the same time, the hero of the 1986 student demonstrations, Fang Lizhi, wrote to Deng Xiaoping also seeking the release of Wei Jingsheng and all other political prisoners. Fang reminded Deng that 1989 was the two hundredth anniversary of the French Revolution and that "liberty, equality, and fraternity" were values shared by people throughout the world. On February 13 a similar petition was sent to the government from thirty-three prominent intellectuals in Beijing. A week later, one of the signatories to this letter, Chen Jun, persuaded others to endorse it. Before he was through, 3,400 people were said to have signed.

Foreign supporters now grew interested, and Amnesty International helped form an "Amnesty 89" working group. Signature campaigns began in Hong Kong, Taiwan, and other places overseas. In Hong Kong the organizers called themselves the April 5 Action Group in memory of the April 5, 1976, demonstrations in Tiananmen that had been honored by Deng Xiaoping. In a foreshadowing of what was to come, dissident groups reflected the same disorganization and lack of focus evident in the government they attacked. Not confining themselves to calls for the release of political prisoners in China, some petitioners demanded democratic elections and a correction of human rights abuses in China; others appealed for the intervention of Western governments; still others addressed abuses in Taiwan and Hong Kong as well as in the

People's Republic. As the campaign gained momentum, one group of signatories called for the further development of capitalism in China. Another denounced the intervention of foreign governments in China's problems and called for the "working masses" to seize control of the political and economic levers of the country.

All this aroused Deng Xiaoping's concern for party discipline and control. Government spokesmen began to complain of those who were "influencing judicial independence in the Wei Jingsheng case." They argued that Wei Jingsheng had been properly imprisoned as a result of his "counterrevolutionary agitation." Deng supposedly told party members, "We should not fear what foreigners say." Democracy, it was said, would be destabilizing to China.

As protests swelled, the government once again talked tough but failed to act decisively. The hesitation encouraged radicals towards more militant action. More and more influential people joined the campaign within China. In the second week of March 1989, forty-two senior scientists signed a petition demanding greater democracy, freedom of the press, and freedom of speech and publication, more money for education, and the release of political prisoners. The petition asserted: "World history and China's experience show that political democratization, including a legal system, is necessary to guarantee economic reform and the whole modernization [program]." Another petition was signed by forty-three well-known journalists and intellectuals.

Partly in response to this campaign, officials at the United States Embassy persuaded members of the White House staff to invite the dissident leader Fang Lizhi to attend a dinner hosted by President George Bush during his visit to China in February 1989. Also invited were prominent members of the Chinese government. In an incident that attracted international attention, the Chinese police intercepted the taxi in which

Fang was riding on his way to the dinner on the evening of February 26, and prevented him from attending.

The decision to stop Fang, it was said, had been Secretary General Zhao Ziyang's. Hard-liners held him responsible for the growing dissident movement. Some of his close allies had encouraged the dissidents, and Zhao himself seems to have realized that political reform would be necessary to keep economic reforms moving. But now to protect himself in high party circles he found it necessary to stop Fang.

On March 28 the government made the point more bluntly. It refused to allow into China a petition on human rights intended for presentation to the Chinese National People's Congress and signed by more than 22,000 people from some thirty nations. Most of the signers were students and workers from Hong Kong and Taiwan. The government also denied entry to a member of the delegation carrying the petition, a Hong Kong journalist named Chong See-ming, who in the past had often criticized the government in a Hong Kong left-wing publication. A few days later, on April 7, the government deported the democratic activist Chen Jun, who was married to a British citizen and held a green card in the United States.

Further evidence of a crackdown came during the 1989 session of the National People's Congress, China's largest and most representative government body. The preceding year many delegates to the congress had engaged in free-wheeling criticism of the government. Now outspoken delegates were silenced and isolated from the foreign press. Dissident members of the Chinese press corps, such as reporters from the Shanghai *World Economic Herald*, were warned not to attend or were told to muffle their coverage.

Among significant issues discussed at the congress was education. At the 1988 congress, Chinese intellectuals had openly campaigned for more funds for education, complaining about the poor condition of the universities. In response,

Premier Li Peng had suggested that the problem of poor pay for intellectuals could be corrected if they would take second jobs to supplement their income. This so outraged intellectuals that a group of students "sarcastically offered to shine the shoes of NPC delegates." In 1989 the central government attempted to be more responsive. In officially published remarks, Deng Xiaoping told a visiting Ugandan delegation that "Our biggest mistake over the past ten years has been the insufficient development of education." But Deng's expressions of concern proved to be only words. The 1989 congress adjourned without making substantive changes in educational policy.

In fact, the government seemed deadlocked over just about everything. Officials spoke about tightening up the economy, but their actions did little but antagonize local interests. They delayed in Tibet, then acted heavy-handedly. They allowed local authorities to respond tactlessly and ineptly to the riot against African students, with dismal results. They decried pornography and dissent but failed to stop it.

Nor were there decisions about political change. In mid-April, on the eve of the student demonstrations that ended in the Tiananmen massacre, reports circulated in Hong Kong of a "dump Zhao Ziyang movement." Leading the charge were conservative party elders Chen Yun, Bo Yibo, Wang Zhen, Hu Qiaomu, Li Xiannian, and Peng Zhen—all men thought to be retired. Two decades earlier, attempting to push an aging Mao aside to preserve party discipline and order, they had set the stage for the Cultural Revolution in which they themselves had been victimized. Now the group was said to believe that Zhao's liberal policies were responsible for the economic crisis plaguing China. They believed Zhao had undermined the party. By sacking him they hoped to reverse his reformist policies. Deng was said to be resisting these efforts, but adding weight to rumors of a power struggle was the postponement of the Fourth Party Central Committee

Plenum, a key leadership organ which had been expected to meet early in the year.

Zhao Ziyang and the people around him acknowledged the crisis. Deep within the bowels of the Chinese Communist party, from the think tank gathered around Zhao Ziyang, reformist intellectuals with good organizational loyalties threw out for public discussion a program they called the "new authoritarianism." This ominous-sounding doctrine, proposed by some of those later to be in the forefront of student protests in April and early May, acknowledged that the reform movement had resulted in a breakdown of much traditional authority. While China adjusted to these changes a new kind of authority would be established to guide the country through the period of transition. China should imitate the model of such conservative Asian regimes as South Korea and Taiwan, where a strong autocratic political system combined with a relatively free economic sector had allowed for continued development. Some argued that the "new authoritarianism" was a necessary stage through which all underdeveloped countries must pass. Others suggested that it was simply a helpful administrative structure, a way of melding the existing political system with a plan for continued economic liberalization and development.

Within the context of Chinese politics the new authoritarianism was considered a reformist idea. Those who proposed the plan hoped that a strongman would emerge in China to guarantee economic rights. Only in this way, it was felt, could China modernize and create the conditions for the kind of democratization that seemed to be occurring in Taiwan and South Korea in early 1989.

The debate reflected the fear of many at the highest reaches of power that a triumph by hard-liners might undermine economic changes and further postpone political reform. The people who proposed the new authoritarianism all had contact with Zhao Ziyang. This theory allowed him to show his critics that reform in China was possible without destroying the political authority of the Chinese Communist party.

Many reformers, however, opposed the idea of the new authoritarianism. Theorists such as Su Shaozhi, whose speech criticizing the party had caused such a stir when it was reported in the *World Economic Herald*, called the idea a proposal for "elite politics" and suggested that neglecting "rule by law" in favor of "rule by man" was always a mistake. A former member of the public security bureau pointed out that "authoritarianism" was "a return to feudalism." The liberal intellectual Yan Jiaqi argued that the best kind of authoritarianism for China would be one based on law.

What these radicals failed to address was the problem of keeping China together under a democratic system. In a way, the problems faced by China in the 1980s were similar to those of the period after the May Fourth incident as represented by Ba Jin in his famous novel *Family*. Although the young broke loose from the hypocritical authority of the despotic old grandfather, when he died they acknowledged that there was no one else to hold the society together. Chinese youth now clearly saw Deng Xiaoping as the tyrant he was, but they offered no person or system to take his place.

Instead, having broken out of Deng's shadow, they began to reassess what had really happened during the Cultural Revolution. They believed that this period illustrated the dangers of an old man, long past his peak, who still exercised power in China, and the influence which a student movement could have on the government.

Now, reformers and liberals were incited by winds of change in eastern Europe and the Soviet Union. In the 1960s Mao had worried that China was becoming the bureaucratic counterrevolutionary state he saw established in the Soviet Union after the death of Stalin. In the 1980s Mao was, in a sense, vindicated as China became an example of liberal reform for other communist countries. But in 1989 Chinese students and intellectuals saw an even freer expression of ideas in the Soviet Union and in the Eastern bloc. They envied plans for new elections in these countries and ogled the legitimization of Solidarity in Poland. They determined that whatever the Russians and Poles could do, they could do better.

Facing a crisis in the reform movement, student and intellectual leaders planned a test of the hard-liners. They made preparations for demonstrations on May 4, 1989, to commemorate the seventieth anniversary of the student movement that had launched the Chinese Communist party and dramatically altered Chinese history. A new wave of student protests had long been expected. In late February an unnamed high-ranking cadre in the party propaganda department had responded to the new amnesty proposals of Chinese intellectuals by suggesting that the government was "worried that this may spread to students." By the spring, everyone knew something was afoot. The reformers who planned these demonstrations believed that the only hope for continued reform was a showdown between them and the now discredited central government. They knew that their plans were dangerous, but they determined to repeat the success of their grandfathers in 1919.

By April dissidents of all stripes as well as reformers within the Communist party hoped and planned for change. They knew they had to act, because in the alleys and courtyards of the Forbidden City, hard-liners also hatched plots. The old men who lived with the ghosts of former emperors exercised their influence over obscure government committees and military units in ways that few outside China could understand. They too did not like what they saw in the country. When pushed, they still had a few tricks they could use.

China was on the point of explosion. The economy had

fallen apart. The social fabric of the country was rent. The government no longer commanded respect. Political infighting had led to multiple centers of power. Everyone, it seemed, waited for a spark. Events came to a head before the May 4 anniversary, triggered by the death on April 15, 1989, of Hu Yaobang.

6

IGNITING THE MOVEMENT

On April 15 the Chinese government announced that Hu Yaobang, ousted secretary general of the Chinese Communist party, had died at the age of seventy-three. Word quickly spread that Hu had suffered a heart attack a few days earlier, during an argument over educational policy at a meeting of the Politburo. The image of Hu clutching his chest and falling to the floor as he shouted at colleagues about higher salaries for teachers and better living conditions for students was a compelling one. Intellectuals, even those not particularly enamored with Hu while he lived, felt saddened by his death. Many had nurtured the hope that Hu, like Deng Xiaoping before him, would some day be brought back into the top leadership of the party.

Groups of students gathered that night to discuss what Hu had meant to them. While in office he had been known more for his words than his actions. His irreverent, off-the-cuff remarks—suggesting, for example, that Chinese abandon chopsticks for more sanitary knives and forks—alienated as many people as they attracted during his lifetime. But death placed him in a new light. He was remembered as the only Chinese leader to have stood up for intellectuals and to have supported new ideas. Everyone recalled how he had been the first major Chinese official to put aside his old Mao jacket and make a regular practice of wearing Western-style suits and ties. They recollected how he had once even remarked, "Marx and Lenin can't solve all our problems," a statement which horrified party elders quickly forced him to modify.

His death, everyone understood, had occurred at a critical juncture in Chinese history. The deadlock between moderates and hard-liners had stalled further reform. In discussion after discussion it was pointed out that even after his demotion, Hu had continued to serve as a voting member of the seventeen-person Politburo. Many feared they had lost the most forceful proponent of continued change at the top level of the government. They worried that one less reform vote in this small body would tilt policy even more in favor of the hard-liners.

The anguish which Hu Yaobang's supporters felt at his death was compounded by earlier expectations for his resurgence: for several months there had been rumors of his return to power. During the meeting of the National People's Congress in late March and early April, television cameras and newspapers had frequently reported on his activities. Secretary General Zhao Ziyang had praised him, and it was said that Deng Xiaoping had agreed with the idea of allowing the former leader to return to office. In retrospect, given the political climate of the time, this move was highly unlikely; the government's hard-line policies towards the National People's Congress made it clear that reformers were continuing to lose power. But the fact that many intellectuals took the idea seriously indicates how widely speculative the Chinese political scene had become by the spring of 1989.

Under these circumstances it was not surprising that many observers alluded to mysteries surrounding Hu's death. His initial heart attack occurred on April 8. When he suddenly took ill again, it was rumored to be under suspicious circumstances. Whether this scuttlebutt was true or not—and it seems quite unlikely—it was another indication of the great distrust which many felt for the Chinese government.

The authorities appeared not to know how to deal with Hu's death. One rumor claimed that the Central Committee had rewritten his obituary four or five times before acknowledging that he had been "a brilliant leader of the party." In the final draft Deng Xiaoping supposedly crossed out Zhao Ziyang's description of Hu as a "great Marxist." But he did allow the party to announce that Hu would be given a full state funeral with a special memorial service to be held in the Great Hall of the People. This was an unusual honor for someone no longer considered to be in good standing with the party. Students quickly took advantage of these mixed signals to advance their own ideas.

Within hours after the report of Hu's death, wall posters appeared on all the major campuses in China, mourning Hu's loss and demanding that the tasks he started be completed. One Beijing University poster, later copied at other schools, read: "Those who die should still live. Those who live should have died."

Particularly hard hit by the news of Hu's death was a small group of graduate students studying in the Department of Chinese Communist Party History at the prestigious People's University. Before the Cultural Revolution, People's University had been the Chinese Communist party's own school. Although it is now under the direction of the state education commission, it was founded to train Communist party cadres. According to campus wall posters, more high-level Communist cadres still come from this school than any other in the country, and as many as 11 percent of its students are the children of high-level government officials, including the grandson of former Chairman Mao Zedong.

People's University is the only school in China that has an official Department of Chinese Communist Party History. This group of students is selected from the entering student body and delegated to study the origin and basis of party doctrine. They are the keepers of the flame of ideological purity. Those engaged in graduate work in this area are often politically ambitious. Many were known to have been close to the people around Secretary General Zhao Ziyang. Rong Jian, who wrote the article in the Shanghai *World Economic Herald* and first proposed the idea of the new authoritarianism, emerged from the closely associated Institute on Marxist-Leninist Thought at the school.

Many of the Party History graduate students and a number of others from People's University had been adherents of the new authoritarianism. In April 1989 they abandoned this doctrine. Like many government reformers, including, apparently, Zhao Ziyang, they realized that further economic reform could not take place without political change. They decided to try to open up the political process.

These views were not monopolized by the Party History Department. People's University had several other strong departments whose members shared this outlook. The school, for instance, had the first journalism department in the country. Students from this department were exceptionally active in the movement as were those from the Chinese department. In all these departments, students were selected because of their ability to write and reflect on Chinese matters. By definition they were not as conversant in English or as knowledgeable about Western society as some students from other schools who later joined the movement.

Not all students from these departments were active in the movement. Nor were most of the faculty. Several senior members of the Party History Department with whom I spoke, for instance, seemed to have no idea of what was happening with the movement. The graduate students were the ones who had the contacts, the ideas, and the ambition.

And it was these graduate students who took the first decisive action. After hearing the news of Hu's death, a group of Party History graduate students talked late into the night. At three in the morning they rode their bicycles downtown to place the first wreath on the monument to the Heroes of the Revolution in Tiananmen Square, mourning the death of Hu Yaobang.

This is the same monument on which the first wreaths honoring Zhou Enlai appeared in 1976 before the demonstrations in Tiananmen that year. In 1976 Deng had encouraged these outpourings of grief for a fallen leader which were combined with disgust for the political process. His support for these protests, later brutally suppressed by the government, gave Deng's opponents the excuse to purge him from office in 1976. When his political power was later reinstated, he reversed the verdicts on all those who had been implicated in this incident. Now, thirteen years later, Deng was on the other side of the renewed Tiananmen protests. In 1989 he was not happy to hear about the new wreaths.

The students who bicycled to Tiananmen late the night of April 15 had ties high up in the party. They were not the young student demonstrators whom the American public later saw on television. The colorful TV personalities did not provide the original impetus for the movement. Leadership came from scholarly members of the Chinese Communist party with high-level connections, an elite corps of students at People's University. They were graduate students in their late twenties and early thirties. Although their actions were impulsive, they were based on a deep understanding of Chinese history and politics.

In placing their wreath, these People's University graduate students also deliberately attached to it their names and that of their school and department—Party History. This was a

BEIJING
SHOWING LOCATIONS
IMPORTANT TO
THE BOOK

TO
SUMMER
PALACE

BEIJING ZOO

BEIHAI
PARK

Dongdan St.

Wangfujing St.

Jianguomen wai

TEMPLE
OF
HEAVEN
(TIANTAN)

Water

Streets

Railways

1 Beijing Foreign Affairs Institute
2 Beijing Hotel
3 Beijing Normal University
4 Beijing University
5 Central Academy of Fine Arts
6 Foreign Languages Institute
7 Friendship Store
8 Great Wall Hotel
9 Muxidi
10 Old Beijing University
11 People's University
12 Railway Station
13 Tiananmen Square
14 Zhongnanhai

daring act. When people saw the name "Department of Chinese Communist Party History, People's University," they realized that behind this demonstration was not merely a gaggle of disgruntled youth but rather protesters with solid party ties and a profound understanding of Marxist theory.

The leading role of People's University students showed, first, that those who started the protests were not the "Western democrats" which the foreign press often made them out to be. They acted because they felt deeply about the Chinese Communist party and were upset by the corruption and bureaucracy they saw undermining it. They hoped to introduce democratic principles to the party and make it more responsible to the people. It is tempting to say that this stance was a result of worldly influence, but in fact it had been a current within the party from its founding. In the past, many of these democratic dissidents had been labeled Trotskyites or rightists.

The leading role played by People's University cadres also illustrated, once again, the importance of political connections in China. Chinese student movements have been most successful when they have enjoyed secret support from the political establishment. As earlier chapters have shown, Chinese leaders have a long history of using student frustrations to advance their own political causes. It is therefore tempting to believe that the protests of 1989 also were instigated by government officials, eager to send a message to their political opponents.

Given the leading role exercised by students from the Party History Department at People's University, this seems a credible assumption. It is one alleged in a general way by the Chinese government, which has sought to prove that the student activities were fomented by Zhao Ziyang, secretary general of the party. But because their actions were taken so quickly, it is unlikely that Zhao had a direct hand in what the students did. The decision to bicycle to the square was made suddenly, only hours after the students first heard the news of Hu's death. Isolated on their campus, away from the center of the city and difficult to reach by phone, the students would have had little time to meet with a high political official such as Zhao. Although I heard rumors that they may have spoken with staff members close to him, the students who took part in this first protest assured me that they acted entirely on their own.

At least in part, their answer was disingenuous. When they placed the first wreath on the square they surely understood the political consequences of what they were doing, even if they did not imagine how large a movement they were about to create. The Party History students comprehended the political struggles then occurring within the Chinese government. They had a good appreciation of political and social developments. They knew how controversial Hu Yaobang had been and understood that in mourning him they were pressuring the Chinese government. They must also have hoped they would influence other groups to take similar action.

Certainly these students were interested in changing the political tide. They knew very well just how large a movement had been ignited by the laying of wreaths in 1976. They had participated in discussions about the planned May 4 demonstrations. They were close to some of those officials around Zhao Ziyang. In light of all this, there may have been a very thin line between their so-called spontaneous actions and those prompted by higher authorities; but given the importance now placed on this distinction by members of the Chinese Communist party—making it literally a matter of life and death—it should be said that the students did not cross the line.

As Communist party stalwarts, they were demonstrating their desire to rid the party of the problems they felt plagued it. They did not believe that these problems would be resolved in a matter of days, weeks, or even months. "We are," one of them told me, "creating a new May Fourth movement. This one will be much more difficult to implement than was the last one. In the 1920s and 1930s it was only necessary to make the masses conscious of foreign invaders about to take over their country. This was relatively easy. They already feared and hated foreigners. But this time we must teach them about democracy. That will be very difficult. It will take many years."

The students also wanted to teach the masses about the danger threatening China from a new bureaucratic ruling class. In suggesting this they drew inspiration from such sources as the Red Guard group Sheng Wu Lian. In the waning days of the Cultural Revolution these radicals had argued that power within the Chinese Communist party had been usurped by a new bureaucratic class, one as corrupt and autocratic as those opposed by students of the May Fourth generation and earlier. In seeking to fight this corrupt class, Party History activists saw themselves squarely in the tradition of generations of students who had risen up against corrupt regimes. Their righteous intent set a tone which influenced the entire movement.

Unlike many students who later joined the movement, however, they were also politically astute. They did not attack leading officials directly or play favorites. Undoubtedly they viewed Premier Li Peng as a man placed in office to guard the prerogatives of the children of the old elite and hence as one of the worst examples of self-interested leadership. As part of their attempt to educate the Chinese people, the students sought to expose government policies and attitudes which had brought this about. But they also assailed the mind-set of officials such as Zhao Ziyang, who had permitted one of his sons to use his father's position to become head of the profitable Hua Hai Trading Company in the semi-independent economic zone of Hainan Island, supposedly accumulating millions through illicit deals. Students genuinely disliked Zhao for his continued failure to discipline his children.

Ironically, Zhao's children were, like those of most other leaders, rotten and dishonest, while those of Premier Li Peng, the students' nemesis, were usually thought to be decent. One explanation for this, put forward by the students, is that during the Cultural Revolution Zhao Ziyang was purged and sent into the countryside. His children spent their formative years on their own, getting by on their wits without the aid of parental authority. Li Peng, on the other hand, as the favorite of the powerful Zhou Enlai, lived a rather uneventful life as a technical expert during this same period. As others fought to survive, he devoted his time to raising his children. But to understand the reasons for the different moralities of these two leaders' children was not enough; the students wanted a system that would not tolerate corrupt behavior by its officials. If people such as Li Peng were not to be allowed office because they protected the privileges of the elite, then people such as Zhao Ziyang must prevent their children from exploiting their positions.

Hence the initial student demonstrators in the spring of 1989 focused on the system, not on personalities. After the first wreath appeared in Tiananmen Square, and as new and more militant posters began to appear on major campuses in Beijing, Shanghai, and other cities, the leaders of the student protests made a conscious effort to rip down or blot out any phrases on these posters that might offend party elders. They were particularly sensitive to criticism that named party officials.

Soon, however, the movement they had begun grew too large to monitor. Within days of the first protests, larger and larger groups made trips to the square to place wreaths. Protesters from different parts of town met at the Monument to the Heroes of the Revolution, talking with one another and exchanging plans for future actions.

While much of what was to occur in the next few days and months seemed spontaneous, this was only partially true. There was not, as the Chinese government has alleged, a "black hand" guiding the students. Rather, the political activities of the previous winter had led to the formation of small action groups of friends, many of them informally linked.

The Party History Department group was one such cell. Another was the unit at Beijing University headed by Wang Dan, who was to emerge as one of the most important student leaders. He had been head of an unofficial society called the Unit for Contemporary Social Issues, which had organized the "democracy salons." Another leader who emerged at this time, Shen Tong, had the previous year been one of the appointed heads of the government-sponsored Chinese Youth League on the campus of Beijing University. He was removed from the organization in June 1988 when, during protests following the killing of a student, he and his friends formed an unofficial student group.

Like the Party History group, followers of Shen Tong and Wang Dan were ready to charge into action and help mobilize others after the movement began in April 1989. They pointed the way for other student activists, providing the organizational basis for decisions that propelled events forward in the early days of protest. As events accelerated, however, each of these small organizations had a different agenda and focus.

And events occurred now with dizzying speed. On April 17, two days after Hu's death, more than five hundred students from Beijing University of Politics and Law marched into town to lay wreaths in his memory, imitating the early actions of the People's University students. They decided to stay on the square that night to make sure the wreaths were not removed as several others had been. That evening students from Beijing University suddenly began to hike to the square. People's University is a short distance from Beijing

University on the route to Tiananmen. When the Beijing students passed People's University at about 1 a.m., they banged on the gates to wake the students up and get them to join the walk downtown. From four thousand to eight thousand students eventually joined, singing the Communist International and other revolutionary songs as they marched.

To everyone's surprise, the police made no effort to stop them. Instead they blocked intersections and spotted traffic. Once again the protesters were receiving the kind of quasi-government support that was to give impetus to their movement.

Many who had followed the call of the initial organizers had little idea why they were marching. More than half dropped out before the march arrived downtown. But those who remained were militant. At the square, one student climbed on top of the monument and shouted to the crowd that the entire Politburo must resign. The students also demanded an official reappraisal of Hu Yaobang to cleanse his name, and a party apology for its past mistakes, such as the campaign against spiritual pollution. In the morning about a thousand students sat down in front of the Great Hall of the People, the seat of the Chinese national government. They refused to leave until an official accepted a written list of their demands, which included calls for publishing the incomes of all leaders, freedom of speech and press, the right to march, more money for education, and higher pay for intellectuals. The students demanded that the National People's Congress, which was still in session, respond to the petition.

One of the leaders at this rally was the Beijing University student Wang Dan, the person who had earlier organized the "democracy salons." As the movement moved into its radical phase, Wang Dan became one of the best-known Beijing student leaders. While many People's University students see themselves as heirs to the revolutionary history of the Chinese Communist party, those at Beijing University feel they have inherited the legacy of intellectual ferment from the May 4 period. Wang Dan and his followers were far more shrill than the somber Party History group, and more critical of the party leadership. Student movements have lives of their own, independent of the interests and ideas of the founders. This one had begun to assume its own shape.

In the short run, the radical tone of those who, early on the morning of April 18, called for the resignation of all members of the Politburo, encouraged more people to join the demonstrations. Crowds in Tiananmen grew larger that day. Mostly they were onlookers, curious to see the wreaths and poems placed on the monument. Some of those who came to look got caught up in the emotion of the moment. More and more students, intellectuals, and even workers put up their own messages, sometimes shouting from the steps of the monument out into the square.

The crowds were encouraged by the government's failure to respond, even to the kinds of insults now being hurled against it. Had officials acted decisively within the first few weeks of protest, they could have stopped the movement with little or no violence. But the government was deadlocked, as it had been throughout the year. Soon it became clear that some officials around Zhao Ziyang supported the students, hoping to use their demands to further their own desires for reform. Faced with this kind of opposition, the hard-liners at first seemed weak and irresolute. The movement grew.

On April 18 another sit-in took place on the steps of the Great Hall of the People. This time students from Beijing University and People's University were joined by scholars from other schools. For the first time a number of workers and city people began to mill around near them.

It was a carnival-like atmosphere. People sang songs and exchanged drinks and cigarettes. It was the kind of sunny day that encourages optimism. Later the scenes became familiar ones on American television. A new group was beginning to dominate the movement. The "happening" had begun.

That evening the number of students in the square swelled to ten thousand. At first, student representatives contented themselves with now-familiar calls for the implementation of democracy, an end to corruption, and the reappraisal of Hu Yaobang. Suddenly, at about 1 a.m., about three thousand students left the square to march on Zhongnanhai, the walled compound where most of the top leaders of the Chinese Communist party live and work. Claiming they wished to deliver a wreath and petition to the leadership, they were halted at the compound gates by a worried band of security police.

While Chinese leaders tried to snooze a few hundred feet away, the crowd shouted, "Long live democracy!" and "Down with dictatorship!" In a more ominous tone they taunted those inside, screaming, "Come out, Li Peng!" This mob included not only students but also groups of unemployed young hooligans similar to those in all Chinese cities. Harsh economic times had fueled their hostility to the government. In the days to come, they provided the impetus that pushed otherwise peaceful demonstrations into violence and confrontation. On this occasion they began to bang on the gate of the compound, determined to fight their way inside. Repeatedly they were driven back by dozens of plain-clothed guards, but each time they tried again.

Eventually, some of the student leaders worked out a compromise. Three leaders were allowed into the compound to present the demands of the protesters. The crowd waited in vain for them to return. As the hours passed, many people drifted away. Finally, about 4:20 a.m., six lines of police appeared and began to clear the crowd. The police provided vehicles for the students and offered to take them back to their campuses. Most refused.

Earlier in the day many students had gathered on their

campuses to replace the official government-sponsored student organization with one of their own, the Autonomous Student Union. At these "elections," individuals put themselves forward as potential leaders, then the list was winnowed down by a vote of the entire group. These poorly advertised and attended forums showed that many of the students who were leading the fight for democracy had little understanding of how it worked in practice. But from these meetings emerged most of the leaders of the movement who were to become known to the public.

Most of these leaders were also present the next day, Wednesday, April 19, which found an even larger and more militant group of students in the square. Joined now by growing numbers of workers and peasants, the crowd estimated at about fifteen thousand rallied through the day, some again sitting in around the Great Hall of the People and others once more moving that night down the street to block the entrance to the party living quarters at Zhongnanhai. "People who do not understand science should not hold high office," they yelled, showing the elitist ideas of democracy that had characterized the 1986 student demonstrators. As the evening wore on, they also grew nastier, shouting curses against many of China's leaders and screaming, "Let Cixi retire." (Cixi was the name of the old Empress Dowager who remained in power throughout the late nineteenth and early twentieth centuries, long after she should have retired—this was an obvious reference to Deng Xiaoping.) Later, several people also heard them yell, "Kill the foreigners!"

The anger of the crowd was experienced by an American reporter who in the early hours of the morning found his car surrounded by a group of young toughs on a street corner near Zhongnanhai. As he sat frozen in his seat, his hands gripping the wheel, the toughs used his car as a battering ram, pushing it through police lines. At the last minute the police lines parted, letting him through, and then closed again on the crowd. After some perfunctory questioning, he was allowed to go on his way.

The police, in fact, seemed remarkably tolerant, appearing unflustered by the constant jeering and screaming. Many who watched doubted that the American Secret Service would have reacted so genially if a similar mob were battering on the gates of the White House in the middle of the night. This was carried to an extreme at about 2:30 a.m. when the police tried to clear the crowd and some of them were pushed back onto a cluster of fallen bicycles. One tough picked up one of the bikes and smashed it over the head of one of the police. He was not arrested.

The person who finally calmed the crowd that night was Wuer Kaixi, a twenty-one-year-old Beijing Normal University student from Xinjiang, later to be elected as the organizational head of the Beijing Autonomous Student Union. Wuer Kaixi caught the attention of students outside his school for the first time during the rally at the Zhongnanhai compound this same night. As others milled around, uncertain of what to do, Wuer jumped up. "I know you're afraid." Wuer said. "I'm not afraid. If you want to say something, write it on a piece of paper and give it to me. I'll read it. I'll read anything."

His presence was electrifying. Soon people were passing messages and notes to him. Wuer alternately read them and cracked jokes. He pulled the group together. After that he became known to all the protesters. So did Wang Dan, the twenty-two-year-old Beijing University history major, already famous with the foreign press because of his democracy salons. He now began to be quoted in Western media, which enhanced his influence with his colleagues.

In contrast, the People's University students who had begun the protests refused to take the limelight. They consciously avoided a cult of personality. Determined to train people, "not to follow leaders," and perhaps worried about their own safety, they constantly rotated positions so that none of them grew to be recognized or to gain celebrity status. This method may have been admirable, but without the more public stances of such people as Wuer Kaixi and Wang Dan, the movement would not likely have grown so quickly. Wang Dan, for instance, now told foreign reporters that the Chinese students would come back onto the streets every day until April 22, the date planned for Hu Yaobang's funeral.

Wang Dan and his fellow students were helped in their plans for April 22 by actions of the police which early on April 20 infuriated Chinese students. About 3:30 a.m. that morning, after Wuer Kaixi had calmed the crowds, the police charged demonstrators on the square and in front of Zhongnanhai, beating and kicking many and arresting others. Later that day the government warned that some protesters were taking advantage of the people's grief over a fallen leader to try to overthrow the government. Authorities cautioned that they were prepared to take "strong" measures to put an end to the incidents.

The early morning police incident became a major issue for the student demonstrators who thereafter demanded a government apology for the police brutality. Violence by the authorities becomes an organizing focus for any protest, but what made this occasion so curious was its unexpected ferocity. The government at first displayed such extreme tolerance towards the protesters, even those who pounded on the gates of Zhongnanhai, that they encouraged an "anything goes" atmosphere. Two weeks earlier, no one would have dreamed of marching on the compound where China's top leaders lived. Now everyone was shocked that demonstrators were beaten and arrested for doing just that.

On the morning of April 20 several thousand people came to the square, though most dispersed when it began to rain. In the evening about fifteen thousand milled around in the square, in the same disorganized, anarchistic manner that had characterized the demonstrations to that time.

These protests sparked by leaders of the Autonomous Student Union were more immature than those led by the somber Party History graduate students. Leaders of the Autonomous Student Union represented a generation who, in the words Jean-Luc Goddard used to describe French students of the 1960s, were raised on Marx and Coca-Cola. Born at the close of the Cultural Revolution, these students had not been scarred by the chaos and infighting of the period. Instead it intrigued them. They had listened to stories from uncles and aunts of their adventures as Red Guards. I have heard some of these stories, too, and they convey a sense of power and excitement. The Guards marched into government buildings and high officials trembled. They were involved in policy-making at the highest levels. What an adventure!

Autonomous student leaders vibrated with cultural, political, and sexual ideas that would have been unthinkable just a few years earlier. Instead of Mao jackets they wore shiny new suits and ties to hastily called press conferences while their followers dressed in outfits ranging from blue jeans to hot pants. Young female rebels later walked in high heels for sixteen hours from the campuses of Beijing and People's universities to Tiananmen in downtown Beijing and then back, not even breaking step as they battled their way through police lines. Looking at this group, it was clear, especially for those who remembered the days when China was called a nation of "sexless blue ants," that "the times, they were a-changing."

Not all of this innovation was for the better. When these students marched, it was not just for idealistic causes but also for their own self-interest. During the 1960s American students were morally indignant about the Vietnam War, but they also feared they would be drafted to serve in that unpopular cause against their will. Chinese students worried about their own kind of draft. They had been assigned to various university departments on the basis of standardized exams. In a survey I took of one group of undergraduate student leaders, thirty of thirty-four had hoped to study something more lucrative than that to which they had been assigned. The way in which the illiberal policies of their government infringed on their lives maddened them.

Freshmen and sophomores were particularly active among the students in this younger generation. This may have been partly a function of environment. When Moses led his people out of Egypt, he kept them wandering around the Sinai desert for forty years. Many modern theologians tell us this was done so that the older generation who had lived as slaves would die off and a new generation who had known only freedom could take power. In China this process took twenty years. Those under the age of twenty were not born when the violent period of the Cultural Revolution ended. They took China's openness for granted. They assumed it could go further.

There was a practical reason as well why this younger group may have been so active. Juniors and seniors were already looking forward to graduation. One black mark on their records, for participating in demonstrations, and they might be banished to a job in some small hole in the countryside for the rest of their lives. They were reluctant to join the protests.

Among both older and younger students, the leadership in fact came from those least knowledgeable about the West, not from those who had studied abroad as was often reported. For instance, the Party History graduate students wore Western-style clothes and were influenced by Western ideas, but few spoke English, and they were contemptuous of those who tried to escape China's problems by leaving the country. They felt it was imperative that they stay in China and focus on their chief concern, the growing strength of hard-liners within the party leadership which, since the previous fall, threatened to undo much of the economic and political liberalization of the past decade.

The first generation of undergraduate students who joined them, although even hipper in appearance, also were those who had been assigned to departments concerned with the study of traditional Chinese values. All these people were of course excited by currents of Western thought and technology sweeping China. But their interest in change came from a concern for China's problems, not because of a fascination with the West.

This repeated a tendency that had surfaced in past Chinese student protests. Even during the May Fourth movement, the most radical participants, such as Chen Duxiu and Li Dazhao, the future founders of the Chinese Communist party, while they were very interested in Western ideas, possessed radical roots that came first from a study of Chinese society and tradition. Like later radicals, their concern for change was a product of a deep passion for Chinese society.

The original May Fourth activists had also been joined by a younger, more Westernized group, excited at first largely by the heat of events. This too occurred in 1989. The Chinese of the 1980s wanted to change their country, but they wanted to have fun doing it. At first many of these younger students, from which this second leadership group emerged, reacted as if they were participating in a panty raid. During the first days of the demonstrations, at all hours of the night, one could see lighted newspapers fluttering out of their dormitory windows—supposedly a political statement. Students had also burned newspapers in early 1987 as a way of showing their contempt for the strictly controlled Chinese government press which refused to print the true story of Hu Yaobang. But it was also simply a prank. Sometimes, when the students ran out of newspapers, they set their clothes on fire and tossed them out the window.

Another favorite stunt: because Xiaoping, Deng's given

name, is also a homonym in Chinese for the word for *bottle*, students could make fun of China's paramount leader by breaking bottles. In mid-April many students had a great time throwing bottles and even canteens from their dorm windows, often narrowly missing passers-by. Many foreign students felt that sometimes the bottles were aimed deliberately at them. Although this kind of activity helped to keep the movement going and got others involved, hard-liners used such actions to inflame Deng Xiaoping. They knew that once he reacted, he would use violence and terror.

By Friday, April 21, the government had had enough. These young, more impulsive students and their worker allies had pushed matters too far when they attacked the living quarters of the Chinese Communist party at Zhongnanhai. The day before, the New China News Agency published an editorial asking people to cool down. Now the government announced that the next morning, Tiananmen, where the memorial services for Hu Yaobang were to be held, would be sealed off, supposedly to prevent traffic problems during the ceremonies. It was clear to everyone that the real reason was to block demonstrators from entering the square. Student leaders such as Wang Dan, who had announced their own plans for an unofficial memorial service for Hu, seemed to have been foiled.

Once again the leadership that concocted the strategy to circumvent the government and bring new force and dynamism to the movement came from the Party History Department at People's University, this time undergraduates as well as graduates. The graduate students had felt uncomfortable in the limelight. They still did much of the planning, but undergraduate students in the same department were to become much more visible in this new action, especially students in the international relations section of the department. Others joined them, notably students from the Chinese Department and the Journalism Department. All the undergraduates were close to the Party History graduate students and shared their political ambitions and, in many cases, their political ties. They also had good contacts with other undergraduates on different Beijing campuses.

As delegates from the Autonomous Student Union on campuses throughout Beijing met on April 21 to decide on a next step, the People's University delegates played a critical role in devising the strategy that would radically transform the student movement and convince others to follow. In a feat of tactical brilliance, the students of Beijing, with People's University flags displayed more prominently than those of any other school, entered Tiananmen Square in the middle of the night and camped there, effectively cutting off the government action. When the troops arrived at 6 a.m. to seal off the square, tens of thousands of students were already there. Without mass violence, it would have been impossible to clear them before the memorial services began.

The action captured the imagination of the city. As word spread of what the students had done, thousands of others poured into the square. By morning, an estimated 100,000 people had joined them in Tiananmen, perhaps seventy thousand of them students. It was the first time that great numbers of the masses had joined the student demonstrations—and they had done so in direct defiance of both a municipal regulation against unauthorized demonstrations and a specific directive issued the day before by the public security department.

The discipline shown by this huge crowd contrasted greatly to what had gone on during the chaotic, ill-mannered demonstrations outside of Zhongnanhai throughout much of the previous week. It spoke well for the organizational skills of those like the People's University students who had organized it. Oddly enough, the police cooperated. In the middle of the square, security forces checked identification cards. Those with a university I.D. were allowed to enter and sit down throughout the next morning, a sign not only of good crowd

management skills but also of the elitist tone of these demonstrators for democracy. Had the police not been there to
separate the crowds, it is likely that tens of thousands of
workers might have joined the students and that the protests
would not have been as orderly.

The students, like their peers who after May 4, 1919, had
organized the Communist party, clearly felt that they, and
they alone, spoke for the masses. Although they called for
the people of Beijing to join their demonstrations, when the
students shouted at the four thousand official mourners,
"Dialogue! Dialogue!" they assumed that a discussion between them and party leaders would allow these government
figures to learn what was troubling the masses.

In the midst of the memorial proceedings, three student
representatives ascended the steps of the Great Hall. Denied
entry, they sank to their knees and began to kowtow in plain
view of the cameras of foreign journalists. Embarrassed
officials finally opened the doors and allowed the students to
enter. They presented their demands to a low-ranking official
who assured them that the safety of the students would be
guaranteed but refused their request to talk with Li Peng.
(The People's University journalism student who was part of
this little delegation, the only People's University student
ever publicly to embarrass the government, was later shot and
killed on June 4.)

Events had not been so orderly in other parts of the
country. Riots broke out in both Xian and Changsha on the
day of Hu's funeral as angry workers and young thugs turned
out in force for protests in those cities. In Xian, an angry
crowd of five thousand threw rocks, burned vehicles and
buildings, and carried on for at least twelve hours. In both
cities, protesters fought back when police charged them.
Hundreds were injured. Chinese television emphasized the
destructiveness of the demonstrators, though some witnesses

claimed that the police had rioted and caused most of the bloodshed.

The government faced a dilemma. As more and more city dwellers joined the protests, the risks of the kind of violence that had occurred in Xian and Changsha spread. The government needed to stop the demonstrations at once, but it was too divided to take decisive action. Hard-liners blocked other officials from giving in to student demands. Moderates prevented the government from using force. Soon, it was hoped, the students would tire, and the demonstrations would end.

Once again, the tactics of Party History students preserved the momentum. On April 17, a few days after Hu Yaobang's death, they had begun boycotting classes. By Thursday, April 20, the strike had encompassed most of the campus of People's University, and the students had organized their own militia to enforce it. By Saturday the ideas had spread to nearby Beijing University. A couple of days later, students throughout Beijing were on strike. By the time the media began to report the strike on April 24, usually crediting it to the students of Beijing University, People's University had already been on strike for a week.

One exception was foreigners. Most foreign students continued to attend their Chinese classes after a wall poster warned them not to participate in the demonstrations because their presence had earlier been used by the government as an excuse to intervene in student protests. One day, at People's University, a member of the student militia burst into one of the foreign classrooms with a camera strapped around his neck and began taking pictures of the traitors who were defying the strike. When he realized it was a class of foreigners, he grew embarrassed and left the room.

Another group that continued to meet were students studying for their TOEFL exam, the test in English proficiency which would qualify them to go abroad. TOEFL students paid extra for their classes, and they refused to abandon them just because of the student movement, despite talk in the Western press that demonstrators were influenced by students who studied overseas.

"I'm not going to abandon an opportunity to go to the United States just for a chance to save China," one TOEFL student told me.

A TOEFL teacher I knew was quite agitated about this situation. "My friends all regard me as a traitor because I continue to hold my classes. But they don't understand that I have no choice. My students insist that I teach them."

Although the TOEFL and foreign students may have continued to attend classes, by Monday, April 24, at least thirty of Beijing's seventy-odd colleges were participating in the strike. This gave tremendous impetus to the movement. It constituted a direct and constant defiance of the government, yet one that was peaceful and almost impossible for the government to combat. It enabled the students to spend all their time organizing and demonstrating.

Rather than stay on the campuses, they now went into the streets to seek support among the masses. Again, this tactic was pioneered by the students of People's University. Shortly after the April 22 demonstration, students from People's University moved some of their posters and demonstrations to a spot just outside the front gate, where they could be seen and heard by crowds of workers waiting at nearby bus stops. They also set up a broadcasting booth at the gate which blasted the students' ideas into the streets. Workers gathered around and began to discuss what was happening. They became friendlier to the students. Beginning April 25, students on most of the major campuses imitated the People's students and began to circulate throughout the city, passing out leaflets, posting signs, and giving brief talks.

On their propaganda tours the students always left the campuses in groups, fifteen or twenty bicyclists riding together, one in the lead carrying a red banner with the name of the school and the department. For a time, one could see them everywhere throughout the city with small crowds gathered around. On street corners they shouted out the message of democracy, emphasizing, at least in their discussions with the public, their opposition to official corruption. And always they repeated that they did "not oppose the government or the party."

I could feel a change in the public mood. On April 21, a cab driver taking me back to the campus had been afraid to enter.

"The students are mad," he explained excitedly. "If they see a car, they're apt to burn it."

I tried to reassure him, but it did no good. He was terrified. Finally I insisted. I had a lot of heavy purchases. He drove through the school gates, but when he saw a crowd of students gathered down the road, he stopped and refused to go further. I had to get out and walk the rest of the way to the foreigners' dormitory.

A couple of days later, when I again took a cab, it was a totally different experience. The driver questioned me about everything that was going on. He supported the students fully, he said. He had even given money to a group of demonstrators on a street corner. His was not an unusual reaction. As I walked and rode around the city talking with people, I could feel the mood changing everywhere.

Events had neared a critical juncture. If city people continued to join the demonstrations, they would be impossible to stop without massive bloodshed. The government's only good news was that in spite of everything, Shanghai, China's largest industrial city, had remained relatively calm.

So far the steps which the government had taken to stop the demonstrations had not worked. The demonstrators, particularly the People's University group, seemed quite adept in their ability to outflank the authorities. They knew just how far to push them and when. They knew how to hold back before they sent things over the brink. But could they keep it up? The ranks of the demonstrators were swelling. More and more hotheads were joining the movement. As more "happenings" occurred, the government might finally take swift and real measures.

The protesters' only hope was to affect policy quickly. Party hard-liners would not make concessions, but perhaps the moderate delegates to the National People's Congress, then still meeting, or the Central Committee might. If these government agencies could be induced to act and offer quick concessions which would satisfy most of the students and throw more power to the moderates, victory could be won and the troops called off. Otherwise it might be too late.

China was at a turning point in late April 1989. Soon the Party History types would not be able to control increasingly radical young students. The bureaucrats could not delay a decision forever. History suggested that they would do whatever was necessary to protect themselves.

7

THE VICTORY OF APRIL 27

As the students scored victory after victory in April 1989, government hard-liners also mobilized. They had lived through the Cultural Revolution, so they understood that student movements, if left unchecked, could bring down governments. They had also taken part in reinterpreting the history of the Cultural Revolution to make the Gang of Four responsible for all the violence of the period. They knew how to discredit opponents with the chaos generated by a student movement.

On April 25 I began to suspect that some of the more impulsive student writings and slogans were being misinterpreted by hard-liners in the party in order to marshal support for their side. On that date I visited an older friend who occupies an important party post and who had just returned from a party conference.

"What the students really want," he declared shaking his head, "is to overthrow Deng Xiaoping."

"I haven't seen much evidence of that on campus," I

argued. The students had jeered at Deng, but he was not the main focus of their movement. It was corruption and democracy. He was an old man. "They are concerned with the next generation," I explained. "To the extent that any single person is a target, it is Premier Li Peng."

"Well, that's what is being said," he answered flatly.

A few days earlier I had noticed articles in the *Washington Post*, the *New York Times*, and the *Wall Street Journal* emphasizing the smashing of bottles that mocked Deng Xiaoping. I later discovered that these articles had been translated into Chinese and reprinted for the party elite, as if to make sure they saw how irreverent the students had become. Perhaps this meant nothing—foreign press clippings on China are routinely translated for internal party consumption.

But the hard-liners were clearly pulling out all stops to mobilize their forces and bring Deng to their side. On April 24 the hard-line Beijing Municipal Party Committee delivered a report to an emergency session of the five-person standing committee of the Politburo, asking that they be "empowered by the Central Committee to immediately check the student unrest." Since Zhao Ziyang, head of the standing committee, was out of the country, the Soviet-trained Premier Li Peng had called the other three members to the session and also allowed Chinese President Yang Shangkun to attend. The Beijing Municipal Party authorities, aware that only the day before the students had met by the ruins of the old summer palace and formed an Interim Federation of Autonomous Student Unions, described the student protest as an "anti-party and anti-socialist political struggle." The standing committee accepted this view and on April 25, the same day I visited my friend, the two members of the government with the most to lose as a result of the demonstrations, Premier Li Peng and President Yang Shangkun, presented a special report on the student situation to Deng Xiaoping. It enraged him.

Deng had probably already decided to get tough on the protesters before anyone came to see him. For after Li and Yang came to his house, Deng in words that he had transcribed and later distributed to the party faithful reaffirmed the need for discipline and order. Rejecting the idea that the student movement was a patriotic one, Deng branded it a conspiracy to overthrow the leadership of the Chinese Communist party and the socialist system. The danger, he explained to Yang and Li, was that the movement might soon spread to workers and peasants, as in Poland, Yugoslavia, Hungary, and the Soviet Union. Showing his distaste for such developments, he praised officials who had ordered the murder of protesters in the Soviet republic of Georgia. And showing the kind of scorn for intellectuals that he had exhibited in the Cultural Revolution, Deng demanded government action while the protest movement was still confined to writers and students. The idea that the students might already have formed their own independent union, he made clear, terrified him, for it sounded like the beginnings of a Solidarity movement in China. This he sought to block before it was too late: he demanded "a clear-cut stance" against this "unrest."

By the next day, word circulated around Beijing that Deng had also said, "We are not afraid to shed blood. We are not afraid to lose face." At the same time Deng arranged for an editorial denouncing the student "turmoil" to appear in the *People's Daily*, China's largest newspaper. Two divisions of the 38th Army were called into Beijing, and warnings were issued on all campuses that students would be met by military force if they marched again.

Deng's views were those of the elderly, terrified elite which still believed that all party business in China must take place behind closed doors. With students mocking his name from their dormitory windows and taunting the country's leaders in front of Zhongnanhai, Deng worried that China faced a crisis similar to that of the Cultural Revolution.

And, in a sense, he was right. The students desired not only to cleanse the party of corruption but also to make it more responsive to the will of the people. If what Deng feared was openness in the political process—and he always had—then he had good reason to oppose the student movement.

The Party History students recognized that party elders might present this kind of obstacle in the near term and suggested that they were in the movement for the long haul. For now they would try to prod the party to change. But long term they hoped to educate the masses to the meaning of democracy. Other, more radical students attempted to avoid this problem by developing their own autonomous organizations. In so doing they were implying that they did not trust the party and wanted to separate themselves from it. At the same time they continually insisted that all they wanted was a dialogue with the government. A dialogue implied that they trusted the party and simply wanted to convince it to change. It sounds confusing because it was. The students were uncertain about their own goals. Sometimes they threw bottles out of their windows, sometimes they went to discussions with serious Party History types. To elder officials it all seemed like a ploy, one that must be ended before it went too far.

With Deng on their side, the hard-liners now were satisfied that the government would meet the demonstrations with force. Spokesmen explained that "a handful of people with ulterior motives" were behind the troubles. "They fabricate various rumors to poison people's minds. They use posters to libel and slander and attack the leaders of the Communist party and the government." They caused others to "storm Zhongnanhai" and to shout "for the overthrow of the Chinese Communist party." Alluding to the Cultural Revolution, commentators announced that unrest once again threatened "reform and modernization." Beginning with television and radio commentaries on the evening of April 25 and continuing throughout the next day, they called for everyone to

understand the "graveness of the struggle" against the perpetrators of disorder.

Meanwhile, the government attempted to get tough also
with the press. When the demonstrations began, the deputy
minister of propaganda had called a meeting of the editors of
all major newspapers in Beijing, at which he had instructed
them not to publish news of the student demonstrations. But
he forgot to invite to the meeting the editor of *Science and
Technology Daily*, a small paper which ordinarily covers only
scientific and technical subjects. Now, however, the paper
began to cover the student demonstrations. When the ministry
finally got around to telling the paper not to publish news
about the protests on the weekend of April 20, it was too
late. One of the paper's editors, Sun Changjian, had been a
close associate of Hu Yaobang. Many of the paper's journalists were closely allied with members of the scientific elite
such as Fang Lizhi. They threatened to strike if their coverage was not printed. On April 23 their issue covering the
events of Hu Yaobang's funeral was quickly confiscated,
though not before staffers delivered copies to campuses all
over the city, where it was placed on walls for everyone to
read. The next day the *Peasant's Daily*, one of China's five
national newspapers, also covered the demonstrations on its
front page.

This did not prevent authorities in Shanghai from cracking
down on the radical weekly *World Economic Herald*, whose
April 24 issue devoted six pages to Hu Yaobang's funeral.
The *Herald* had published comments by radical reformers,
including the Marxist critic Su Shaozhi and the advocate of
the new authoritarianism Rong Jian. It had already established itself as a bone in the throats of government hard-
liners. Now, in its pages, some of China's leading intellectuals made a strong indictment of those officials who in 1987
had forced Hu to resign. Yan Jiaqi, a scholar known to be
close to Zhao Ziyang, lamented that in China's political

process, "A handful of people can just talk among themselves and put aside the interests of the Chinese people, and then reach an unpopular decision." These people, Yan complained, "have no right to mourn Hu Yaobang's death, because they trapped him." But officials made sure Yan's words did not reach the streets. The hard-liner party boss of Shanghai, Jiang Zemin, banned the issue, dismissing the paper's editor, Qin Benli, and confiscating the 300,000 copies already printed. Before the censors arrived, staffers sent copies of the paper to virtually every foreign journalist in China and to many radical students and intellectuals as well.

Lines were now drawn. Dissident intellectuals, long itching for a fight, had joined the students in defying the government. Hard-liners had shown their patience was at an end. The fun and games seemed to be over.

Tough talk and government action scared some of the flashy young student radical leaders who had brought so much enthusiasm into the movement. The April 26 editorial authorized by Deng in the *People's Daily* had called the demonstrations "illegal." Fearing he would be targeted for arrest as rumors spread through the city that the army had been called out, the newly elected head of the Interim Federation of the Autonomous Student Unions, Zhou Yongjun, a student from the Chinese University of Politics and Law, backed down. On the campuses of Qinghua University, Beijing University, and Beijing Normal University, many of the radical undergraduates who had been at the forefront of the struggle voted not to participate in the march planned for the next day, April 27. The main student organization at Qinghua University withdrew from the Autonomous Student Union.

But others who had remained on the sidelines were now angered by the government's truculence. The vast majority of students had been willing to let their classmates front for them, but now they seemed determined to show the government that it was not, as they said, only a "minority" who supported the demonstrators. They announced they were ready to march.

Once again Party History students stepped forward to lead them. This time they were encouraged by a letter, signed two days earlier, by 159 faculty members from People's University. It criticized the mass media's reporting of the student movement and backed the students. Party History students made it clear they would demonstrate with or without the young radicals. The night before the march, their representatives went from campus to campus spreading the word. To show their determination, a group of about thirty students sat down and wrote out their wills. So did a number of other students at Beijing University. The next morning they informed friends and family that they expected to be killed—but it would be for a just cause, for China and democracy.

Many students took more practical measures which showed they still had a deep faith in the party. Some of the children and grandchildren of very high cadres and military officers called home, informing their startled parents that they planned to march in defiance of government directives. "If the troops are ordered to open fire, they will be firing on me," they announced. These students were, as NBC news commentator John Chancellor later put it, "serpents' teeth." They were boring from within, using their power in the old system to try to change it.

As the students made their presentations, a desperate but ineffectual government worked to stop them. Faculty meetings were called and teachers urged to pressure their students. "They must not march!" the teachers were told. The faculty complied, relaying the message to the students. But they also laid out their own terms. "We will join the student strike," the faculty at People's University warned the administration, "if the government uses weapons against the students."

Both students and faculty, it seemed, were trying to work with the government even as they struggled against it. But the government continued to labor feverishly to stop the students. Few people on or near most of the large campuses in Beijing got much sleep on the night of April 26. Throughout the evening and into the morning, officials blasted out their message on campus loudspeakers: "This is a warning! Do not leave the university gates! Go back to class!" Tension was high.

The morning of April 27, activity began early at People's University. As students congregated, administrators tried a new tactic. "Last night," campus loudspeakers announced, "student leaders decided that demonstrations will not be held this morning. Everyone should return to their classes." For a moment a few of the students looked confused. Then everyone began to laugh. No one was fooled. By 7:30 a.m. thousands of students had joined in the formation that they had first used so successfully on the march into the square the night before Hu Yaobang's funeral, and that would soon characterize student marches throughout China—arms linked, striding like Roman centurions, flags flashing through the rows! They were set to win or die. This time they looked rugged.

"Holy cow! They sure have their shit together now!" I heard one foreign student gasp as he saw them for the first time. Everyone sensed that this demonstration would be unlike any that had happened in China for many, many years. I remarked to an older professor that although the students looked fierce, they were not very well armed for a fight with soldiers and policemen. "Chinese students," he answered prophetically, "don't fight with weapons. They fight with their hands and their feet."

The students strode around the campus several times. "We will win!" they shouted in unison. The chants were deafening, and the air was electric. The dorms emptied. Those who had hesitated now realized that history was about to be made. They ran to join.

After more than an hour their enthusiasm was pitched. But something was wrong. Students from Beijing University and Qinghua University, a few miles to the north of People's University, had not yet arrived. The route to the square from these two schools passes right by People's, and the People's students had agreed to wait for their colleagues from the other two schools to join them so that they would all march to the square together. But it was growing late. Scouts were sent out. They reported back that several rows of police blocked the road in Zhongguancun, preventing the Beijing University students from meeting up with their colleagues. The Beida and Qinghua students were afraid to cross the police lines. It looked like the students might not march that day after all.

As soon as they received this news, the People's University students roared through the school gate, past the security forces and officials trying to hold them back. Party History students formed the lead phalanx. They headed north, away from the square, seeking a rendezvous with their compatriots. When they came up against police lines at Zhongguancun, they pushed their way through, meeting up with amazed students from the other schools. Then they all marched back through the police lines toward the square, passing Beijing Normal University and most of the other major schools in Beijing on the way to ensure that students from these schools marched in the same formation.

Throughout the day, city residents watched in awe as the big red flags emblazoned with the legends "People's University," "Graduate Students, People's University," and "Department of Party History, People's University" spearheaded the four-mile-long column of students, followed by similar flags from the students of Beijing University, Beijing Normal University, Qinghua University, and other schools. They broke through line after line of police set up to stop them. Before it was over, some eighty thousand students had joined the march. At times as many as 200,000 people may have walked alongside the students, some just observing, others acting in support of the protesters but prevented from joining their ranks because of their linked-arm formation.

It was during this march that the people of Beijing declared themselves for the demonstrators. They gave life to the government's worst fears and justified the students' faith in their cause. For most of the eighteen hours the students marched, crowds lined the path cheering and flashing victory signs, as if they were watching a liberating army. They stood on sidewalks, looked down from the windows of high-rises and from shop doorways, hung from lampposts. Some wore Mao buttons as a sign of their disgust with the authorities. Many pressed money and food into the hands of the demonstrators.

One student later told me how, at the end of the march, a worker insisted that a group of students take a break and come to his house. His family fed them dinner, loading them up with all sorts of delicacies. When they left, the worker pressed twenty yuan into their hands. Everyone had similar stories about the half-million or more people who enthusiastically lined their route. Well after the movement had been crushed, student leader Wuer Kaixi admitted to an American reporter, "The only time when I thought we might succeed was on April 27, when those of us who marched to Tiananmen Square in response to that harsh *People's Daily* editorial found ourselves supported all along the route by tens of thousands of ordinary people."

I experienced the fervor of the crowd firsthand when I watched the students return to People's University late that night. It was an emotional scene. Students from nearby Beijing University and Qinghua University came by in small groups on the bicycles, buses, and trucks that city workers had provided them. But the People's University students had refused to split up and walked together in formation the long way back to the campus.

About 1:30 a.m., as the demonstrators finally struggled toward the gate, still walking with arms linked and flags flying as they had been when they left eighteen hours earlier, the crowds shouted, "Long live People's University! People's University has won!" I followed in back of the marchers, hoping to catch sight of the fireworks that were waiting to be set off at the entrance to the campus. I also wanted to hear any speeches that might be made.

But I had stepped into the street too early. Screaming, chanting crowds still lined the way and took me for a marcher.

"Thank you! Thank you, foreign friend!" they shouted, cheering and clapping for me. I felt like a fraud. I tried to step out of the road, but when I moved close to the edge of the sidewalk, the people would not let me through. They grabbed my hand to shake it and thank me. To the side I heard someone say, "Look how strong that foreigner is. He doesn't look tired at all after marching all that way."

Up ahead someone was videotaping the students. Realizing there was a foreigner there, they swung the spotlight onto me. I couldn't get out. I had to continue walking in back of the students through the gate.

Although it was well past midnight, the cooks and workers of the school had reopened the central dining hall and were serving the famished students a late dinner. I watched them file in, their enthusiasm undiminished. Some jumped on tables and screamed. They shouted slogans. Seeing me standing by the door, one exhausted student literally fell into my arms.

"The government said we couldn't do it. But we did it anyhow, and we won," he whispered into my ear. "Excuse me. My voice is hoarse. I have to go eat now."

The students had indeed succeeded in defying threats from

government and police. Many felt that they had finally broken with the old authoritarian patterns of the past. Like the May Fourth activists they sought to imitate, they saw themselves as breaking with tradition. But, in fact, like the May Fourth protesters they won at least in part because some of those in power had no interest in stopping them. For the police and militia units stationed along the route of the march had not tried fiercely to block them. The security forces were unarmed, scattered, and poorly placed. Often, when the students pressed up against lines of police and militia in the middle of key streets throughout the city, gangs of young toughs attacked these same forces from the rear, throwing bottles and attempting to shove them aside, so that they became too weakened to resist the students bearing down on them from the other direction. The students pushed them aside without much trouble.

Many who watched, myself included, felt almost as though the situation had been staged to make the students think they had won a big victory, and hence gain greater support and momentum. This, in turn, might allow government moderates to suggest to the hard-liners that force would not work against the protesters, and that it was time to make concessions.

In suggesting that the march was staged, I do not mean that the police were told to pretend to block the demonstrators and then let them through. Such a charade would have been discovered by hard-liners and would have infuriated them. Rather, I believe that whoever planned the dispatch of the security units that day did not have their heart in it. The police were obviously under orders not to use excessive force. There also were too few police to handle the crowds, and those used were not the best-trained or disciplined teams. In designating the units they did, the security people in charge clearly did not attempt to be as firm as possible with the students.

According to some reports, Qiao Shi, the head of security

and a member of the standing committee of the Politburo, made a last-minute decision that the troops were not to use guns or clubs to stop the students. Whoever made the decision, the word traveled very quickly to People's University. Some of the People's University students, though probably not most of the other groups, apparently knew what kinds of troops were to be sent out and had thought about how to deal with them.

It is, of course, possible that those around Deng Xiaoping had such faith in the authority of the party and the government that they believed the students would back off when faced with any police and militia units blocking their way. But Deng should have known better. During the Cultural Revolution, supporters defied him even after he had personally visited some of the campuses. Perhaps this time he and his minions had not counted on the planning and foresight of the People's University contingent. Each time these students advanced into the lines of the security forces set up to block them throughout the city, the police were quickly forced to fall back, often to the surprise of onlookers.

Whether planned or not, the impact of the march was similar to what had occurred a few months earlier in Tibet. The people of the city had witnessed the government talk tough but act soft. They sensed a student triumph at hand. Once again the government had shown itself to be weak and ineffectual. Workers, angered by an economy raging out of control and by rampant official corruption, shifted their allegiance to the students.

Links between the upper and lower levels of Chinese society have always been weak. In 1911, when runaway economic and social change undermined the structure of the old regime, provincial and district organizations based on close social, political, and family ties simply drifted off. Now, in a similar time of change, the government again appeared to be dissolving, and smaller living and working units were prepared to take up the slack, at least in Beijing. The people of the city, seeing that the students had not been scared by the government's troops, lost all pretense of loyalty to the old administration.

The students, however, were still cautious. They took care during the march to ensure that their relations with the forces of violence remained cordial. As they surged against lines of police and militia, they shouted to the confused troops, "People love the People's police! The People's police love the people!" When they passed columns of soldiers in Tiananmen, they chanted at them, "Welcome 38th Army!" They also passed out leaflets to soldiers, explaining to them the purpose of their movement. At one point, after the marchers had broken through the last line of barricades lining the square, some of the soldiers were cornered and vastly outnumbered by mobs of youths who clambered onto their vehicles. Worried that local toughs were about to start an incident, the students rushed to the soldiers' aid, persuading the angry, pushing crowd to back off and allow the soldiers to leave.

The students left the square almost as soon as they had arrived. At this point in the movement they had no interest in occupying Tiananmen. They preferred to march around the city to influence as many people as possible. They wanted Beijing to understand that they had won. The fears of the morning had vanished.

Even before the march was over, the government began to make concessions. By late afternoon of April 27, even while the students still marched, most of the security forces had been pulled back. The only place they were still in evidence was at the steps to the Great Hall of the People. Then, on the evening news, the government announced it was agreeing to the students' demand for a meeting with high officials. "We are prepared to talk with the students anytime," a government spokesman said, adding that this would occur only if the students returned to their campuses and adopted "a calm and reasonable attitude."

At this time the students had begun to emphasize three issues. The first was talks with government officials; the second was an apology for the beatings and arrests of April 20; and the last was an accurate reporting of the student movement in the media. Although it did not specifically address any of these points, by agreeing to a meeting the government showed it was willing to make concessions on the first point. At the same time the government emphasized that the students' aims, especially their desire to wipe out corruption, "were in accord with the wishes of the party and the government."

The government soon appeared to capitulate to the students on another point, publishing a list of imported luxury items which it said it wished to limit. The list included everything from perfume to cars, goods which many of the top leaders had no doubt already stocked.

Now, for the first time, a dialogue seemed about to take place with the authorities. The students felt they were on the verge of a transformation of Chinese society. The morning after the march of April 27 a huge banner appeared above the cafeteria entrance on the People's University campus. It read: "April 27 is the day People's University was reborn, the day the new May Fourth Movement began."

This banner signaled the students' feelings that a spirit of change and leadership had returned to People's University, the school which had been founded in the caves of the Chinese Communists' guerrilla base camp at Yanan to train revolutionary cadres. Now the students felt they were returning to the revolutionary tradition that had begun with the May Fourth movement and led to the overthrow of the old Chinese order and the victory of the Chinese Communist party in 1949. Like their predecessors, they were breaking with the authoritarian, bureaucratic traditions of the past. Although few students at other schools cared very deeply about People's University, most also wanted to revive the mission and dynamism of the Chinese Communist party. This was especially true at Beijing University, where the students saw themselves as heir to the intellectual experimentation of the New Culture movement in the early 1920s. Students at these two schools and at most others all had the same sense of the importance of the role they were playing. They believed their generation had created a new movement, as influential to China as May Fourth.

Chinese students in 1989, like those of the May Fourth era, ardently desired to see China once again become a major actor on the world stage. To accomplish this they knew that China must develop its own identity. Like student revolutionaries before them, they opposed a slavish fascination with foreign goods. But they also hoped that import restrictions on some products, as the government now suggested, would not become the xenophobia that characterized the country during the last years of Mao Zedong. They wanted China to take its place in the family of nations as a proud, modern, but independent country.

In agreeing to talks and accepting the validity of some of the students' demands, government leaders appeared to have decided to work with them to confront China's problems. But if this was so, what about Deng Xiaoping, who just the day before had come out so vehemently against the students? Some observers have suggested that the hard-liners were leading the students on, conceding to some of their demands but not making enough concessions to satisfy them. In this way they hoped to convince government hold-outs of the students' unreasonableness and the need to crush the student movement.

This analysis is plausible, but it attributes a high degree of advance knowledge to a group of leaders who at other critical junctures seemed to have had little idea of what was happening. Certainly there were people within the government who bitterly opposed any concessions to the students. They no doubt dragged their feet and sought to surrender as little as possible to the moderates. But there seems little question that at this point such hard-liners were a minority. Most in authority thought a compromise necessary and forced others in the government to go along.

Whether this means that Deng Xiaoping temporarily bit his tongue, as he had done so many times in the past, or that he was simply ignored, is not clear. One report has it that he moved toward the moderates because of entreaties by members of his family. His exact feelings probably do not matter. For a long time the Politburo and the Central Committee had voted one way, and Deng Xiaoping or the hard-line, military-backed President Yang Shangkun had simply overruled them. Now Deng's way had not worked, and he was mum, so the others felt pressure to seek an end to the situation without violence.

Deng's talk on April 25 with Yang Shangkun and Li Peng had been reported to party members and had infuriated most middle-level cadres. They saw it as interference in party affairs from someone who, according to the constitution, held no formal position in the top level of the party. They feared that the result of this talk and the subsequent April 26 editorial would be the end of reform. A considerable portion of Deng's talk had been directed against Hu Yaobang's "irresolute" stand against "liberalization" and supposed advocacy of "double-digit growth." Many saw these words as an attack on Zhao Ziyang. Under pressure from the masses to institute honest government, they determined to help Zhao.

The next day, April 28, the government announced still further concessions to the students. Government spokesman Hu Qili, a member of the standing committee of the Politburo allied with Zhao Ziyang, told China's major newspapers that they could begin to cover the student demonstrations freely.

The masses would be allowed to decide for themselves about the students' conditions. Over the next few days an amazing change came over the Chinese press as it opened up.

The conflict might have been resolved at this point. Both sides tried. The fact that they got nowhere was because by this time they were speaking different languages. The government wanted the students to trust "good" individuals. They wanted the students to have faith in them. They wanted them to believe they understood the problem. For some students this may have been enough. But now that they had achieved a major victory, most of the students did not wish to rely on individuals, they wanted the power to form their own independent union.

On the same day the government was freeing the Chinese press, the chief unofficial student organization, the Interim Autonomous Student Union, disbanded and was replaced with a permanent organization of the same name. Wuer Kaixi, who unlike the previous leader had backed the march of the day before, was elected its new head and immediately began a signature drive on the various campuses to demonstrate that the group represented the ideas of a majority of students, hoping this would convince the government to recognize the union.

The government had agreed to talk with official student groups, but the students considered these official groups tools of the Communist party and rejected their representation. Three days earlier, on April 25, when several government leaders had attempted to initiate a discussion with members of the official student union from Qinghua University, they had been forced to cancel these talks; students had objected that the official association did not represent their views. Now that the students had demonstrated an impressive show of strength, they were less inclined to accept talks with delegates they saw as government stooges. On April 29, the day the talks were to be held, the students began to create a special Dialogue Delegation. These were specially selected, highly articulate students who met to train for the upcoming discussions with the government.

The students were not offering the government ideas but groups, and nonofficial ones at that. Perhaps if the students had rallied behind one group they would have had a better chance for success, but they were unable to do that. In later attacks on the student protests, the government gave the students credit for a much more unified organization and strategy than in fact they had. The students were strategically mobile not because they had a strong central organization with a well-considered plan, but because they had many different subgroups constantly responding in new and creative ways to the changing situation. These various groups provided the movement with the kind of organizational framework that allowed it to mobilize quickly against the government. But this also proved to be the movement's undoing, for each of these subgroups pursued its own goals and interests. Instead of creating concrete proposals for elections, for example, the students spent much of their time trying to get the authorities to accept a constantly changing cast of leaders, each of whom was said to represent the real ideas of the students.

While the government tried to meet student demands by offering them a meeting, they did not do so graciously or intelligently. They stubbornly invited a number of students whom the others plainly did not support. In fairness, about one-third of those present were members of the Autonomous Student Union, but the government insisted that they come to the meeting as individuals, not as representatives of an unofficial student organization. When pressed, officials even asked Wuer Kaixi to attend, but then informed him that he could not participate in the dialogue.

If the government was confused, so were the students. They professed to want a dialogue with the government because they believed the party could be reformed. All they wanted, they implied, was to sit down and reason with party officials. But what they were really pushing for were political organizations separate from the Communist party. They did not say so because they did not wish to alienate the government and were still uncertain how these organizations would be selected or function, or how they would relate to existing institutions. In spite of their desire to break with authority, they still depended on it. And because their demands were unclear, the government was understandably fuzzy about what to do for the students—or so it could claim.

In the end, the delegation which the government selected to meet with it consisted of some of the older leaders and some of the newer ones. Had they worked together, members of the movement might have been able to establish an agenda for these delegates. Instead, those who agreed to meet with the government were immediately denounced by their fellow students as government pawns. Those who finally went announced that they were attending only as individuals, not as part of any group. Several showed their displeasure by walking out in the middle of the dialogue. Few stopped to consider how far the government had gone in accepting their demands.

The students had asked for a meeting that could be seen and heard by the Chinese and international press. They got it. The government broadcast the discussion on television and radio throughout the country, repeating it a number of times. While millions, probably hundreds of millions, watched and listened, student leaders interrogated government spokesman Yuan Mu and a group of other panelists. The officials defended themselves reasonably well. They did not, as the students had hoped, concede to the demonstrators' points. But though the students did not always like Yuan Mu's tone and were not able to air all the issues they would have liked, they did speak to quite a few. The nation watched its leaders being berated about corruption, government distortion of the news media, the misreporting of the student demonstrations, the beatings administered to demonstrators, even the deployment of troops and the isolation and hobbies of its leaders, all broadcast over government-controlled media. At one point a student demanded, "We call on Prime Minister Li Peng to come out. Why can't the people's Prime Minister meet the people?"

These remarks about Li Peng, shown even in the first edited version of the television broadcast, led many Chinese to believe that he had been discredited. Until this point Secretary General Zhao Ziyang had been out of the country on a trip to North Korea. Thus he had not only avoided responsibility for the student activities but had been able to watch while Li Peng increasingly became the direct target of the demonstrators. Now Zhao was in a position to benefit from events. He saw a way to improve his own shaky position in the government.

On May 30, the day after the government talked with the students, Zhao returned from North Korea by train and, in speeches to members of the government, supported the students, contradicting the April 26 anti-student editorial. As a result of his encouragement, in the following days the Chinese press became increasingly strident. Convinced of victory against hard-line elements in the government, Zhao, in early May, for the first time told several government gatherings that, as he put it in a talk with a Turkish delegation, political and economic reforms "support each other."

In acknowledging that greater democracy was necessary to China's development, Zhao moved a long way from the idea of the new authoritarianism. But he still refused to recognize democracy as a value in its own right. He saw it rather as a tool with which he could pursue reform and preserve his own position. Both Zhao and the students were handicapped by their failure to understand that democracy demanded institutions in order to be successful. It could not be equated, as many seemed to believe, with "moral government" or the triumph of one political faction.

In discussions, the Party History people showed a better grasp of democracy than most other students. But as Zhao's power seemed to grow more secure, the Party History group faded from the protest scene. They realized they had scored an impressive victory; they saw what they had done in beginning the education of the Chinese people. But they did not appear to feel that the time was ripe for more direct action.

Once again their attitudes and temperament contrasted to those of their fellow student leaders. For one thing, the self-effacement of the Party History students seemed out of place with a protest that was increasingly becoming a media event. Other students were loud and raucous, holding press conferences and declaring their self-importance to anyone who would listen.

One day in early May an attractive foreign student told me how she had been approached by a self-proclaimed Chinese student leader who told her that he planned to hold a press conference in her dorm room later that night. He advised her to get dinner ready for him because he would be hungry. That same day I witnessed a Reuters reporter trying to obtain some comments from the Party History group about their role in the movement. They insisted that they put up the first wreaths in Tiananmen simply as a patriotic gesture, without any idea of what would follow. And Party History flags had been displayed so much more prominently than those of other schools in the big demonstrations because they had many of them left over from recent relay races!

Once the Party History group faded from the scene, the movement factionalized in a way familiar to observers of American student politics in the 1960s. One group would suddenly call a press conference, then others would cancel it.

On May 1 and 2 new elections for student leaders were held on the various campuses. The debates and discussions were acrimonious, and some of those not elected claimed they would leave the movement. Several times, in full view of the foreign press, student leaders fought each other for control of the microphone. There were even charges—some of which turned out to be true—that money collected for group use was being put to personal gain.

The dialogue with government officials on April 29 should have been interpreted as a student victory. The next day even the hard-line mayor of Beijing, Chen Xitong, and the city's party secretary, Li Ximing, invited a delegation of students for a discussion. Li disclosed his private income to prove he was not corrupt. But the students did not see this as a victory. Nor did they believe they had worked out an accommodation with the government. Instead they worried that by pushing too much they had alienated party leaders. To protect themselves, one of the students' major demands, as articulated by Wuer Kaixi on April 28, had been no punishment "after the autumn harvest," that is, when the demonstrations ended. Since they had not received even this agreement, they worried that the government was about to prosecute them.

By the end of the first week in May the campuses were gripped by a fear that the students had gone too far, that a backlash was inevitable. Some began to worry that when they went home for summer vacation they would be quietly seized by the police. A young teacher with whom I spoke told me that five of the most active of his students had all suddenly been called home. Two had received telegrams that their grandfathers had died, one had gotten a letter that an uncle had passed away, and two had taken phone calls that told of relatives who had suddenly become ill. Cynically, my friend told me he could not be sure if the parents were acting to get their children out of danger, or if the students had secretly written their parents asking for an excuse to leave the campus

At Beijing University, the parents of activist Jia Guangxin were more candid. They showed up on campus and told him to pack his bags and come home. Even Wuer Kaixi, elected leader of the Autonomous Student Union, disappeared briefly in early May, having gone into hiding because he feared arrest.

When it became clear that the government was not cracking down, most of the activists returned. On May 3 more than sixty students, led by the Beijing University history major Wang Dan, rode bicycles to the center of town to deliver a petition to the government demanding a new dialogue open to the press. They asked that the students be represented by delegates they had chosen themselves, and they insisted that the government be represented by a member of the Politburo, a vice chairman of the People's Congress, and other high-level policymakers. If the demands were not met, a May 4 march would take place.

Everyone had already done a good deal of talking, and another discussion with the government was of questionable value. At the same time the government had no reason to refuse the request. Instead of humoring the students, however, spokesman Yuan Mu irritatingly rejected their demands. He repeated the charge that "a handful of people" were behind the protests, suggesting links between the students and activists in the United States. He also alleged that Fang Lizhi had a hand in the disturbances. Although he also affirmed that government police would continue to be unarmed in dealing with the May 4 march, he expressed the impatience of many in the government by saying that China had "had enough social turmoil." He made it ominously clear: "The government has the ability and the determination to overcome the current disturbances."

The government rejected the students' own elected union because it still feared a Solidarity-style movement. In its April 26 editorial denouncing the students, the *People's Daily* had insisted, "No illegal organizations are allowed in China. No visiting of students to factories, countrysides, or schools." Officials worried that if they publicly recognized student-organized unions and delegates, they would be subjected to demands from countless other groups throughout the country who wanted similar freedom. In fact, most people who watched the televised dialogue of April 29 probably believed that the government had already capitulated on this point; so the government's distinction seemed trival and meaningless.

What no one said was that another discussion would accomplish nothing. What was needed was a procedure to ensure elected student representatives. But the students themselves had not been able to conduct real elections on their own campuses, and they seemed to have no idea how to make these concrete proposals.

Hence when the huge demonstration was held the next day, May 4, this time led by students from the Autonomous Student Union, it lacked the earlier excitement. This was not because the march was slightly smaller than the one of April 27—more than a hundred thousand were nonetheless on hand. Moreover, many workers joined students in the march despite warnings they would be fined. Yet both sides acted as if from a script. Once again the students linked arms and walked in formation. Once more, for reasons that are baffling, police were scattered at intersections throughout the city, and the students pushed through their lines showing how they could defy the authorities. But there was little of the tension that existed on April 27. The ranks of the security forces parted easily each time the column of students approached. The students marched, but it was unclear why they were marching.

Mostly the students displayed a general disgruntlement with the government. Many carried signs which mocked the saying attributed to Deng Xiaoping that had been the mainstay of the reform movement: "It doesn't matter if the cat is

black or white, as long as it catches mice it's a good cat."
The students' version read: "It doesn't matter if the cat is
black or white, neither can catch mice." This pretty well
summed up the feelings of the day.

Meanwhile, on May 2 six thousand students had marched
in Shanghai in sympathy with their Beijing colleagues. When
I flew there on the morning of May 4 to see what was
happening, I heard again and again from people in the streets
that the student demonstrators were not Shanghai students but
natives of other cities. The townspeople seemed to want to
distance themselves from the protesters.

In the morning the protests in Shanghai were small. As the
day wore on, however, the students picked up support just as
they had in Beijing. Several times they walked the short
distance from People's Park to the Municipal Building, tying
up traffic in the center of town as they marched. The police
worked hard to keep nonstudents from joining the protests,
checking identification cards of all who entered the park. Still
the demonstrations swelled. By evening, as more and more
people poured out of the campuses, at least twenty thousand
had joined the protesters.

The feelings of the crowd had undergone a measurable
change as well. They jammed the sidewalks and the windows
of buildings along the line of the march, clapping and
cheering wildly for the students. It had become a people's
demonstration. Moreover, there were similar, smaller protests
in Nanjing, Wuhan, Fuzhou, Guangzhou, Changsha, and
many other places in China and abroad.

The biggest change from April 27, however, was not in the
spread of protests to other cities but in the reaction of China's
journalists. Many now marched alongside the students. In
Beijing several hundred gathered in front of the official New
China News Agency to demand the reinstatement of the
editor of the *World Economic Herald*. They also protested the

biased and inaccurate reporting of the news that had characterized the Chinese media.

This was an astonishing turn of events, one which was to have a great influence on China in the coming weeks. Earlier I noted that journalism students at People's University had been among the most politically active students in the school. Throughout the course of the demonstrations the press had become freer and freer in its coverage, both in response to student pressure and liberalized government policy. Now the press itself declared it would cover events openly.

A few Western journalists with whom I spoke were stupefied. One Reuters correspondent noted that he had just seen some writers whom he had previously taken to be party hacks carrying banners and shouting for freedom of the press.

Because many people were used to interpreting party policy by gauging press accounts of different issues, this change in the press gave new legitimacy to the student movement. As the press became free to discuss events, many Chinese assumed that the movement had gained official endorsement and felt freer to give it their support.

This then was a significant victory. But realizing they could do little more without a clearer agenda, the next day students at People's University announced an end to their boycott of classes. Students at most other major schools also prepared to resume their studies, but not everyone agreed. A noisy group of young protesters at Beijing University declared they would maintain the boycott.

The students had helped to unshackle China's press and television. They had put the reform movement back on track, allowing Zhao Ziyang at least a temporary victory. And they had forced the government to back off from earlier attempts to label the students "unpatriotic." The government had been forced to treat them seriously, but the students had won no guarantees that their movement would persist. After Propaganda Minister Hu Qili, on April 28, told newsmen they could cover the student demonstrations, journalists had moved into a vacuum left by a weakened power structure to demand a freer press. Perhaps the students could have insisted that the National People's Congress remain in session and establish government bodies that would define and ensure democratic procedures. But they did not do this. The closest they came to a concrete proposal was on May 4, when the leaders of the Autonomous Student Union suggested that democracy on the campuses become a model for the rest of the society.

Meanwhile, all they could do now was return to campus, hoping that Zhao was back in power and that he would work to create the kinds of reforms he had promised. This seemed to be what many, including the Party History students, still hoped. But the radicals would not accept this. Their actions continued to rattle the power structure and ultimately forced the hard-liners to move.

After the April 27 march, students felt they had finally broken with the restraints of the old culture. "We marched to Tiananmen Square when they told us we couldn't. The workers came out to support us. We delivered the declaration of the new May Fourth movement," said Wuer Kaixi. Like his colleagues, Wuer had been influenced by the television documentary *River Elegy*, which had explored the authoritarian nature of China's traditions. "The emperor told us not to march," many students repeatedly observed, "But this time we didn't listen to the emperor. The emperor tradition is now dead." It was not the first time in this century that Chinese students had broken with authority figures, but then or now they were unable to offer a substitute for this authoritarian structure. Ultimately, they still wanted the government to say that what they did was right.

THE HUNGER STRIKE

It's ages now I've been asking you:
When will you come away with me?
But all you ever do is laugh at me, 'cause
I've got nothing to my name.

I want to give you my hope
I want to help make you free
But all you ever do is laugh at me, 'cause
I've got nothing to my name.

When will you come away with me?

The ground is moving under your feet
The waters of life are flowing free
But all you ever do is laugh at me, 'cause
I've got nothing to my name.

The Chinese youths who marched in April and May 1989 knew these lyrics by heart. They come from a song by Cui

Jian, the lead singer in Beijing's best-known rock band. Cui Jian and his group usually sang these words while dressed in the army fatigues and peasant cottons favored by Communist cadres during the Yanan period of the Chinese revolution in the 1940s. In 1989 young people such as Cui Jian looked back to the caves of Yanan—neither with the reverence of an older generation that had turned that era into a symbol of revolutionary flowering, nor with scorn. Rather, Chinese youth recalled this time as an age of audacity, when people were willing to try to make something of their lives without regard for what had gone before.

During April and May, Cui Jian's lyrics came to be the symbol for a generation that refused to give up the struggle. They represented the feelings of those who felt that the "ground is moving" and the "waters of life are flowing." As another Cui Jian song put it:

> *Twenty years and all I've learnt is patience, holding on.*
> *No wonder all the comrades said my head was in the clouds,*
> *I got myself together, made myself stop dreaming,*
> *Now I'm awake and I can see*
> *This world's as weird as weird can be.*

During April students set out to change the weirdness that had become China. They came closer than anyone dreamed possible. With "nothing to [their] name," they had, as Cui Jian urged, run off. Now they were unwilling to stop. When older intellectuals entreated them to be reasonable, they were not inclined to listen. They believed in themselves in a way that earlier groups of students never had. They were sure they were about to do something their elders had never accomplished.

For generations Chinese students had struggled for their own freedom and for the economic development of their country. Each generation saw its hopes postponed. The radicals of 1898 suffered a harsh government crackdown, then, after their seeming triumph in 1911, they witnessed the disintegration of Chinese government and society. The May Fourth activists watched their movement overtaken by the horrors of the warlord years, the fratricidal fighting between the Communists and the Guomindang, and finally the invasion of their country by the Japanese. The radicals of the 1930s had their lives unhinged first by World War II and then by the civil war. And the students of the Cultural Revolution lived through a movement that collapsed into violence and terror.

The student radicals of 1989 had experienced none of this. By the end of the 1980s China had enjoyed its longest tranquil period in more than a century. From 1969 to 1989 Chinese society steadily improved. Children raised during this time of hope and prosperity never fully understood their parents, who grew up during an age of hardship and bitterness. This was not because of a difference in values between the old and the young. Most student activists were the children of liberal intellectuals and Communist party members; their parents shared their hopes for change and democracy. The gulf between the young students and the older generation was one of experience. Disappointment had taught the parents to postpone their dreams and desires. Again and again, the young had been reminded both at home and in school how bad times had once been—the horrors of life under the Gang of Four and the misery of the old society before 1949. They were told this so many times they were sick of it.

They were fed up with being lectured about how grateful they should be to Deng Xiaoping for removing the horrors of the past. They no longer wished to hear of how much people had suffered before. They wanted to talk about what to do now.

Compared with earlier generations of Chinese children, they had grown up in affluence, but they still felt poor. They were the first generation in China in more than a century not scarred by poverty and fighting. While China was developing rapidly, they still felt it was too slow. They felt they could change the present in a way the old would never understand. They did not feel they had to wait for the future to win the values for which successive generations had struggled. They *were* the future.

Their sense of this future was not simply ideological. Students were comfortable with the technological and economic advances that had occurred in China in the previous decade in a way that the older generation was not. Their ability to take advantage of these new methods and opportunities greatly enhanced the movement's tactical agility. When I lived in China at the beginning of the 1980s, few people had telephones in their homes. Even the most sophisticated Chinese were usually awkward on the phone. Conversations were kept short, and they rarely conveyed important information. People often yelled into the phone, believing it was the only way their voices could travel such a long distance.

By 1989 telephones in China, though still not as widespread as in America, were commonplace. In urban areas many private homes and apartments had installed phone lines. The volume of long-distance calls had increased 280 percent during the decade of the 1980s. It became possible to dial directly into China from foreign countries, including the United States. The young were comfortable with telephones.

This detail was important to the development of the protest movement. Students on different campuses used the phone to coordinate their plans. They called friends in other parts of the city and country to keep them abreast of events and to help spread the word of what they had done. Before newspapers in China began reporting on the protests, many students learned about what was going on from friends abroad, who would call to tell them what the media in Hong Kong and foreign countries were saying about events in their own country. Others listened avidly to the Voice of America and the BBC. By 1989 many students had their own shortwave sets. Because the Chinese government had ceased jamming broadcasts from overseas, they were able to tune to these stations freely.

A relaxation in travel restrictions also helped them. Because people no longer had to put up with complex procedures in traveling from city to city in China, many Chinese in the provinces hopped on trains and flooded into Beijing to take part in the movement. Their bodies added weight to the protests in the capital. Later some of these students went back to their hometowns and persuaded their friends to imitate what was going on in Beijing.

The students also took advantage of the new economy. Street vendors and private entrepreneurs were among the first city people to support the students. They did not need to fear being fired or reported by a work unit. They had money and time to give the movement. By late April student leaders were able to use some of these donations to purchase battery-operated megaphones—the kind of item that would have been undreamed of in China a decade earlier. Now they were readily available in stores. Other new products of the reform era were also put into the service of the movement, such as the public address systems and tape recorders that allowed the students to bring their message to the masses. By the end of the protests some student leaders even had walkie-talkies, cellular phones, and beepers. The students deployed these tools with an ease and proficiency that amazed many of their elders.

The item that drew the most attention when used by students was the facsimile machine. Fax transmissions of news from abroad helped the protesters know what was being written about them in foreign newspapers. Many of these machines were lent to the students by one of the largest of the new private enterprises, the Stone Computer Company. (Some of the megaphones and loudspeakers mentioned above were also financed by Stone.) This company alone probably gave the students tens of thousands of dollars, some say hundreds of thousands of dollars, of equipment.

People coming from abroad also brought aid for the students. By 1989 complex visa application procedures to enter China had become a relic of the past. Many in Hong Kong simply hopped on planes and set down in Beijing a few hours later with money and supplies for the movement. These were channels which the students knew their elders would never have believed possible.

The new world in which the students had grown up had not only made them more familiar with technology than their parents, it also had given them a radically different culture. They dressed and acted differently. Their clothes and behavior often had less in common with older intellectuals than with the urban toughs who hung around the periphery of the movement. Such groups have been a feature in Chinese cities for many years now. *Liumang,* as the Chinese call them, are usually seen as the antithesis of normal middle-class Chinese values. But in the late 1980s, though few would admit it, the line between toughs and students began to blur. Students began to dress like *liumang* and even began to cut their hair like them. By the gates of every university, one could see students and underworld types interacting. They joked with each other, made deals together, and sometimes, as in June 1988, fought together. Often I could not tell them apart.

It used to be that undesirables were those without jobs. But in the late 1980s many who could not find jobs became private entrepreneurs or worked for nonofficial companies. A new world grew up in China, one populated by many who were not associated with official government work units. In some ways, those engaged in illicit activities became role models for the students. They made a lot of money. They handled black-market currency deals. They sold the illegal tapes and pornographic books that the students sometimes bought. They dressed in fashionable Western clothes, some of which they also sold, having bought them on the sly from licensed joint-venture factories established in China. Some of these underworld types were in fact former students or dissidents.

Even when they were still distinguishable, it was clear that attitudes toward the undesirables had changed. Occasionally when I referred to some obvious toughs as *liumang,* I was corrected by young Chinese friends who preferred to refer to them as *shimin,* or city people. For many, some of these *shimin* commanded respect because of their success in a culture where everyone had been told that "to get rich is glorious." They also attracted students because they showed that, in the new world, it was not the old government which knew how to succeed but precisely those anti-establishment, subterranean elements which their parents had always warned them against.

These *shimin* were often the first to act out the students' fantasies. In the early days of the demonstrations it was the *liumang* who shouted out the slogans against Deng Xiaoping and Li Peng. Later the students imitated them. The *shimin* were the ones who in late April attempted to break down the gates to Zhongnanhai where the party leaders lived, flouting the leaders of the Chinese government and radicalizing the students' actions.

An alliance between radical students and underworld types is not a new phenomenon in Chinese society, although it may have been out of fashion for some time. One of the most famous traditional Chinese novels, *Shuihu zhuan,* or *Water Margin* (translated by Pearl Buck under the title *All Men Are Brothers*), romanticizes a Robin Hood–style gang of bandits. For centuries this theme has been a major focus of Chinese fiction, one avidly devoured by generations of Chinese youth. In more recent times one of the fans of this genre was the young Mao Zedong. As a revolutionary Mao developed a military strategy which modeled itself after that of the bandit and rebel forces in the Chinese countryside. As late as the 1960s, during the Cultural Revolution, the line between gangsters and Red Guards often blurred.

This anti-establishment theme also characterized the rock music that was a constant part of student life. The daring and individualism of the music portrayed the feelings of a generation certain that their way of life would break the molds of the past. The importance of this music was emphasized in September 1989 when the exiled student leader Wuer Kaixi electrified scholars gathered in Boston by telling them that Chinese rock had been more important to student protesters than the ideas of reformist intellectuals. Especially Wuer singled out the Taiwanese singer Qi Qin and the Beijing group headed by Cui Jian (whose lead guitarist was a Hungarian student staying in the foreigners' dormitory at People's University).

To illustrate his point, Wuer sang the Qi Qin ballad that begins, "I am a wolf from the North, a wolf from the North, wandering in the boundless desert." Like the Bob Dylan song of the 1960s, "Highway 61 Revisited," Qi Qin's tune speaks of an individual wandering alone through the bleak landscape of the present. Wuer used this image to illustrate the individualism of his generation, which he said dared to speak out "against authority," unlike the intellectuals of the past who "have given up the idea of reform."

Wuer's lines could just as easily have been spoken at a meeting of American radicals in the 1960s. As if from a set play about that period, no sooner had Wuer finished speaking than an older Chinese woman jumped to her feet to denounce him, arguing that his ideas did not represent those of Chinese society. She even mocked his manners. Had he been more conversant with American songs from the sixties, Wuer might have replied, "Something is happening, and you don't know what it is, do you, Mr. Jones?"

This generation gap was part of what stood between the government and movement leaders in early May, when high-level members of Zhao Ziyang's camp contacted student leaders and urged them to return to class, assuring them that the struggle had been won. Older students were willing to accept such assurance, but the new generation did not share the same respect for authority. They were a generation that wanted hard results. What the students had won was not yet clear, and no one was at all certain that Zhao could bring them victory in any case.

Although many believed Zhao to be a sincere reformer, nothing he had done had assured the students that he would be able to move beyond the authoritarian party culture of the past. Yes, in several speeches—notably the one on May 4, to the governors of the Asian Development Bank—he had expressed agreement with the students' "radical demands" and suggested that they sought to correct "certain defects" in the party rather than to oppose China's fundamental system. For Zhao this had been a daring step. He had implicitly contradicted the party's official April 26 editorial denouncing the demonstrators as perpetrators of "turmoil." Chinese President Yang Shangkun was later to denounce Zhao's speech as "a turning point...that entirely exposed the different opinions of the standing committee of the Politburo." The speech became one of the reasons for Zhao's later removal from office.

But even Zhao's worst enemies have never proved that he engaged in anti-party activities. For Zhao never stated what he was willing to do concretely for the students (and this is of course why the students still distrusted him). Instead he had merely suggested that "imperfections in the socialist legal system and democratic supervision" were due to the party's "lack of openness." The most Zhao had offered the protest movement was to say that "reasonable demands by the students should be met through democratic and legal means."

While suggesting that dialogues be pursued with many different groups, Zhao had made no definite commitment.

In spite of Zhao's promises, no dialogues developed. In early May Zhao never formally met with any student group to declare himself on their side. At no point did he suggest what he was prepared to do to advance democracy. If he was supporting the students, he remained a remote leader. Students would have liked to trust him, but he had given them nothing to affirm their faith in him. His deeds characterized him as just another member of the old culture, part of the problem rather than part of the solution.

Moreover, it was never clear whether Zhao had the power to deliver what he implied he wished to give. The day after his speech to the Asian Development Bank, the harder-line Li Peng spoke to the same forum and suggested that while many student demands were in line with those of the party, the government nevertheless disapproved of "some actions of the students."

Word had come down that the student movement had helped Zhao improve his standing within the party; but if that were so, he was not using his new power decisively. Like most members of the old culture, he was reluctant to act without the approval of his leader, Deng Xiaoping. A poster hanging on Changan Avenue, next to Tiananmen, expressed the feelings of the students toward all of China's top leaders. It read, "Notice of Missing Persons: Deng Xiaoping, Zhao Ziyang, and Li Peng."

Beset with these doubts, radical student leaders nonetheless moved to cut back their protests. After the May 4 march, students at all schools except Beijing University and Beijing Normal University returned to classes. The protests did not end altogether. Posters denouncing the government continued to appear on the campuses. The loudspeaker system at People's University still functioned and attracted huge crowds of workers and city people with its radical rhetoric. The newsletter published by the Autonomous Student Union continued to be printed. At Beijing University as many as 70 percent of the students honored the strike, though most of these students seemed interested only in having the government consider the rather mild demand of the union for a new dialogue with government leaders.

In the short run what they got was not dialogue with politicians but lectures from intellectuals associated with Zhao Ziyang's brains trust. On May 5 a group of reformers, many of whom had been writing for the banned Shanghai weekly *World Economic Herald,* began a lecture tour of the major campuses in Beijing. The group included such intellectual luminaries once known to be close to Zhao Ziyang as the journalist Dai Qing, the dissident Marxist theoretician Su Shaozhi, and the respected intellectual commentator Yan Jiaqi, as well as a number of younger scholars. These intellectuals had been encouraged by Zhao's May 4 speech. Now they mobilized to support him.

They urged the students to press for more freedom of the press, the promulgation of a constitution that would guarantee equal treatment under the law, and an end to rule by personalities. Politics, they insisted, was directly related to continued economic reform. A loss of party discipline and widespread corruption had undermined people's faith in the government and made the continued promulgation of economic adjustments difficult.

The most outspoken intellectual was the journalist Dai Qing, whose family connections gave her a firsthand knowledge of the political intrigues at the highest levels of government. At a speech at People's University on May 5, Dai said, "I feel that April 27, 1989, like October 1, 1949; June 6, 1966, and April 5, 1976, before it, is a most important day in the history of the People's Republic of China, because every one of these days has accomplished something important in the history of the People's Republic. Don't you know that, beginning April 27, 1989, the authoritarian rule, which has reigned over China for over one thousand years, is coming to an end?''

June 6, 1966, marked the start of the Cultural Revolution. In this speech, Dai, someone with close ties to Zhao, acknowledged that Mao's struggle against Deng Xiaoping, Liu Shaoqi, and others during the 1960s had been a blow against autocracy. This thought was heretical in Chinese official circles. Only a few weeks earlier Dai had advocated the new authoritarianism. Her speech showed how much members of Zhao's camp had changed their public stance as a result of the student movement. At least one important Chinese intellectual now appeared to endorse the Cultural Revolution.

With some of his closest supporters making these kinds of radical statements, why didn't Zhao Ziyang arrange a direct conversation with the students? Because Deng had not told him he could do so. Rather than defy his mentor, Zhao preferred to sit tight and push from behind the scenes. He was using the students to help maneuver his way up through government circles. In so doing, he was showing that he knew little about the kind of open government he had endorsed. He played by the old rules, but there were others within the government who could play by these rules better than he.

About May 8, Deng Xiaoping and a group of other party elders all in their eighties, none still holding formal high party positions, are said to have begun to meet secretly. They decided then that they must continue to back the April 26 editorial and began to plot the eventual military suppression of the demonstrators. The hard-liners galvanized the Beijing Municipal Committee. Before the Cultural Revolution this group had been the stronghold of anti-Mao forces; Mao touched off the events of that era with a purge of Peng Zhen, then the leader of this group and now one of the old-timers who met with Deng. In late April, Beijing officials had been instrumental in the events leading up to the anti-student April 26 editorial. Now the two leaders of Peng's old Beijing organization, the Mayor Chen Xitong and the party boss Li Ximing, suggested to other party faithful that Zhao's May 4 remarks to the Asian Development Bank had been his personal views, not those of the party. The two also confronted Zhao face to face on this issue. Zhao is reported to have told them, "I'll be responsible for what was wrong in my speech."

According to Chen Yizi, the former head of Zhao Ziyang's economic think tank and the highest-ranking Chinese official to have escaped abroad, at a May 8 meeting of the Politburo's standing committee Zhao made a series of radical proposals to investigate corruption and establish an independent press and judiciary. Li Peng refused to accept them, shouting that they did not represent the party's official position. Chen Yizi relates that Zhao then left the meeting to visit the students on the square. Li Peng followed him to his car and yanked the door open, warning Zhao that if he met with the students he would be held responsible for splitting the party. Zhao drove off, but when he arrived at the square he had his driver circle it three times, not daring to leave the car.

In the end, rather than meet the students, Zhao contented himself with talk, not action. Throughout the first week of May, even as his intellectual supporters toured the campuses, Zhao had made a number of public statements in support of the students. When confronted by the Beijing party officials on May 8, Zhao made his strongest comment yet, suggesting in televised remarks the same day that "political restructuring" would support the economic reforms. Zhao's language stood in sharp contrast to the opinions expressed by hard-liners. But Zhao still hesitated to meet directly with students.

In early May, on cue with the actions of the hard-liners in Beijing, a new major presence was heard—Jiang Zemin, head of the Shanghai Communist party. Jiang had antagonized many students and intellectuals in late April when he had banned the *World Economic Herald*. Partly because of his actions, journalists had joined in the May 4 demonstrations, and growing freedom of the press had become one of the few achievements of the movement. To preserve this gain, on May 5 several Chinese legal scholars began a lawsuit against Jiang on behalf of the *World Economic Herald*. They argued that Jiang not only had acted illegally against a private paper but had slandered the reputation of Qin Benli, the paper's editor. If upheld, this charge would have set a precedent for other newspapers who wished to limit party interference with the press.

While Zhao Ziyang made no comment on this issue, Jiang moved aggressively to defend himself and the hard-line establishment for which he worked. First, in a speech before a reported ten thousand cadres in Shanghai, Jiang argued the necessity of closing the paper. Had he allowed publication of the April 24 issue of the *World Economic Herald,* the one carrying a series of incendiary articles about Hu Yaobang, Jiang suggested that the already explosive situation in China would have been greatly aggravated. Then on Sunday, May 7, three days after the May 4 demonstrations and Zhao's speech to the Asian Development bank, Jiang banned the paper once more, demonstrating that he was one official in China who did not back down under pressure. The paper was banned a second time, it was said, because those who wrote the latest edition had printed a statement denouncing as illegal the party's action in removing editor Qin Benli from office several weeks earlier. Jiang's actions, coming as they did just before the hard-liners met, were to make him the hero of the old guard.

Both sides were stirring. Zhao had to pick his issues carefully. He was walking a delicate tightrope. In order to win his battle within the Politburo, he needed to keep the pressure on his opponents. But if the students pushed events out of control, a fear of chaos might lose Zhao support at the upper levels of the government. In discussions within the Politburo, Zhao's ace in the hole was the idea that he alone could peacefully resolve the student problems. He had to keep the students in his camp by encouraging them, but he also had to show the party that he could bring them under control.

As the struggle between moderates and hard-liners intensified and the government still stalled its plans for a dialogue, protests at the universities remained sporadic. On May 7, even after calls from the Autonomous Student Union to end the strike, Beijing University students voted to continue it. On May 8, the Beijing University Preparatory Committee formally voted to continue a limited boycott to ensure that their demands for a dialogue were met.

The next day a few of these students returned to the streets. On May 9 more than a thousand Chinese journalists from thirty news organizations, responding to Jiang Zemin's actions in closing the *World Economic Herald,* submitted a petition to the government calling for greater freedom of the press. As the journalists presented their petition, a group of about a thousand students demonstrated outside the building. Later they staged a short march to Tiananmen Square, banging on the gates of the *People's Daily* on their return.

The issue of press freedom had become a cornerstone of the student movement. The victory which had apparently been won on April 27 was now jeopardized by Jiang Zemin. The students determined not to let it rest. On May 10 about five thousand students staged a bicycle parade, protesting in front of the offices of China's major newspapers to support the journalists. For the first time they wore colorful headbands, adorned with Chinese characters, which they had copied from pictures of South Korean students. By the offices of Chinese TV, the students shouted, "Central People's Broadcasting turns white into black and truth into lies!" At every stop, they yelled, "Support the journalists' petition!"

Later about fifty well-known Beijing writers, poets, and novelists, all on bicycles, linked up with the student protesters. The writers called for freedom for all media and wore T-shirts supporting the movement.

Events now began to move quickly. The visit to China of Mikhail Gorbachev, secretary general of the Soviet Union, was less than a week away. Because relations between China and the Soviets had been broken for thirty years, this scheduled meeting of top-level leaders of the two countries was expected be a personal triumph for Deng Xiaoping, ushering in more stable relations between the two nations. Everyone assumed that the government would want to bring the protests under control before Gorbachev's arrival to avoid a major international embarrassment.

As his arrival grew imminent, Gorbachev became a symbol which the students used against their own government. Before the April 27 march, Deng had made it clear that he feared the escalation of the student demonstrations into the kind of chaos already sweeping Poland and the Soviet Union. Throwing this back in his face, the students demanded they be given the same rights as Polish and Soviet citizens. Chinese students and journalists now contrasted Gorbachev's youth and energy with those of Chinese leaders. They pointed out that Gorbachev was considered an honest politician. His children, they noted, had become doctors, not officials or businessmen dependent on government connections.

In fact, students exaggerated Soviet liberties. In talking about freedom of the press in eastern Europe, no one pointed out, for example, that the Soviet press had not been allowed to give a full account of the Chinese demonstrations. Nor did students discuss the obstacles that Gorbachev faced within his own government. Nonetheless, on May 11 students at Beijing University announced that they would petition Gorbachev to come to their campus and exchange ideas about socialism.

Meanwhile, the students discussed how to take further

advantage of the Gorbachev visit if the government continued to avoid a dialogue with them. At first the Autonomous Student Union proposed that the students march into the square and then leave. Then a group of radicals, who had studied the tactics of Mahatma Gandhi, advanced the idea of a hunger strike. Chai Ling, a Beijing Normal University graduate student in psychology whose husband had been one of the three students who kowtowed in front of the Great Hall of the People on the day of Hu Yaobang's funeral, was one of the chief proponents of the idea. She convinced some students from her school to join her. In the beginning, movement leaders like Wuer Kaixi and the Beijing University history major Wang Dan were dubious, and the idea had little support on the other campuses. But after Chai gave a moving speech at Beijing University, a number of students got behind the proposal, and it won acceptance. Ultimately, several of the top leaders of the Beijing Autonomous Student Union, including Wuer Kaixi and Wang Dan, attached their names to a list of hunger strikers; soon more than a thousand had signed. On May 12 they issued an ultimatum: if the government did not respond immediately to their requests for a dialogue, the next day they would begin a hunger strike in Tiananmen Square.

The government did not respond. More than three hundred Beijing students gathered at Beijing Normal University and announced that they would fast until the country's leaders agreed to an open dialogue with them. "We are young, but we are ready to give up our lives," they declared. Led by Wuer Kaixi, they marched into Tiananmen Square on May 13 wearing headbands that read FASTING and coats that announced WITHOUT DEMOCRACY, WE WOULD RATHER DIE. At the base of the Monument to the Heroes of the People, they sat surrounded by fifteen to twenty thousand supporters and onlookers who chanted and screamed slogans backing their ideas. The fast began officially at 5:20 p.m. At the start it was high drama, but no one realized how successful it would be in reviving a flagging movement.

It seemed a desperate bid by what in the words of Qi Qin's popular song were a few hard-core "wolves from the North," a group which seemed to be a perfect symbol for the new counterculture. Although they tried to act like Gandhi, their headbands had been copied from South Korean student radicals known for extremism and rampant violence. Just a few months earlier, Korean students had incinerated a policeman trying to dislodge them from a protest site.

Student radicals, worldwide, have often identified themselves with the image of students as bohemians, appropriating a hodgepodge of ideas and customs from peers in other lands in order to express their revolt against their own tradition. During the last years of the Qing dynasty, student radicals had shown their disavowal of the old society by cutting their hair short, a feature they copied from Western students of the time. Now, in 1989, they wore it long, fastened with a headband.

By fasting they hoped to contrast the moral righteousness of their behavior with that of the corrupt and despotic government against which they protested. "We love democracy more than rice," they shouted as they camped at the very center of Tiananmen. A welcoming ceremony had been scheduled nearby for Mikhail Gorbachev in forty-eight hours. Now the students sat at the exact point where Gorbachev was expected to lay a wreath honoring China's revolutionary martyrs. Their action galvanized China and the world.

They also thought it would make their government act. Few of the initial hunger-strikers imagined that they would have to continue their fast for very long. Most believed that by camping in the middle of Tiananmen Square on the eve of the Gorbachev visit, they would either force the government to dislodge them or make concessions. Most knew that a few days earlier, on May 10 and 11, an emergency meeting of the

FORBIDDEN CITY

Changan Avenue   To Beijing Hotel →

Great Hall of the People

Museum of Chinese Revolutionary History

Site of Hunger Strike and Protesters' Camp

Monument to the Revolutionary Martyrs

Mao's mausoleum

TIANANMEN SQUARE

Qianmen Xi Avenue

TIANANMEN SQUARE AND ENVIRONS

Politburo had reportedly backed Zhao Ziyang's call for a dialogue with student demonstrators and the implementation of more democratic procedures. Zhao had reportedly also submitted a letter agreeing to take action against two of his sons accused of corruption. The government was already capitulating to the students. On May 12, at Zhao's behest, a lead story in *People's Daily* praised democracy, human rights, and "a balance of power within the government," the first time such a pronouncement had ever appeared in the official press. Perhaps a little more nonviolent pressure would bring matters to a head.

Now that he had victory in hand, the students demanded that Zhao act. He hesitated. Although Zhao had received the Politburo's endorsement, Deng Xiaoping had failed to attend the meeting. Zhao therefore wished to move cautiously. At this point cautious leadership would not work.

Zhao's style was so different from that of the students, it is unlikely they ever could have gotten together. His was the slow, ponderous manner of the government bureaucrat. On May 12, the day after the Politburo meeting and the same day the students announced their planned hunger strike, the party's Central Committee finally established a Dialogue Preparatory Group, which announced that it would begin to develop procedures for a discussion with Chinese journalists. On May 13, as the hunger-strikers occupied the square, Zhao called on them to be reasonable during the Gorbachev visit. He informed the students that the issues they raised would be placed on the agenda of the mid-July plenary session of the standing committee of the National People's Congress. In the hours before the hunger strike there were more government offers of dialogue, but they were rejected by the students as insincere.

Other official appeals followed. The next day the hard-line mayor of Beijing, Chen Xitong, and the chief of the state education commission, Li Tieying, came to the square and personally promised that a dialogue would be held. They too asked the students to leave.

Meanwhile, Yan Jiaqi, Su Shaozhi, Bao Zunxin, and other members of Zhao Ziyang's so-called brains trust wrote a dramatic poster proclaiming "We Can No Longer Remain Silent," which they posted at Beijing University on the evening when the students first occupied the square. The next day many of these same establishment intellectuals broadcast an appeal that declared the student movement "a patriotic democracy movement" and demanded that the Autonomous Student Union be legalized. The words of these "twelve famous scholars and authors" were reported in the *Guangming Daily*, one of the country's major national newspapers, and broadcast over the government-controlled television station. The significance of such open protest was not lost on Chinese readers, normally accustomed to seeing in the media only what the government approved. In their message the intellectuals described "how upset" they had been since the students began their hunger strike. They brought new attention and sympathy to the students, enhancing their credibility and popularity.

But while trying to see that the students' demands were satisfied, these intellectuals who were also backers of Zhao worked frantically to move the students off the square. Before the hunger strike began, Zhao seemed to have won. Everyone hoped that a little more pressure would make the government grant the students the dialogue they wanted. Instead the students' actions gave the hard-liners credibility and jeopardized Zhao's victory. Seeking to help him, the intellectuals called on the students—"for the sake of the long-term benefit of the reforms" and to ensure a harmonious summit between China and the Soviet Union—to "temporarily leave Tiananmen Square." If they did so, the intellectuals said, the government would have a genuine dialogue with them. If there were no dialogue, they promised to join the struggle with the students.

These middle-aged intellectuals had little idea of what was going on in the students' minds. They were still trying to persuade them to respect the party's authority and to trust its bureaucratic decision-making process. The intellectuals may have had a better understanding of political realities than the students, and certainly they had a better grasp of the workings of democracy, but they understood nothing about the psychology of the rebels. While the students saw themselves as defying tradition, the intellectuals still spoke about respecting the rules of the party—in ways not dissimilar to those once expounded by Liu Shaoqi and Deng Xiaoping when they tried to contain an earlier generation of student radicals in the initial stages of the Cultural Revolution. The students knew where the efforts of Deng and Liu had led; they had no interest in following others who walked the same path.

But the intellectuals were not the only members of Zhao's camp to present a doomed, last-minute effort for compromise. That same afternoon two officials sympathetic to the protesters' demands, chairman of the state education commission Li Tieying and minister of the United Front Department Yan Mingfu, met for several hours in a building across the road from Zhongnanhai with about thirty students, including Wang Dan, Chai Ling, and Wuer Kaixi. The officials apologized that it had taken them so long to arrange a dialogue; they cautioned that if the students pressed their demands too far, they would provide an excuse for a crackdown by hard-line officials. The meeting went affably until time for the 7 o'clock evening news, when it became clear that the talks would not be broadcast. An angry crowd of students gathered at Zhongnanhai demanding that their compatriots leave the talks. The talks broke up at 7:20 p.m., the students feeling the meeting had been a charade. Once again the government, even the most decent and moderate among them, were playing by the old party rules. Having rejected the April 29 dialogue, there was no way the students would accept this one. If they were to win, the students decided they would have to speak with Zhao Ziyang and Li Peng. They should have said Deng Xiaoping.

The Gorbachev visit was now less than a day away. One can imagine the desperation and fear of government officials, worried about what might happen if Gorbachev arrived while the students still occupied the square. Zhao knew that his legitimacy within the government depended on his ability to get the students to see reason and leave peacefully. But he also feared to defy Deng by going to meet directly with the students. By trying to persuade them to place their faith in the system, Zhao and his allies showed little understanding of this new generation. Perhaps they still thought they were dealing with Party History graduate students rather than a younger generation of radicals who enjoyed defying authority. As long as no one in the government was prepared to do something concrete for them, these students would stick to their guns.

The futility of government efforts was evident later that evening, when members of the public security bureau ordered the students to leave the square by 8:30 the next morning because of Gorbachev's visit scheduled for that day. Yet it was clear that the government had no way to enforce this order short of a bloodbath, which would have cast a pall over the Gorbachev visit, to say the least. The students remained.

Their movement swelled. The first day, May 13, there were twenty thousand supporters on the square. By the second day they had grown to thirty thousand. It was blistering hot during the day and cold at night. Toilets overflowed. Garbage piled up. The square began to stink. During the midday heat of the first day, several fainted. The strikers began using the latrines in pairs to ensure that those who went did not fall down from hunger. When the first ten strikers were sent to the hospital, the students gained even more sympathy from the masses. Five hundred students bicycled eighty miles from Tianjin to join the strike. The hunger-strikers' ranks swelled from three hundred to three thousand. Smaller demonstrations broke out in small cities and towns throughout China. And in some of these areas, such as Jiangsu province, government officials met in a public forum with journalists and protesters.

By 8 o'clock Monday morning, May 15, the students had defied the security orders and remained on the square, humiliating Deng Xiaoping and forcing the welcoming ceremony for Soviet leader Gorbachev to be switched from the square to the airport. Now the movement begin to career wildly out of control. That day almost eighty thousand people crowded into the square. The world media, including Dan Rather of CBS News, arrived in Beijing to cover the summit and set up their cameras in Tiananmen Square, where they were to have reported Gorbachev's arrival. Instead, they focused world attention on the students.

There was no longer any question that the students had directly challenged the government. It was clear to sophisticated observers that party elders and Zhao could not compromise their differences. It was a time to choose sides. Yan Jiaqi's group of intellectuals, many of whom just the night before had signed a letter urging the students to leave the square, finally stopped trying to reach a compromise and instead took action. They formed their own Union of Intellectuals and marched into the square to endorse the student movement. They also asked the media to make the movement public, demanding, even at this late hour, that rumors of behind-the-scenes attempts to incite the students be denied. Later that day teachers from universities throughout Beijing also poured into the square to show support for their students.

The actions of all these prestigious and influential figures helped to change the event on the square from a student protest into a mass movement. The students welcomed others into their ranks. There was no more linking arms to prevent workers from joining directly with them. Work groups and factories throughout Beijing mobilized to show their public support for the students. The next day, May 16, more than 150,000 people surged onto the square. The press of the crowd was so heavy that in the evening, at the dinner given for Gorbachev in the Great Hall of the People located off Tiananmen, guests had to be brought in through a back door.

For the first time protesters came not just as individuals but as part of work units, their flags and banners waving in front of them. Schoolteachers came, as did government officials and factory workers. Journalists paraded under the flag of such papers as the influential *People's Daily* or even broadcasting stations such as CCTV. People saw the official media advocating freedom of the press and democracy, screaming for the resignation of Li Peng and Deng Xiaoping.

Even Zhao Ziyang now realized he must move. At his televised meeting with Gorbachev, Zhao revealed what was supposed to be a party secret: he confirmed that all major decisions within the Chinese Communist party were still ultimately determined by Deng Xiaoping. "Since the Thirteenth Party Congress," he admitted, "we have always reported to Comrade Deng Xiaoping and asked for his advice while dealing with the most important issues." This statement, for which Zhao was later to be criticized, surprised many foreigners who seemed baffled by Zhao's intent, perhaps because most of them were still so reluctant to believe ill of Deng. Only in retrospect did Zhao's implication become clear to the outside world—it was Deng who, in spite of the Politburo's decision, had hampered accord with the students. As in Mao's day, Zhao was saying, China was still ruled by a "helmsman." As the party later charged, Zhao "deliberately directed the fire of criticism at Comrade Deng Xiaoping."

At the same time, Zhao offered further concessions to the

students. At 5 o'clock in the afternoon Yan Mingfu, the United Front Department minister who met with students earlier, made a desperate trip to the square by himself. They must, he told them, go home. In an important accommodation he announced that there would be no settling of accounts after the autumn harvest, offering to take their place as a hostage to guarantee this. Although Wuer Kaixi and Wang Dan were inclined to accept the offer, the others hooted them down, and Yan left. At 2 o'clock that morning, Zhao tried again, sending the students a message from the standing committee pledging to "work out concrete measures to enhance democracy and law, oppose corruption, build an honest and clean government, and expand openness."

But there was no holding back the movement now. When people turned on their television sets they saw pictures of *People's Daily* reporters demonstrating against the government of Li Peng. In the papers they saw pictures of the students and of television reporters and even members of different official ministries marching with slogans supporting the students and carrying such anti-government slogans as "Step down Deng Xiaoping" and "We don't care if the cat is black or white as long as it resigns." Several times the Chinese media seemed to exaggerate the number of people demonstrating with the students. The country was gripped with the drama of hunger-strikers being taken to hospitals in ever increasing numbers.

To those used to reading between the lines, it appeared that the entire Chinese political and economic establishment had shifted loyalties. But this is different from saying the Chinese press was free to talk about everything. For example, there was no hint in the press or on television of a power struggle within the government. There were no reports from Zhongnanhai about what was going on at the highest levels of the party.

Many of the elite also seemed to know only what they read. For many, the demonstrations meant that the government was shifting. They scurried to get on board the new regime. In mid-May one of China's leading military officials was said to have sent representatives to the students offering to help Wuer Kaixi overthrow the government if he so desired. Perhaps it was a trap; more likely it was a genuine offer from those moved by what the students were doing and anxious to be on the winning side. The students, committed to nonviolence and afraid to deal with political brokers from within the government, turned them down.

The demonstration on May 17 turned out to be the largest mass rally since the Cultural Revolution and possibly since the founding of the People's Republic of China. More than a million people, by some estimates more than two million, came to Tiananmen Square, most of them marching with their work units. Outside the gates of People's University, eight miles away, the entire wide avenue that passed by the front of the school was clogged from early morning until late at night with marchers heading downtown. Throughout the city, marchers from different directions met at every street corner. One parade would sometimes have to wait for hours until another passed.

The vast, hundred-acre Tiananmen Square was not large enough to accommodate all the protesters. One demonstration would march in and immediately march back out as another took its place. The road running next to the square, Changan Avenue, reputedly the widest street in the world, was clogged its entire length with marchers going to and from Tiananmen. In the midst of this mass of humanity, one lane remained open for ambulances needed to take hunger-strikers to hospitals. Students joined hands to monitor the traffic. In spite of the mass of these surging throngs, there were no traffic accidents involving the ambulances that sped by throughout the day.

Workers at the Foreign Ministry marched. The propaganda workers marched. Peasants marched in from the countryside.

Policemen in uniform marched. Even a thousand uniformed cadets from the People's Liberation Army marched. The list of marching government units alone would take up a whole page.

As the city of Beijing poured into the square, the culture of the students became the culture of the people. Tens of thousands of people began to wear headbands. Others put on the pointed hats that intellectuals were made to wear during the Cultural Revolution. Workers, showing their disgust with the corruption of the 1980s, carried Mao and Zhou Enlai posters. Folksingers came to the square. Acrobats came. *Liumang* swilled beer.

A city with its own government and garbage disposal units grew up on the square. Later, as the occupation continued, a couple was married there. Others fell in love. People danced and flew kites. Rock singers, including Cui Jian, performed. The pickpockets normally busy in any crowd in China suddenly took a holiday. The Western press began to refer to the event as the Chinese Woodstock.

Now that the irons were in the fire, Yan Jiaqi and his group of intellectuals finally stopped issuing calls to be reasonable. They signed a May 17 declaration which called Deng Xiaoping a "senile and fatuous autocrat, who acts like an emperor who does not wear the crown." "Important issues," they complained, "have to stop at this old dictator. If he does not approve, no one can negate the April 26 editorial." They demanded that the people repudiate Deng and begin to rely upon themselves.

Rebellion was in the air, and Deng Xiaoping was not about to take it lightly. As the people loyal to Zhao congregated on the square, the five members of the standing committee of the Politburo were summoned by Deng who told them that in his capacity as head of the Central Military Commission he had begun to summon the military to deal with the situation. Li Peng and economic planner Yao Yilin immediately agreed. The other two, security chief Qiao Shi and propaganda minister Hu Qili, bowed to the inevitable. Only Zhao openly opposed Deng.

In the early hours of the morning of May 18, still outwardly maintaining unity, four of the five members of the standing committee of the Politburo finally went to the hospital to see some of the students who had collapsed at the hunger strike. The oldest of the group, Yao Yilin, was too tired to go along.

That evening saw one more effort at reason. The long-awaited dialogue between students and government leaders finally took place. About a dozen students, including Wuer Kaixi and Wang Dan, met with Premier Li Peng and other top officials, though not Zhao Ziyang. Knowing that the officials were not prepared to repudiate the April 26 editorial, Zhao had sent Deng Xiaoping a letter of resignation, hoping word of this would increase his support against Deng. Although Deng refused to accept it, Zhao did not attend the dialogue he knew would fail.

The meeting probably would have been a disaster no matter which government leader attended. Li Peng came in a Mao suit, the students in various states of dishevelment. Wuer Kaixi, who had spent the morning in the hospital, was dressed in a pair of striped pajamas. Li Peng warned that "in Wuhan, students have already stopped the trains for three hours." He noted ominously that "we will not sit idly by, doing nothing." When Li tried to talk about his warm feelings for the students, Wuer angrily interrupted him, shouting, "Stop playing games and get down to business." A testy Li snapped that he should not be impolite, and Wuer responded, "Impolite? You've got a million people on the streets and you're calling me impolite?" Calming down, Li asked that the students end the fast and insisted that the meeting concern itself only with how to rescue the student hunger-strikers. Asserting that the government should not be so worried about saving face, Wang Dan, Wuer Kaixi, and others argued that Li should disclaim the April 26 editorial.

But they admitted that people might not leave the square regardless, for the leaders could no longer control their followers. The two sides were at an impasse.

In another futile gesture later that evening, the government televised part of the dialogue, leaving out the worst of Wuer's challenges to Li Peng. This did nothing to assuage student concerns. But it did give Chinese their first glimpse of the student leaders. Many viewers were impressed by how articulate they were and how well they compared with government leaders such as Li Peng.

In the next few days the numbers on the square continued to swell. People from the provinces arrived by train. In small cities and towns throughout China, smaller demonstrations in sympathy with the Beijing students erupted. Even heavy rains on May 18 could not keep several hundred thousand people from coming to the square, including many workers from some of the city's most important factories. On several of the days more than a million people arrived.

By May 19 the entire middle and lower levels of the government had deserted Deng Xiaoping and Li Peng. At this point, had he acted decisively, Zhao Ziyang might have been able to step into the power vacuum. Zhao was head of the party and had the support of most of its officials. A vote of the Central Committee or the National People's Congress, the two major official political bodies in China, would almost certainly have gone in Zhao's favor. Had Deng Xiaoping and other retired officials not intervened, it is probable that even the small executive arm of the Central Committee, the Politburo, would have continued to support Deng. Ranged against Zhao were a few high-level officials, including a majority of the five-person standing committee of the Politburo and a group of retired officials such as Deng Xiaoping, none of whom occupied any high-level official or party position. Under these circumstances, many thought the government should ignore the old men.

On May 19 a group of officers are said to have gone to Zhao Ziyang and offered him military support. According to the rumor, he considered it for four hours, but in the end he was afraid to move against the man who had put him into the job—Deng Xiaoping. He was a child of his culture, and so he allowed the opportunity for a decisive change in the Chinese political and social system to pass.

Zhao's situation was like that of reformist Chinese leaders in the 1920s. Again recalling the novel *Family,* only the young generation were willing to defy the grandfather. The elders still feared this symbol of the old regime, even when they had sufficient power to overthrow him. In the end, when his younger siblings ran off to join the new culture in Shanghai, all the older brother could do was wish them well.

This is what Zhao Ziyang now did. The standing committee of the Politburo met on the evening of May 18 to obey Deng and plan a crackdown. After the meeting adjourned, at 4 a.m. on the morning of May 19 Zhao made a sudden trip to the square to visit the fasting students. It was an unofficial visit said to have been opposed by Deng Xiaoping. In a moment of history filled with absurdities, this was one of the most bizarre. As Zhao embarked (on what was to be his last public appearance), Li Peng got word of what Zhao was doing and followed him out of their living quarters in Zhongnanhai in a separate car. When Zhao stepped up into the parked bus placed on the square by municipal workers to shelter some of the hunger strikers, Li Peng rushed in after him to make sure he would not miss anything. But Li Peng needn't have worried: Zhao was not there to overthrow the government. Instead, with tears in his eyes, he announced: "I have come too late." He told the students that things were difficult to resolve. It would, he now admitted, take a long time. He asked them to end the hunger strike. And then suddenly he showed that he did, after all, understand what it was they were all about. "We were once young, too," he admitted, "and we all had such a burst of energy. We also staged demonstrations and I remember the situation then. We also did not think of the consequences." When he finished speaking, the students, finally truly moved by one of their leaders, surrounded Zhao and asked him to autograph their clothes and books. Li Peng stood and watched silently for a minute and then left without speaking.

It seems clear that Zhao Ziyang realized he was through. Because he had not acted more decisively earlier, he was about to lose a showdown battle with Deng Xiaoping. In a final effort later that day, he is said to have proposed that the government officially retract the April 26 editorial and begin to deal with corruption by starting with his own and Deng's son. But if indeed he made this suggestion it was of no use. Zhao had waited too long.

The students realized that events had come to a standstill. With Gorbachev about to leave China, there was little additional moral pressure which they could bring to bear on the government by continuing the hunger strike. It would only risk lives. By late in the day some of the students had already heard of an impending crackdown. On the evening of May 19 the students therefore voted to end the hunger strike, though most agreed they would continue to sit in the square.

Early in the morning of May 20, about four hours after the students ended their hunger strike, radio and television broadcasts were suddenly interrupted to show Li Peng addressing a meeting of senior party, government, and army officials. Zhao Ziyang was not present. Supposedly he had been asked to give the speech Li was now presenting and had refused. Slurring his words and speaking in a loud, somewhat deranged voice, Li blamed the students for causing turmoil and declared that martial law in Beijing would commence at 10 o'clock the next morning. He was followed by President Yang Shangkun, who announced that troops were moving into Beijing, not, he claimed, to deal with the students but to maintain order.

The announcement that martial law was about to be declared galvanized the city even more than before. A day earlier some city workers, in a move that might have helped spur government hard-liners to action, had formed a Beijing Workers' Autonomous Trade Union. Members of this group later hung big pictures of Mao Zedong in the tents they pitched on the square. They talked openly and boldly about the good old days of the Cultural Revolution. Mao, they felt, had the right ideas, although he sometimes used the wrong tactics. Now they determined to use what they considered the right ones. Originally this group had called for a one-day strike in support of the students. Now they began to talk about a general strike.

The city too was infuriated. People poured into the square not just to watch and demonstrate but to make preparations to defend the students. They marched in an orderly fashion, defying the ban placed on such activity by the martial law authorities. Meanwhile, in the light of day the student leaders, who upon hearing of the declaration of martial law had decided to resume their hunger strike, reversed themselves once again and called it off, though some groups continued to fast. With troops about to bear down on them, most concluded that the strike no longer served a useful purpose.

In retrospect, student leaders who escaped to the West have criticized the decision to concentrate all their "symbolic and physical resources" in defending Tiananmen. But at the time they had no choice. The decision was mostly made in the lurch. Students who had come into the square from the provinces had no place to go in Beijing and could not suddenly leave town even if they had wanted to do so. Thousands were still pouring into town even as Li Peng was speaking. Those who might have had time to hop trains would have found themselves cut off from the center of the protest and perhaps exposed to criticism from angry local leaders. They were joined in their decision to stay by the masses who came to the square to help protect this now holy space and those who occupied it.

In effect, the leaders of the Autonomous Student Union who had led the hunger strike were now confounded by a new generation of radicals—in much the same way they themselves had earlier confronted the Party History group which had begun the movement. Although the union leaders might at this point have been willing to settle for what they had gained, declare a symbolic victory, and go home, those whom they had now radicalized would *not* settle. Like others before them, they still believed that victory was in sight.

In the short run they were correct. As military convoys moved towards the city, crowds of people clamored into the streets of Beijing to stop them with their bodies, with buses appropriated from the city, and with commandeered cars and trucks. At the edges of the city, carriers loaded with troops crawled to a halt. The soldiers were harangued by citizens who quickly learned that these units had been kept isolated without television or newspapers for days and knew nothing about the democracy movement. They did not even know why they were being sent into the city. Some had been told they were about to film a movie.

The battle of Beijing had begun. Toughs and students were now one. Scruffy-looking young entrepreneurs on newly purchased motorcycles formed "Flying Tiger Squads" which acted as the Paul Reveres of the town. With their girlfriends seated behind them, they scurried around town on vehicles that a few years earlier had been rare on the streets of Beijing. They delivered the news of troop movements, rousing residents into the streets in different parts of the city at the first sign of trouble and keeping student leaders abreast of events. For several days the troops were marooned on the edge of town, the surrounding crowds not permitting them to move. Each time new forces were brought up, they were halted.

The protesters blocked all major roads and crossroads. Barricades were set up on intersections at the edge of town. Old ladies and children sat and lay down in front of troop carriers. On street corners throughout the city, students and workers gave speeches. Networks of neighbors developed. People worked in relays to guard their streets and to prevent troops from charging through their districts. A "Dare-to-Die" squad formed among the roughest young men pledged to keep out the troops at all costs. For a while it appeared that the government was genuinely stymied.

Throughout vast areas of the city, the masses had taken the governance of Beijing into their own hands. It was the kind of spontaneous urban revolution that Karl Marx had said would inaugurate a communist society. And it was precisely the kind of spontaneous mass movement that has always terrified the rulers of communist states.

For a brief time in late May 1989, Chinese leaders were forced once again to confront their own ideology. The Chinese Communist government had come to power as a mass movement. Although its officials had displayed a wanton disregard and distrust for a continuation of this movement immediately after seizing power, nonetheless the people and authorities of China had grown up giving lip service to the idea of mass protest. As a result, it had been difficult for authorities to justify suppressing a genuinely widespread movement.

It was this ambivalence toward popular protest that Mao Zedong was able to use to his advantage in beginning the Cultural Revolution. In 1976 those who suppressed the Tiananmen demonstrations did so to their later regret. For by characterizing those demonstrations as a mass movement, Deng Xiaoping was ultimately able to use the actions of the authorities against them, implying that those who crushed these protests were counterrevolutionaries or ultra-leftists. Hence when the 1989 student movement arose and soon burst the bonds of the limited measures applied against it, no leader wished to be the first to put it down.

In the latter stages of the Cultural Revolution, Revolutionary Red Guard groups such as the Hunan organization Sheng Wu Lian had turned the Marxist ideology of the regime against it, suggesting that the entire Chinese bureaucracy had become a new class of power-holders. By 1989 many of the Chinese people shared this analysis. As they poured into the streets of Beijing, the people's words and slogans often echoed those of earlier radical groups. But the people have never controlled the "people's army." As Mao Zedong once declared, "Power grows out of the barrel of a gun." Now that the people had shown their true feelings, the elite turned to their guns. The leaders might well have remembered another of Mao's sayings: "It is anti-Marxist for communists to fear the student movement."

9

THE CRACKDOWN

Traditionally, the Chinese political and social order has been composed of small, diverse groups held together by a strong central power at the top. When this power is questioned, the society loses its central focus and the groups begin to quarrel with one another. In the twentieth century there have been various attempts to meld the country's units into a new style of organization. But all these efforts have had one thing in common with the past: each time order has been restored only when a new emperor-like authority has emerged.

In 1989 Chinese students once again encountered this same pattern. In their music and culture they regarded themselves as rebels who had broken with the old order. Yet although their technology was new, their ideas were really little different from those advanced by student radicals for almost a century. As early as 1898 Kang Youwei and Liang Qichao had advocated a democratic constitution, a purge of corrupt officials, greater social and economic change, and increased freedoms. And Kang was only one in a long line of advocates of such ideas. Similar calls were echoed by Chinese students at the time of the 1911 revolution, the May Fourth movement, and the Cultural Revolution.

This may have been the first generation to enjoy Western rock music, but the themes of individualism and social alienation that reverberated through this culture are ones that have appeared repeatedly in radical Chinese student movements, beginning in 1898. The social and sexual experiments of the May Fourth students were in no way less revolutionary than those of the students of 1989. Even complaints about the educational system by earlier generations of students sound remarkably like those of 1989.

In the past, as now, students studied doctrines at odds with the values of their own society. In the past, as now, the students' Western learning often undermined the traditional elite's sources of prestige and power. In the past, as now, Western-educated students had difficulty finding employment, and this helped turn their alienation into rage. Similarly, Chinese students found themselves expected to study at inadequate teaching facilities with poorly equipped instructors, while few in China understood the new material the students demanded to be taught. Then, as now, one of their reactions to these frustrations was to launch a radical attack on the foundations of traditional Chinese culture.

Perhaps most important, then, as now, the students rarely seemed able to act without first gaining legitimacy from institutions which were anathema to their ideals. In spite of the radicalness of their proposals, Kang Youwei and Liang Qichao nonetheless looked to the emperor for help in implementing their program. The anti-Qing activists of the early 1900s sought help from the gentry. Warlord-supported politicians and educators provided support for May Fourth actions. And, of course, it was Mao Zedong who gave the Red Guards much of their initial impetus and legitimacy during the Cultural Revolution.

Chinese student rebels have often sought government backing because, in spite of their radical behavior, they have taken for granted many of the cultural assumptions against which they rebelled. Although they advocated democracy, most never fully appreciated the ideas of individual rights which are the basis of this doctrine. Traditional Chinese individualism was the spontaneous and naturalist way of the Taoist who refused to recognize any of the conventions of society. Taoists could revolt against the political and social institutions of the outer world, but when they came to reconstructing a new society in the here and now, they never offered an alternative to these institutions. They ended up simply trying to put better people into them.

In modern times few Chinese have articulated a notion of individual worth such as that developed in the West, which specifies limits beyond which a society cannot interfere with an individual. When Chinese speak of individualism, they generally see a way of unfettering the creativity of individuals so they can be more productive members of society, or giving individuals the freedom to withdraw from society. Even the most wild individualists have tended to believe that when operating within Chinese society, they must submerge their individual energy to that of the group. During the May Fourth period of the 1920s, Chinese writers developed a romantic individualism which had many ideas in common with the 1989 pop culture of Chinese students. But when these romantic individualist writers turned political, they submerged their own frenzied outbursts into the actions of the Chinese Communist party, believing that within society individuals must harmonize with the group. The idea that one could be political and still act as an individual was anathema to Chinese individualists in the 1920s and again in 1989.

When the hunger-strikers attempted to implement democracy among themselves in 1989, they saw it as an all-or-nothing proposition. In an exaggerated interpretation of democracy that placed a skewed emphasis on group harmony, they decided that no decision about leaving Tiananmen Square could be made without a unanimous vote of all students. Similarly, though they defied authority by rebelling against what they considered immoral leadership, they refused to give up on the larger organization, the state. This does not mean that none of them understood democracy. Some certainly did. But they had no idea of how to achieve it within the context of Chinese society.

By contrast, the Party History Department students who began the 1989 protest movement were at least clear about their desire to reform the party. They had a realistic idea of the potentialities and limitations of the organization. They were succeeded by a second group of flamboyant, new-culture student leaders who took charge of the protests in late April and who seemed quite disillusioned with the party—but they lacked any realistic alternative model, and they never tried to create one. Not only did their own organization, with its standing committee and central committee and its reluctance to allow workers to participate, mimic the organization of the party, but the students' attitudes also imitated the sexist, patriarchal, authoritarian nature of the party leaders they opposed. In their revolutionary headquarters at Beijing Normal University, for instance, leaders such as Wuer Kaixi plastered their walls with pictures of pin-up girls. Wang Dan, the "intellectual" of the movement, openly bragged to an American reporter about the love letters he had received from enamored Chinese women.

In the heavily macho atmosphere of the movement, the men turned to a mother figure to heal their quarrels and stop them from fighting in late May. Chai Ling, a Beijing Normal University graduate student, was selected the general director of the Safeguard Tiananmen Square Headquarters because, unlike all the male students, her ego did not seem to be involved in her decisions. She was the only one everyone could respect, for she seemed to have an almost maternal interest in the care of the students, whom she called "children." But this was not, as it might seem, a nonsexist choice. Chai Ling simply held the feuding "boys" together; she could not develop alternatives to the existing state. The students remained in the bizarre position of asking government leaders to implement a new system of which they themselves had only a very imperfect understanding, and which would have eliminated the power of the very officials to whom they appealed.

In emphasizing these attitudes it should not be overlooked that similar undemocratic and sexist ideas as well as political feuding can be found in Western democratic societies. Still, this aspect of the movement illustrates the way in which the students continued to embrace the authoritarian patriarchal values of the society against which they rebelled. Their identification with the government left them ill prepared to respond to the ultimate government crackdown. Because they had not developed alternative institutions to those of the government, they were ultimately dependent on the authorities.

Not only did student attitudes echo those of the government; they both showed a similar weakness. Just as the students could not shake their abiding hope that the government would provide answers to their problems once they demonstrated their persistence, so the government continued to believe that the people would ultimately accept and obey what it was telling them once it demonstrated a modest amount of force and authority. When the crackdown came, its severity was in some ways determined by the government's mild response in the early stages of the protest. The ease with which the students had defied government efforts to stop them led many to conclude that no matter what they did, the government would not treat them harshly. The people grew to believe that their protests were aiding moderate forces within the government, forces which were protecting them and would eventually be able to throw off the influence of the hard-liners. But as the government grew frustrated by the snubs to its authority, it finally determined to show the people that it indeed meant business.

It took the government more than a little while to make this decision. As late as May 20, when poorly trained and ill-prepared troops were sent into the city, the authorities probably expected that the mere presence of these troops would now finally halt the demonstrations. It would have been difficult for any government to imagine the courage which the Chinese people were to show in the face of the advancing troops. Less than a decade earlier, in late 1981, there had been a similar situation in Poland at the time of the suppression of the Solidarity trade union. Before General Jaruzelski's declaration of martial law in that country, the entire populace of Poland seemed mobilized behind Solidarity in much the same way that the Chinese population was marshaled behind the Chinese students in the spring of 1989. In Poland at the time, and abroad, there was considerable talk that the army would find it impossible to take over the country without facing a widespread rebellion by the masses. But when actually confronted with the armed might of troops, the Polish people offered almost no resistance. Having observed events in eastern Europe closely, Chinese leaders were no doubt quite surprised when their own workers and students formed dare-to-die squads and the people linked arms to prevent troops from entering Beijing.

But this turn of events may also have been due to the less than enthusiastic support of many military officers for the orders they had now been given. In the days after May 20, when the troops were stalled by the students, many observers felt that the moderates were again trying the trick that had worked so well on April 27. Crowds then had easily pushed aside unarmed and poorly motivated troops, police, and militia units, and an effort was made to convince hard-liners that force would not work against the movement.

More likely, most military officers were reluctant to fire on the students because they could not figure out how to carry out this order without causing needless civilian casualties and, most important, without destroying their own careers. At least one general was said to have checked himself into a hospital rather than have his troops open fire on the people of Beijing.

In late May 1989 the final outcome of the protests was still quite ambiguous. Only a few days earlier, as already noted, several military men had been so sure that Zhao Ziyang and the students would win that they had reportedly offered to help them overthrow Deng Xiaoping. Even after the declaration of martial law, any general called upon to support an unpopular, eighty-five-year-old embattled dictator would surely have responded slowly. Memories were still vivid of what had happened to those who had helped the government intervene in the Tiananmen incident of 1976. And no one had forgotten the fate of many who became involved in the factional fighting of the Cultural Revolution. The situation was especially tricky this time because the troops were being ordered to suppress the sons and daughters of the elite, people who in some cases may have even been the generals' own children or their children's friends.

The military's fear of the situation can be seen in the way the troops were isolated and kept in ignorance before they were ordered into the city. When officers ordered the first troops into Beijing in late May, they gave them no orders to fire. No wonder these troops, poorly trained and lacking understanding, quickly halted after meeting citizen road-blocks. Since the first troops sent into the city were part of the Beijing garrison and were already familiar with the people of the city, they were easily persuaded to put down their weapons and stop their advance. Within a few days their leaders, probably feeling they had gotten themselves off the hook, ordered these troops back.

At this point the students had two choices. The first was to declare victory and leave the square. The government had proven itself to be weak. Having scored a moral triumph, the students could have gone home and waited for the government to change or collapse. The other choice was to remain in the square even after the government had declared martial law and begun to send troops into the city—in effect, this meant revolution. It meant that the students would have to move to take advantage of the further erosion of the government's authority. This was possible, even if unlikely. Despite the declaration of martial law, hundreds of thousands of people still came to Tiananmen every day. Had the students wanted, they might have used the "Dare-to-Die" corps or the "Flying Tigers" to storm Zhongnanhai, arrest Li Peng and some of the other hard-line leaders, liberate Zhao Ziyang, and declare a new government. At least they could easily have stormed several government buildings and occupied them. Deng seems to have been concerned about just such a possibility. There are reports that he beefed up his personal security staff because he feared an attack on his residence and was no longer sure whom he could trust. He also left the city before martial law was declared, urging other leaders also to take precautions.

Even in retrospect this possible scenario is nothing more than speculation. There is no way of knowing how successful a daring revolutionary act by the students might have been. But given the disintegration of the political process in the days after martial law was declared, it seems that the students might have had a chance. So few people within the government had any idea of what was going on at this point that top leaders and generals were calling their children and friends of their children in the United States to ask what they knew about the situation in China. A decisive action by the students might have produced a very different kind of political situation.

Zhao Ziyang, the head of the party, supported them. Most of the ministries had demonstrated for the students. Even the majority of the provinces were refusing to acknowledge martial law. A majority of the Central Committee, the most important official organ of the Chinese government, if allowed to vote, would have supported the students. Those who opposed them were a few high-level officials such as Li Peng and Yang Shangkun and some old retired leaders who officially occupied no important government or party positions. Under these circumstances, had the students acted they might have been able to gain administrative control of the country.

Yet there were practical reasons for the students to hesitate. Had they attempted to install a new regime (or, more accurately, had they acted to retain the regime which Deng and his allies were ousting), the government reaction would probably have been even more severe than it was.

Still, the students' failure to consider such a plan is striking. They were willing to indulge in individual acts of self-expression, exemplified by the student who stood naked on a building, shouting, "I am what I am." But they did not choose to try to overturn a government which had clearly marked them for arrest and detention. Although they had no way of knowing that the government's response would eventually be as deadly as it was, the fact is that for all their talk about being rebels unprecedented in Chinese history, in the end they simply waited for the elders and their henchmen to act against them.

What this demonstrates is the students' abiding faith in government authority. Although they were rebels, the students remained such an intrinsic part of the old society that they spent their time trying to prove that they were not counterrevolutionaries, rather than attempting to figure out how they might build a new government.

The students had declared their total disgust with the government. The government had replied by declaring martial law. The students and the people had organized to oppose this government policy, even blocking government troops from entering the city. Yet no one wished to take the next step and declare a new, independent political institution.

And no one thought (or dared) to secure the television studios or the newspaper offices. As a result, on May 22, troops who arrived singly and in civilian clothes posted themselves outside these institutions to ensure that they remained loyal to the party. Editors and writers reacted naively: upon seeing the troops, they threatened to strike if the government interfered in any way with their ability to carry out their jobs. It was tough talk, but not the kind they could sustain when people with guns pointed at them were standing outside their doors. Within a few days the press and other media considerably quieted their coverage of the student movement. On May 22, two days after declaring martial law, Li Peng announced that he would personally take over the instruments of propaganda from former Zhao Ziyang loyalist Hu Qili.

In the first few days after the declaration of martial law, the papers still sometimes managed to run articles that they slipped through the hands of the censors. For instance, on May 21 the *People's Daily* published a front-page article on the resignation of the Italian government, hinting in an unsubtle way that it was time for the Chinese government to follow suit. The next day the paper printed another front-page piece about a Hungarian leader who had suggested that army troops could not be used to solve domestic problems. But the fact that the media now used innuendo to express their views indicated the kind of pressure they felt. The press had ceased to be an organ favorable to the students and was soon again turning out propaganda for the government.

Within a few days the government succeeded in forcing editors to submit advance copies of all publications to a special press group and to begin running officially written articles unfavorable to the students and to Zhao Ziyang. Soon it seemed to many as if the rhetoric in Chinese newspapers was reminiscent of the late sixties and early seventies, with its attacks on "bourgeois liberalization" and "foreign influences" and its discussions of Zhao Ziyang as having created a "struggle between two headquarters." By late May one had to look to see if TV anchormen read the news with their eyes downcast to detect even a glimmer of displeasure with the official lines.

Yet despite this clear display of authority and intention, the students continued to concentrate not on how to replace the government but on how to get the government to change its mind and return such moderates as Zhao Ziyang—who just a few days earlier had not been a student favorite—to power. Their waiting, defensive stance was ironic—although the organization of citizens against the troops was impressive—because the protesters had no institutions of their own to protect. "Desperados" and "kamikazes" gathered towels for use against tear gas and buckets of cement to make roadblocks. They divided into those with white headbands, who agreed to take the front lines against the troops, and "deputies" wearing red headbands, who took fewer risks because they had families to protect. But after the students stopped the first line of troops, they did not attempt to persuade them to come over to their side and turn their guns on Zhongnanhai. Rather they waited for them to withdraw. Meanwhile they told the soldiers stories of how the "People's Army loves the people." They were solicitous, feeding the soldiers and worrying lest foreign reporters get too close to them. Somehow they seemed to feel that if they were pleasant to the troops, the officials who had sent them into action would change their minds and decide to support the students. They did not consider how to prevent the officials from sending new, more vicious troops into the city.

Although the students continued their rebellion, it became

transfixed with rumors and pipe dreams of salvation centered on party officials. For example, within a day or two after the declaration of martial law, more than forty members of the standing committee of the National People's Congress were said to have agreed to an emergency meeting of the congress. The rules of the committee provided that ten members could call an emergency meeting at any time with the permission of the presidium. Otherwise, eighty members, a majority of the body, could call a meeting whether or not the presidium approved. For a long time there was much talk among the protesters about how this would be a legal way to overrule the martial law forces and reconstitute the government. Everyone looked for help to Vice Premier Wan Li, a Politburo member then visiting the United States, who was known to be a moderate and thought to side with Zhao Ziyang. Wan Li was the president of the National People's Congress, and it was hoped that if he returned to China he would not only add to the anti-Deng forces on the Politburo but could use his position in the National People's Congress to convene that body and reverse the martial law order.

All this talk ignored the obvious fact that the Chinese elders were not about to allow the National People's Congress to act. Even if this body somehow managed to overturn the order for martial law, no one in the government would have paid the slightest attention to such a directive. Had China been a country that respected institutions, Zhao Ziyang, as China's highest official, would have prevailed. But Zhao and the Politburo had already been overruled by Deng Xiaoping. When decisions of the secretary general of the Chinese Communist party and of the Politburo had already been nullified by a single individual willing to act decisively, there was no way that a more ambiguous body, such as the standing committee of the National People's Congress, would be able to change anything in the real world. Nor was there any way for Zhao Ziyang to make a quick comeback, as was also rumored in the days immediately after the declaration of martial law. What was needed at this point was not another meeting of another group but decisive action by those opposed to Deng—something that, once again, no one contemplated.

In any event, Vice Premier Wan Li never had the chance to be a white knight, even if he so wished. On May 25 he cut short his visit to the United States and returned to China. Although he had planned to go to Beijing, his plane landed at Shanghai, and he remained there for several days. When finally he emerged into the public eye it was to articulate his support for the new martial-law government. Realizing who exercised power, Wan Li had no intention of risking his skin by flouting that authority.

But Wan Li was not the only figure whom people somehow hoped would disavow Deng, even though the nation's highest and most powerful officials had already refused to do so. There was also much talk about Deng Yingchao, widow of deceased Premier Zhou Enlai and the supposed stepmother of Li Peng. Deng had been a high party official in her own right and remained a member of the Central Advisory Commission, the group of supposedly retired officials still pulling the strings behind the scenes. Shortly after the declaration of martial law, word circulated that she had written to the party suggesting that if the troops moved against the students, she would resign from the party. In fact, Deng Yingchao's letter called on the students and others to *trust* the government and the party, advising them that the army intended only to restore order.

Even if Deng Yingchao had written a letter opposing the government, it would have had no real consequences, because other old people with even more power, especially Deng Xiaoping, would have opposed her. But many persisted with this faith in authority. In a report which received considerable publicity in the United States, the well-known

Chinese writer and journalist Liu Binyan, who was visiting
the U.S., stated that in telephone discussions with Chinese
friends he had learned that ten government ministers, including the foreign minister, had threatened to resign; that only
three of China's provinces had declared their loyalty to the
central government; and that three of Zhao Ziyang's closest
aides had demanded an immediate meeting of the full National People's Congress to discuss the "coup" at the top of the
government. These cracks, Liu Binyan implied, meant that
the government's power was tenuous and that Li Peng would
soon be forced to resign.

It is not that Liu Binyan's sources were wrong, for they
were probably right. But once again they meant nothing.
They demonstrated the continued naivety of reformers such
as Liu who, in spite of all of his reportorial skills, did not
seem to understand the sources of political power in China.
After all, the hunger strike demonstrations had already revealed
cracks within the government. What they had not shown, and
what rumors still did not show, was that anyone was willing
to seize the political levers from Deng and the other elders.
Since Zhao Ziyang himself had refused to act, aside from
voting and speaking, why would anyone else?

These rumors demonstrate an important aspect of life in a
system where the government monopolizes the flow of information. In the absence of fact, people resort to speculation.
As events throughout late May and early June demonstrated,
even those who knew better continued to believe some quite
absurd ideas because they had no other sources of information. As these rumors were running rife in China and in the
West, the government was continuing to make its case against
Zhao Ziyang and was slowly purging more and more of his
supporters. Had the leadership been genuinely worried about
threats to its power, it would have had no time for such
luxuries.

A far more serious and credible threat to the government

was a letter from seven former high-level military officers. The signers, including a former defense minister and a former army chief of staff, formally attacked the government's plans to bring troops into the capital to suppress the student democratic movement. Observers thought this letter would have considerable influence within military circles, for it was supported by a large number of lower-ranking officers. The letter demanded that the army "not shoot the people" and that it "not enter the city of Beijing." As a group, these high-level officers were not only sympathetic to the students' demands because many of their children and grandchildren were involved; they also worried that the government's intended use of the military violated a long-standing tradition of not using field armies within the capital. They also seemed aware of the ramifications of a crackdown. As senior officers who had been present in 1976 and during the Cultural Revolution, they understood how repression could ultimately reverberate against the military.

But the officers who signed this letter never followed with any indication of positive help for the moderates. Neither Zhao nor the students, after all, had seemed interested in offers of military aid when it would have made a much greater difference. At a time when Deng was mobilizing units in his favor, it was unlikely that the efforts of this group could have much effect without decisive action by the students. As it was, however, the letter was never published in *People's Daily,* China's premier newspaper. And so this pipe dream too evaporated. As Zhao Ziyang had shown earlier, many wanted change, but few were willing to encourage it.

The students' only realistic option was to disband the movement and return to their campuses, hoping to salvage what they could of their lives and futures. Some students seemed to realize this right away. For example, at 3 a.m. on Monday, May 22, just forty-eight hours after martial law had been declared, Wuer Kaixi declared in a speech that the democratic movement was lost. He asked the students to retreat from Tiananmen to the embassy area—and then he fainted.

Wuer's immediate concerns for safety may have been premature, but his long-term view of the movement was correct. The students were in imminent danger from the military. The protesters who had initially occupied the square had already begun to leave, anxious to return to their campuses for exams and baths. Both Wuer and Wang Dan had, in fact, originally recommended evacuating the square on May 17, in response to government offers of compromise. But as they had informed Li Peng during their dialogue, the leaders no longer controlled those on the square. The students who had just arrived, many from out of town, were newly excited about the movement. Seeing the protesters win victory after victory, they did not believe that they could lose and so they refused to budge.

After his speech Wuer was bitterly attacked. The standing committee of the union immediately acted to remove him as chairman, and Chai Ling, head of the students' security, now assumed even more power. Once more, even as the students demonstrated for democracy, they took on many of the characteristics of the government they opposed.

In the days that followed, many other students began to come to grips with the reality of their circumstances. By the end of May, aware that their movement had stalled, most of the Beijing student leaders had begun to advocate that students abandon the square. On May 30 they voted to leave.

But the newly radicalized students persisted. Finally, realizing that even they were no longer radical enough to satisfy the demands of these students from the provinces, the Beijing leaders quit. Among those who resigned at this time were Wang Dan and Chai Ling.

Students from the provinces who remained in the square now decided to postpone their departure until June 20, the day on which the Central Committee of the National People's Congress was scheduled to convene. As Chinese student radicals, they too focused on the government. They still believed that the government would eventually reverse itself and decide in their favor.

On May 30 the "goddess of democracy," a twenty-seven-foot-tall statue which bore a striking resemblance to the American Statue of Liberty, was erected in the middle of the square, opposite the huge portrait of Mao Zedong. The statue had originally been intended as a farewell gesture by those leaving the square. It was created after three days and nights of frantic effort by students from the Central Academy of Fine Art. They had based their statue on a figure of a Chinese peasant man grasping a wooden pole in both hands. The bottom part of the staff had been cut off and the top part changed into a torch, so only the hand above the man's head grasped this symbol of freedom. The students had also lengthened the hair, changing the male figure into that of a woman. On the evening of May 29 the sculptors brought their creation to the square in sections aboard tricycle-driven carts. They were forced to do this after the public security bureau phoned the academy and warned that any truck driver who carried the statue would lose his license. Working frantically through the night, the students assembled the statue at the square, completing it by noon of May 30.

The statue immediately became another affront to the government. Most of the media did not even dare refer to it by name, calling it instead the "goddess of something-or-other." It had been transformed from a final statement into another defiant symbol of opposition. The goddess rallied the flagging spirits of the Chinese democracy movement as hundreds of thousands flocked to the square to see what the students had done. But it did little to alter the political situation which headed inexorably toward a climax.

Increasingly sinister signs of a crackdown began to appear.

Shortly after midnight May 30, several members of the newly
formed Workers Autonomous Union were arrested near the
Beijing Hotel. Scared officials of the union borrowed tents
and set up camp next to student headquarters in Tiananmen
Square to protect themselves.

But being in the square did not guarantee safety. Chai Ling
had been persuaded by the bickering students to resume her
leadership role. Her abilities clearly bothered the government. At 3 a.m. on June 1, three men who had passed
themselves off as students from outside Beijing, along with a
fourth person, attempted to kidnap her and her husband as
they lay sleeping in their tent in the square. They failed, but
later that night two loudspeakers on the Monument were cut
off, as was the only telephone that connected the students
direct with their headquarters. The students were being increasingly isolated.

At the end of May the government had begun to try to
organize people against the students. On May 31 it bused a
group of peasants to a stadium south of Beijing to demonstrate with slogans announcing "Oppose Turmoil" and
"Resolutely Uphold Li Peng's Important Speech." Effigies
were burned of the dissident Fang Lizhi. Another such
demonstration took place in the northwestern section of the
city on June 2. Thousands of peasants were paid ten Chinese
dollars each to march through the streets wearing anti-
American costumes and shouting their support of Li Peng and
Deng Xiaoping. In response, students staged a satire parade
at which they donned the tall paper hats of Cultural Revolution
"counterrevolutionaries."

Meanwhile, a well-known pop singer, Hou Dejian, and
three prominent intellectuals began a seventy-two-hour hunger strike in Tiananmen Square. These hunger-strikers were
led by Liu Xiaobo, whom the government later accused of
being "the vicious manipulator" of the student demonstrations. Liu, on a year-long appointment to the East Asian

Institute of Columbia University in New York, had returned to China at the end of April to take part in the protests. Asserting that it was "not yet too late," he hoped by his actions to convince the students and the government to rethink their positions. It was a well-conceived effort, but few people joined these new hunger-strikers.

By the morning of June 2, rumors were flying that 200,000 troops had surrounded the city. In Beijing large concentrations of soldiers had infiltrated the city and were stationed at the television station, the radio station, the telegraph office, and the post office. People were growing accustomed to having soldiers in the city.

Late that evening a police car racing through the city struck four people, killing two of them. Thousands of citizens agitated by the incident raced to Tiananmen Square to demonstrate over what had happened. En route they discovered troops coming into the city and quickly alerted others to this news. From five to ten thousand unarmed soldiers who had jogged into the downtown area of Beijing were halted at the edge of the square. The troops were young boys, tired and exhausted. After being stopped they wandered in a daze, trying to climb lampposts and hide in alleyways out of the way of the citizens who grabbed them, interrogated them, and then turned them loose to be stopped by someone else farther down the road.

The newly aroused populace were being drawn back into the square. Worse yet they were arming. The troops who had been stopped were unarmed, but behind them were buses filled with gas masks and machine guns. The weapons were seized. Most were put on display by the students to contrast their own peacefulness to the government's violent intent. Some efforts were made to return the weapons to the police, but the police refused to accept them. Instead the government announced that guns had been taken from the troops by hooligan elements in the city. In retrospect, some believe that government forces deliberately abandoned their weapons—some of which were later shown to be defective—to the students in order to justify the coming massacre. But this is unlikely. The police did not accept the weapons because in this situation, in which all normal lines of authority had broken down, they had no authority to do so.

The government in fact seemed to be so alarmed by what had now transpired that on June 3 it broadcast a "mobilization order for action." Throughout the day troops attempted to regain their armaments from the students. At about noon, armed personnel rushed out of Zhongnanhai and began throwing tear gas bombs and clubbing the crowd, attempting to seal off the surrounding streets. In the nearby Xidan area, where the Democracy Wall posters had hung in the late 1970s, the troops used rubber bullets and tear gas on the crowds. An estimated ten thousand troops even rushed out the rear of the People's Hall around 2 p.m. and tried unsuccessfully to close the intersection there. According to a later account by Chai Ling, one student tried to reason with the troops over a loudspeaker, shouting, "The people's police loves the people; the people's police do not beat the people." A soldier ran over to him and kicked him in the stomach, asking, "Who the fuck loves you?"

Shots first were heard about 11 o'clock on the evening of June 3, near the area of the Xinhua News Agency. The violence did not begin everywhere at the same time. Convoys entered the city around 9 or 10 that evening and were once again halted by stone-throwing civilians who set up blockades and barriers which forced the troops to stop. This time, however, the military determined not to be embarrassed as in the past. Stung by resistance, the units were ordered to open fire. When they suddenly did so it was with unexpected ferocity.

By midnight armed troops with tanks and heavy equipment were moving through the city, firing indiscriminately as they went. They soon reached the square, having blasted anything and anyone in their path. Men, women, and children sitting on their balconies, and sometimes deep in their apartments, were slaughtered by the random and uncontrolled gunfire of the soldiers. Old men and women, young girls and boys who tried, as they had in the past, to sit down in front of the tanks, were brutally run over. Others who kneeled down in front of individual soldiers, pleading for mercy, were machine-gunned. What the Chinese government had earlier done to Tibet, it was now doing in heightened fashion to the people of Beijing.

One of the worst incidents occurred in the Muxidi area of Beijing, west of the square near the site of the car accident the night before. This area contains one of the most exclusive housing developments in Beijing, one sheltering the families of the high elite. The troops had been stopped there at about 9:30 p.m. They waited and watched as the people alternately pleaded with them and screamed curses. When the orders to advance came, the troops suddenly raked the crowds with stun grenades, automatic weapons, and armor-piercing bullets. On the street a dozen or so people were killed. Several more were murdered as they sat in their apartments, when soldiers turned their guns on the windows of the buildings. Since many of the people who live in this area have children and family members abroad, many details of this slaughter in Muxidi are known. There were many other scenes of murder and mayhem throughout the city, not as well documented.

In its efforts to cover up the massacre, the Chinese government has insisted that there were no killings in Tiananmen Square. Many have disputed this official account of what happened when the tanks rolled into the Tiananmen area. However many people were or were not killed in Tiananmen Square, there is no question that the Chinese army carried out a major slaughter in the streets of Beijing on the night of June

3 and was still killing citizens in the streets of the city several days later.

One of the reasons events in the square have seemed unclear is that the advancing troops immediately cut those in the square off from the mass of people on Changan Avenue who were attempting to defend the Tiananmen area. This also prevented most foreign cameramen and journalists from witnessing what was to happen to those who were forced by the soldiers back towards the area of the square between Mao's mausoleum and the Monument to the Heroes of the Revolution. Huddled together, the demonstrators had to decide on their response. In an account recorded on June 8, student leader Chai Ling described the students' frightened reaction to the onslaught of the troops. The students decided it would be folly to attempt a violent response to the soldiers and at first simply waited for them to arrive. But after the four hunger-strikers crossed the square and found an officer in charge of the forces now ringing the area, most of those left in the square were apparently allowed to leave peacefully, their arms linked together as they had been on student marches throughout April and May.

Before their withdrawal from the square could be completed, however, Chai Ling reported that the troops fired several rounds directly at those on the Monument to the Heroes of the Revolution, aiming, according to other witnesses, so that their bullets would strike the protesters but not damage the monument. The only casualties Chai Ling herself reports were not those shot on the monument but those crushed by tanks while remaining in their tents on the square. According to Chai Ling, "about twenty or thirty people" from "the Workers Autonomous Union all got killed" this way. These people were the hard-line Maoists. They had pledged to stay on the square and fight.

Chai Ling also reported that just after they left the square a tank rolled towards the students, crushing ten of them so badly that their bodies were split into pieces. Other observers have said that troops opened fire on those at the end of the long column of students just before they left the square. Some accounts have told of students from Nankai University in Tianjin who elected to remain in their tents and, like the workers, were crushed by tanks. Although there were casualties galore at the edge of the square and throughout the city, no one, including Chai Ling, has conclusively confirmed that people were indeed flattened in their tents. Some independent observers confirm the government's account that no one died in the square itself.

Once the students finally escaped from the area, Chai Ling talks of seeing a city which had just gone through a war. The dead not yet carted off by the army lay on the streets, the wounded screamed, and others cried over missing friends and murdered children. In the midst of this the students returned, arms linked all the way, as if in a dream, to the campus of Beijing University, where they apparently remained.

As brutal as was the onslaught of the troops, what happened in the next few days, after the city had already been stunned into silence, was in some ways even more horrifying. The world was moved by a photograph taken on June 5 of a lone man running into the streets to stop a moving row of tanks. There were many such scenes of bravery and despair, but few of the soldiers or tank drivers showed such compassion for those who got in their way. Numerous civilians, including children, continued to be beaten and killed because they said the wrong thing to a passing soldier or sometimes because they looked at him the wrong way.

The final death toll of the slaughter will never be known. There were reports of soldiers later incinerating bodies on the square and picking up other corpses throughout the city for cremation on the edge of town. Before their access to hospitals was cut off, foreign journalists confirmed that several hundred had been killed. Most sources have put the final total at one thousand to three thousand with many more wounded, though others have suggested that as many as ten thousand were slaughtered. And this is only in Beijing. Troops also killed large numbers in Chengdu and perhaps smaller numbers in crackdowns throughout the country.

In brutally moving the military into the center of Beijing, some observers have suggested that hard-liners within the Chinese government may have been more interested in making a point to their dissident colleagues than in suppressing the student demonstrators. Before the troops plowed their way into the city, clearly the hard-liners were having difficulty implementing their policies. Although martial law had been declared several weeks before, the policy had been ineffective before the weekend of the massacre. Moreover, there were persistent rumors that official attempts to remove the moderate party chairman Zhao Ziyang, who had shown sympathy for the student protesters, had bogged down because forces sympathetic to Zhao still had sufficient votes to prevent his ouster.

By moving forces into the center of Beijing, hard-liners may have sought to influence the way in which certain members of the party hierarchy voted. With their houses surrounded by troops who had already murdered and maimed innocent civilians and students, these leaders may have thought twice before casting votes in party meetings against those who controlled this military. But it was not the ensuring of votes that concerned the party. Deng Xiaoping had already shown what he and the other older leaders thought about the importance of votes within government bodies. What these party leaders could not abide was dissent. They may have welcomed the brutality as a way of teaching a lesson to dissident party members, many of whom had openly supported the students and were now shuffling their feet instead of supporting party policy. And by acting quickly, the hard-liners prevented forces sympathetic to Zhao from interfering before it was too late.

The leaders also may have ordered the troops to move quickly and brutally in order to discourage anyone else—students or military dissidents—from moving against them. The government realized how vulnerable it was. It feared that when word of troop movements leaked, the students or military units loyal to the moderates might move.

Like many autocrats, Deng had long been paranoid about his own security, refusing to live in Zhongnanhai with the rest of the elite. Supposedly he worried that a single bomb could kill them all. Although Deng himself had probably long since abandoned the city before the troops moved in, reportedly for more secure headquarters in the Western Hills outside of Beijing, others may not have. Just after the forces moved in, tanks put themselves in positions to defend Zhongnanhai. Later there were reports of long lines of limousines removing Chinese leaders from the city to better-protected headquarters.

The troops were also brutal because the hard-liners were so desperate. They had watched in frustration for months while the government had talked tough but failed to act decisively. Meanwhile, the students still occupied the square and kept postponing their decision to leave it. When the hard-liners finally made their move, they were determined not to botch it.

The leading government player in this drama was Yang Shangkun, the eighty-two-year-old president of China and the vice chairman (under Deng Xiaoping) of the Central Military Commission, the supreme military body in the country. Before Yang's assumption of the office, for much of the past decade the post of president had been largely a ceremonial one, occupied by a senior military leader to show the military's support for the government. But Yang used the presidency skillfully to augment his power in the months leading to the crackdown.

He advanced not only his own power but that of his entire family. His younger brother, Yang Baibing, was also a senior military leader; in the fall of 1989 the younger brother joined the older brother as a member of the Central Military Commission. What seems to have happened on June 4 was that Yang Shangkun called the bluff of moderates within the military. It was he who ordered the troops into the city, where they took up positions from which they could also exert pressure on those who ostensibly controlled the central government. In this way Yang showed that he was the man in charge. Having seen the government fail so many times, he determined to advance into the city with the utmost brutality to teach the citizens and his fellow soldiers a lesson. After the way the party had been laughed at for days and months, he was demonstrating that the party still controlled the gun and knew how to use it.

Finally, some in the government may have feared mass retaliation against the troops if they were not sufficiently brutal. For weeks the people had kept the army at bay and had developed methods to stop the soldiers. When the army did come bursting into the city, there were Molotov cocktails thrown at tanks and soldiers killed by civilian defenders of the city. The violence on the part of the populace was not as great as the government described—showing over and over again the photograph of a soldier who was lynched and then burned by an angry mob after he reportedly killed several innocent people. Moreover, the fear of popular violence certainly did not justify the government's vicious response. But it probably did contribute to the troops' desperate plunge into the city.

After the army entered the city, widespread rumors illustrated the continued trust shown by even the most disillusioned Chinese in their institutions, which they should now have seen to be thoroughly discredited. Many people seemed inclined to believe that the military action had been carried out by the evil connivance of a few leaders with the support of "outsiders." Even those who should have known otherwise reported that the troops sent against the city were not ethnic Chinese but Mongols. What made this idea particularly absurd was that the Chinese government trusts its Mongol minorities so little that it would never allow them to have their own army divisions. When drafted, Mongol soldiers are integrated into Chinese units. What gave rise to the rumor was the fact that parts of the 27th Army had been based in Inner Mongolia before they marched into Beijing—but they were not Mongol troops.

Other, more credible rumors involved an imminent clash between Chinese armies. The talk was that supposedly moderate Beijing garrison units, said to be the best-trained and best-equipped forces in China, had moved themselves into the city just after June 4 and had begun to engage units of the 27th Army in combat. This indicated, presumably, that the moderates would not allow their city and the central government to be taken over so easily. But while small clashes may have occurred between individual units of angry soldiers, the talk of imminent civil war after the Beijing butchery was just talk. Generals do not like to fight when they can count the number of guns and bullets on both sides and know that defeat is certain. A loss of troops means a loss of power.

Moreover, it turned out that it was not just the 27th Army that had entered the city so brutally. Elements of other armies had joined them, including the supposedly pro-student 38th Army. These armies had all joined not only in the slaughter of Beijing citizens but also in shooting into the hotels of foreigners and blasting out the windows of some of the compounds where diplomats and their families lived.

The government's continued willingness to use the murder of the weak in order to restore order was demonstrated a few days after the crackdown when it began a series of highly publicized executions of "troublemakers" who had supposedly disrupted the functioning of the government. Those who received bullets in the neck were workers and unemployed youths, not students. Those killed had no ties to anyone with influence. At least one of those killed in Shanghai was reported to have been mentally retarded. The government was scaring the people into submission by killing the defenseless.

The "emperor" had returned. But by acting as brutally as it did, the Chinese Communist party lost its credibility. The students of the 1980s were, in effect, faced with a situation similar to the one their grandparents confronted in the 1920s. In 1898, as again in the 1960s, Chinese students placed their hopes for change on a single individual—the emperor in 1898 and Mao Zedong in the 1960s. In both cases they were disappointed. Aware of past failures, the May Fourth students, like those of the 1980s, no longer trusted their leaders, but they had not lost all faith in the old political and social system. It was not until this system too failed them in 1919 that former students began to construct their own organization, the Chinese Communist party, to replace the old government. In retrospect it would appear that in building this party they brought into it too much of the culture they had opposed.

In trying to change this culture, were the students of 1989 attempting a revolution or a rebellion? The answer is neither. At first they were simply trying to reform the party. They had experienced sweeping economic and technological change. They truly believed that these advances had so altered the people's consciousness that they were ready to accept sweeping political transformations as well. In making their good-hearted efforts, the students were naive. The twenty years of peace and prosperity in which they had grown up had lulled them into a false sense of security. They had a feel for technology but not for their own past. They were a generation that knew less about their history than any that had come before them. They had gone so far that they could not imagine the difficulties they would have in taking the final steps. They seemed truly to believe that even as they attacked, somehow, someone in the government would come to their aid.

They did not understand how much they resembled the students who had gone before them, or how similar were their demands. Most of all, they did not understand that political power in China does not yield easily. Although the students claimed to imitate the May Fourth movement, they forgot where that movement had led—into the formation of a revolutionary party which provoked a bitter and cataclysmic upheaval. This upheaval transformed the economy and society of China, but its politics remained unchanged.

10

AFTERMATH

Throughout the twentieth century, Chinese students have demonstrated for democracy, national strength, and an end to bureaucratic corruption. Attuned to ideas of liberation and freedom and sensitive to new forms of technology and science, they have often believed themselves to be born into a world radically different from that of their parents. Repeatedly they have seen themselves as the first generation to break sharply with their past.

Their protests succeeded in inspiring and awakening the nation. But mostly they failed to achieve their goals. They failed because they were not clear about what they wanted. They failed because they rarely understood the individual rights for which they often demonstrated. They failed because usually they saw democracy not as something that would protect the rights of the individual but as something that would advance the strength of the state. They failed because without an army of their own they were often highly dependent on official sanction.

When former students finally succeeded in establishing the Chinese Communist party, most found it necessary to compromise their revolutionary principles to work with the warlord culture and feudal peasant traditions. Like other party leaders, they began to view new generations of students as simply another popular element to be manipulated or repressed, depending on the needs of the party.

From 1977 to 1989 party leaders such as Deng Xiaoping lectured the students on how their peers had been exploited by Mao Zedong and the so-called Gang of Four during the Cultural Revolution. But in the late 1980s the students ceased to believe it. Reassessing the legacy of the Cultural Revolution for themselves, they sympathized with the desire of those Revolutionary Red Guards who in the 1960s had hoped to eliminate bureaucracy and corruption and return the party to its earlier revolutionary heritage. They agreed with the analysis of those Red Guards who had begun to see the leaders of the Chinese Communist party as a new class perched above Chinese society. They believed that much of the openness and decentralization that had occurred in China since 1977 had been made possible because the Cultural Revolution weakened the Party and forced the government once more to appeal to the masses to retain its power. The powerful example of the Red Guards gave students of the 1980s the courage to work for change in Chinese society, but without the mistakes and violence of the 1960s.

The students did not view the Cultural Revolution uncritically. Some, in fact, could see no positive legacy from that period. Others who felt differently nonetheless recognized that for many it had been a period of terror. They understood that Mao Zedong had misled and used the students. They determined not to be fooled by more recent power-holders.

By 1989 Deng Xiaoping no longer was taken to be the Chinese Gorbachev, a man who would bring democracy and reform to the Chinese Communist party. Deng had presided over a decade-long effort to reform the Chinese political system and vastly improve the quality of Chinese life. But in 1987 Deng and his cohorts, unwilling to allow power to pass from their hands, had crushed the student movement that year. Over the next couple of years the economy deteriorated as reformers and hard-liners struggled against one another. After that most students had little faith in Deng, though many still believed that the new political and social structure which Deng helped to create would ultimately be capable of reform.

After Hu Yaobang's death in April 1989, it was a group of students deeply committed to party values who began the protests, hoping to bring China in accord with its own ideals and return the party to its revolutionary heritage. This time they had a better chance of succeeding than any of the generations that had come before them, because now they had allies who supported much of their vision. The reforms of the 1980s had empowered an independent class of city dwellers who backed the student leadership with force.

Workers, hoodlums, clerks, and urban entrepreneurs joined hands with the students. Together they played a role in the movement parallel to the one which Karl Marx has claimed similar groups once played in France and England at times of revolutionary upheaval throughout the eighteenth and nineteenth centuries. Like their earlier European counterparts, the Chinese activists of the 1980s wanted to check arbitrary rules and rulers and acquire a share in the making of future laws. As in these earlier struggles, the people of Beijing were aided by social and economic changes that shifted central power to local interests.

Despite these sources of strength, students and city dwellers suffered together from government repression. After its crackdown in June 1989, the government quickly asserted its authority over urban populations, moving to curb small businesses and private entrepreneurs. Earlier attempts by hard-liners to reinstate power over the various enterprises and groups that had thrived as a result of reforms underlay much of the social tension that touched off the student demonstrations. Once their guns had silenced the resistance, the old leaders creaked ahead with their plans.

Before April it had seemed to many that in spite of what had happened in 1987, Deng Xiaoping might ultimately come down on the side of the reformers and attempt to salvage his image and the policies for which he had been credited. After June he made it clear that this was not to be. Out of sight since he met Gorbachev on May 16, Deng reemerged into the public eye on June 9 when he gave a speech which later became required reading in schools and work units throughout China. In an attempt to show the infallibility of the state whose citizens he had just murdered in defending, Deng began in Bonapartist fashion by glorifying "China's great wall of iron and steel," calling for a moment of silence for the soldiers "killed" during the events in Beijing. He then paid homage to the old autocrats who ruled the party from the center, noting how fortunate China was to "still have a group of senior comrades who are alive... who took part in the revolution at various times. This is why it was relatively easy for us to handle the present matter."

Having made the point that the feeble old autocrats of the state were indispensable, Deng went on to belittle the urban masses who had just been crushed. According to Deng, the old "core cadres" understood that what they "faced was not just some ordinary people who were misguided, but also a large quantity of the dregs of society." The goal of the protesters, Deng asserted, "was to establish a bourgeois republic entirely dependent on the West." Deng acknowledged the advantages of "reforms and openness." But aware that the economy was in for hard times, he also ominously suggested that China return to the "plain living" of the past, declaring that he was now "in favor of putting the emphasis on capital industry and agriculture"—these, of course, being that part of the economy under the state's direct control. Throughout the 1950s and 1960s China's leaders had been obsessed with increasing steel production, just as "iron and blood" had been the concern of militaristic, autocratic rulers in the nineteenth century. Deng showed that he was still a product of this tradition, dwelling on China's need "to improve our existing facilities and increase production by 20 million tons" so that the country "could reduce the amount of steel we need to import."

Even if Deng did not not intend the homage he was paying to Bonaparte, Bismarck, and Brezhnev, he was certainly signaling that the country would allow the old guard to maintain its control and perks. His approach called for rebuilding the economy by reducing imports and exerting production controls, emphasizing state enterprises and restricting the dynamic new businesses that had contributed so much to the Chinese economy. This would curb the growth of the small businessmen and entrepreneurs who had aided the students. It would put the workers who had joined the demonstrations back under state control. And it would slow the runaway inflation that had plagued Chinese cities—but only by throwing the country into a recession.

The result of Deng's policy is likely to be similar to this description by Stan Sesser of what occurred in Burma after the military took over the economy in 1962: "As they took over manufacturing and trade, they got the perks—the house, the car, gasoline, a telephone. But nine times out of ten they didn't know what they were doing. The Burmese were having enough trouble making their industry operate without having this intervening layer. Your boss was always someone from the military, and he was in it for the plunder, building on Ne Win's premise that you couldn't trust the Burmese Ph.D.s who had been educated in the West."

In China the people who have so far suffered most from the new economic policy are those in urban areas. They are the same people who showed their disrespect for the country's rulers, and they are being punished for it. In the fall of 1989 the government announced that grain production was still well below 1985 levels despite better weather and an all-out effort, which for the first time in two years included cash payments to the peasants for what they produced. This cash was raised largely from urban workers, whose salaries were cut by as much as one-fourth. In lieu of the cash owed them, these laborers were paid with government bonds. As a result, the number of I.O.U.s distributed to the peasants were far fewer than in the past.

While Deng and other old hard-liners have their revenge, their solution does not bode well for the long-term health of the Chinese economy. As the government cuts urban salaries it destroys worker morale and discipline, making it harder to improve the very industries Deng wants to emphasize. The simultaneous limitations placed on new industries that developed as a result of earlier reforms make a Brezhnev-style stagnation all but inevitable for China's cities. Even if the government continues to milk urban areas to help the countryside—which is unlikely unless the country's leaders are willing to tolerate a return to the industrial dark ages—in the long run agriculture is likely to suffer even more.

Experts have estimated that without a drastic change in agricultural policies, Chinese grain imports will increase from about 15 million tons to more than 40 million tons a year by the end of the 1990s. The figure could well go much higher if China is plagued with the usual mistakes and slip-ups. Since current economic policy bodes poorly for a growth in Chinese exports, this means a greater currency drain and increased cash shortages. The government has already indicated its unwillingness to keep loosening the economy in order to encourage more initiative and growth, so it will find it necessary to resort to increasingly draconian solutions to keep the masses quiet. Even before the 1989 crackdown, the hard-liners had announced new taxes on peasants who produced fruit, fish, and other nonessential items for the free market, in order to force these people to return to grain production. In the coming months, harsher measures may follow.

This is unlikely to mean a return to the collectivization of the past, but it does mean a reversion to the kind of police state now being abandoned in eastern Europe. The smallest decision will be channeled to higher authorities, to be answered after an interminable delay by those with little knowledge of the actual situation. Normally cautious bureaucrats will naturally become more so. Responsible Chinese officials are likely to grow increasingly wary about contacts with countries of the West which are seen to be infecting China with the disease of democracy.

The ineptitude which the hard-liners have shown even in that area of the Chinese economy that has performed best—agriculture—may be a sign of things to come. There could well be a return to the situation that existed in China from the time of the Communist victory in 1949 until 1976, when, with the exception of only one year, 1957, per capita food consumption did not reach even the meager levels that had existed in the country before World War II.

Given the desire to increase the authority and power of the state, it is not surprising that the two men selected to head the current government are Soviet-trained technocrats who favor a return to central planning and placing curbs on small, independent enterprises: Premier Li Peng and the new party boss, Jiang Zeming. Although real power is still held by Deng Xiaoping and the other old men who helped him carry out the crackdown, none of whom held formal high-level office in the party, their choice of successors is nonetheless ominous. Jiang Zemin, whose selection to replace Zhao Ziyang as secretary general of the Chinese Communist party was formally announced on June 24, was the former Shanghai party boss who banned the *World Economic Herald*.

As rumor has it, Jiang was selected as the new party leader by Deng because he had run out of other candidates he could count on to be personally loyal to him. Although he is a political hard-liner, Jiang was more willing to tolerate some of Deng's earlier economic reforms than most of the other candidates for the job, and will probably try to ensure that not everything is reversed by the newly centralizing state. In some ways, Jiang seemed the perfect choice for the doddering old fossils who had now reemerged in charge of party business. Jiang had distinguished himself less for his competence than for his hard-line attitudes and his ability to flatter his superiors. Being from Shanghai, he was not directly linked with the Beijing butchery, but he had showed himself to be ruthless nonetheless.

After the June 4 crackdown in Beijing, Jiang's Shanghai organization quelled unrest in the city by ordering the arrest of those responsible for burning a train which on June 7 plowed into a crowd of demonstrators lying on the tracks, killing six people and injuring another six. A few days later the Shanghai party publicized the execution of three of those arrested, all workers with none of the political connections that some of the students might have had. One of those who received a bullet in the head was convicted of providing the match that others used to burn the train. The man was said to have been mentally retarded and not to have understood why the match was wanted, but that did not prevent the government from carrying out his sentence with remarkable dispatch. Executions in Shanghai were followed by similar spectacles in other cities, spreading terror throughout the population and halting demonstrations in urban areas.

Although Jiang is fluent in English, French, and Russian, a cosmopolitan gloss which China's leaders no doubt hoped would make him more acceptable to Westerners, he was also the man in charge of propaganda following the crackdown, when some of the official statements about foreigners sounded like slogans manufactured in the Ayatollah's Iran. It was also Jiang who instituted study of Deng Xiaoping's speech of June 9 and was probably responsible for the growing personality cult that developed around China's real "helmsman" with the production of a film and several new books about Deng in the summer of 1989.

Jiang's propaganda policy seemed designed to return China to the ideological controls that had characterized the country in the past. Mandatory political study sessions were again introduced in offices and factories. People allowed to study abroad were screened to prevent "flies and worms" from infesting the country. University enrollments were cut considerably, and those who were enrolled were required to join the army for periods of up to one year before settling into their regular curriculum. Books and magazines that once circulated freely were now withdrawn from the shelves. Newly produced films were canceled. Neighborhood watch committees were redeployed to report dissident behavior. Even cheek-to-cheek dancing was banned.

More worrisome, however, were the arrests of dissidents, students, and workers which continued inexorably in the wake of the crackdown. Tens of thousands of people throughout China were detained. Pictures and names of others were flashed on television screens and printed in the newspapers as neighbors and family members were urged to turn in miscreants.

One of the most bizarre indications of the new government's mind-set was its attempt to implicate Zhao Ziyang in what has been called the Soros Affair. George Soros is a billionaire American investor of Hungarian Jewish origin who has established foundations in Hungary, Poland, and the Soviet Union for the promotion of "openness." The Soviet foundation, for example, includes Raisa Gorbachev on its board and mostly finances cultural and art projects. In 1986, at the urging of Chen Yizi (then Zhao's think tank director) and several other progressive officials, Soros established a similar foundation in China. He endowed it with a million dollars, only about $400,000 of which was ever used. Since the Beijing massacre, according to Chen Yizi, one principal charge against Zhao Ziyang has been his association with that foundation, which is said to be controlled by the United States Central Intelligence Agency. Chen Yizi has claimed that this "evidence" of treason on the part of the former secretary general of the Chinese Communist party was used by Li Peng and his associates at a June 28 Politburo meeting to demand that Zhao be put on trial and his assistant Bao Tong sentenced to death. In the end it appeared that Zhao would simply be stripped of his offices.

The government showed that it too understood how to utilize the world of fax machines and camcorders. Surveillance cameras bought in Japan to monitor traffic were set to produce detailed records of student and foreign interactions on public street corners. People were warned that such future associations would be remembered. The satellite feed of an ABC videotaped interview with a man in the street, who claimed to have seen mass killings, was played on news programs with a subtitle calling for the "rumor-monger's" arrest and identification. The next day he was shown on TV being booked and apologizing for the "lies" he had spread. A few days later he was sentenced to a long jail term.

One saving grace was that the government lacked the power or will to carry out this surveillance policy as fully as it might have liked. In south China many turned a deaf ear to government appeals for ideological orthodoxy, often mouthing prescribed ideas while ignoring them in practice. Some of the most prominent of those students and intellectuals being sought by the government managed to go into hiding or flee the country, where they formed an exile organization dedicat-

ed to continuing the movement they had begun. The dissident
Fang Lizhi found refuge in the American embassy. Others
were protected by powerful groups or institutions. Few arrests, for instance, were made of People's University students. Government alumni closed ranks around the school,
preferring to have its protesters dealt with by school officials
than by outside authorities. Indeed, the first vice president of
the school, Wu Shuqing, was named head of Beijing University.

As always in China, powerful local units were able to
negotiate their way around government proclamations. Since
there were still elements in the army and in the government
sympathetic to the moderates, optimists hoped that in the
near future these people would form the nucleus for the
creation of a new, softer government. On the other side,
however, was the increased prominence of such hard-liners as
Long March veteran Wang Zhen, who advocated that China
radically curtail relations with the West and institute even
stricter autocratic policies.

Despite a continuing behind-the-scenes power struggle,
both moderates and hard-liners joined to lie about the June
crackdown. A series of pamphlets, articles, and videotapes
have repeated the government's line about the "truth" of
what happened on June 4 in Beijing so endlessly that it has
become difficult for many in China to remember what really
occurred. According to the government, a small group of
hooligans instigated by dissident intellectuals and conspirators in the West attacked the People's Liberation Army,
burning its equipment and killing several soldiers. This Western-
backed "rebellion" was quashed by a heroic army which
never used greater force than was absolutely necessary. A
few people were killed accidentally in the process of quelling
the uprising, "some knocked down by vehicles" or "stray
bullets," but it was fewer than two hundred. And none were
killed in Tiananmen Square. Only thirty-six students were
killed, according to this official account, all of whom "ignored

warnings issued by the municipal government that night" to return to their campuses. Prime Minister Li Peng went so far as to claim that Chinese troops had to use real bullets on the demonstrators because they did not have enough tear gas, rubber bullets, or usable water cannon. In any case, the problems, the government has maintained, all were caused by "counterrevolutionaries."

In some ways this is the most damnable lie of all. It may be debated whether the reforms attempted by the students and their allies were revolutionary, but there is certainly no question that government leaders were the real counterrevolutionaries. The Chinese students stood in the tradition of Chinese revolutionaries of the past.

Although many hope that the present government will come to its senses when it realizes the economic damage its reforms have caused, this is unlikely. As the Sheng Wu Lian Red Guards correctly diagnosed in the 1960s, the Chinese bureaucracy has become what Marx would have called a class, one which cares more about its own power than about developing the country. When the fossils that hold this class together die, the bureaucracy may begin to fall apart, but this may take much longer than most people now believe.

This fossilization of revolutionary zeal has set in deeper and deeper during the course of modern Chinese history. When the Chinese Communist party was seeking power, it praised the revolutionary spontaneity of youth; but once it seized power, it began to emphasize the need for students to have greater discipline and to learn more from the older generation. During the Cultural Revolution, Mao Zedong attempted to return to the party's older, revolutionary view of the students. Since the 1989 crackdown, however, the party has again stressed the need to discipline youth. Ideological training is emphasized, especially for the young. The old culture and its authorities are defended, and works such as the movie *River Elegy,* which attack this culture, are criticized. The party has even brought back old speeches made by Deng Xiaoping in 1961 to the Chinese Communist Youth League, calling for work to be done so that children are again "polite" and show "concern for the collective undertaking and old order."

These actions underscore government fears of students who have grown up in a world of fax machines and computers and have used this technology to spread their movement; students raised on rock-and-roll who see themselves as liberated in ways older generations do not understand. Terrified by the alliance formed by youth with "hoodlum" elements, the government has seized on this relationship to claim that "local hooligans, ruffians, and criminals" were behind the protests. Emphasizing these "outlaw" elements, the government seeks to win the support of older Chinese who detest these groups.

But the effect on youth is to make them still more disillusioned with the government. Already many of those who have fled the country have begun to talk of buying guns and organizing to overthrow the regime. Inside China one hears of terrorist incidents directed against soldiers and the police. Although the party was itself once heir to the great revolutionary tradition of the May Fourth movement, it has already lost touch with this past. Soon it may lose everything. The longer it waits to reform, the more it will forfeit even the possibility of maintaining its power.

What has happened in China will have ramifications throughout the world. First off, the world economy will suffer. A major element of unpredictability has been introduced into that economy, one that will show up first in the stock and commodity markets. For the past few decades Chinese leaders have reacted to political crises by assuaging the stomachs of their people. This may mean that we shall see short-term Chinese grain purchases. But over the long term, as China's foreign currency reserves become tighter, these purchases may become slow and erratic.

The most frenzied reaction to the Chinese crackdown has shown up in Hong Kong. This British crown colony is scheduled to be returned to China in 1997. The decision was made without a plebiscite from the inhabitants but with guarantees from the Chinese that after taking control they would allow the city to retain its own laws and economic institutions. These promises have now been shown to mean nothing.

The student democracy movement greatly touched the people of Hong Kong, raising political consciousness in the city as nothing before had ever done. Students and business-men alike marched into the streets, collected money, and gathered support for the protesters. They were not only swayed by what the students in China were doing, but they saw it as a way of guaranteeing that after 1997 their own rights and property would be protected.

These hopes were crushed on June 4. The people of Hong Kong reacted with outrage. The financial markets collapsed, and the number of those seeking to emigrate rose sharply. As a major world financial center, one which is intricately tied to the Chinese economy, Hong Kong has and will continue to suffer financially from the crackdown, and this will produce reverberations worldwide.

More important, the western world now faces the prospect of seeing six and a half million people being turned over to a regime which has already shown its willingness to murder and abuse its own citizens. In his speech to the military, Deng contemptuously put down the people of Hong Kong, remarking: "I was told a million people paraded in Hong Kong. Do not be scared. Compared to a billion people, a million is nothing. By 1997, Hong Kong will be returned to us anyway, and it will be prosperous. . . ."

Unless Britain changes its attitude on the return of Hong

Kong soon, the people of Hong Kong may have only one hope. It is a hope they now share with the rest of the Chinese people: Bonapartist regimes rarely last long. Although the students of 1989 repeated many of the same mistakes of those before them, they also showed how much China has changed. The activities of workers and students revealed the new urban culture that has been created in China. New ideas about sex, about music, about technology have changed the face of China. The extent to which most of the government and the work force of Beijing were willing to join the students shows that the democratic values which they espoused achieved a certain resonance within the Chinese urban community. Among these groups, the Chinese Communist party has now lost credibility. It is unlikely that even the idealists at People's University still believe that reform of the old party is possible.

One way or another, the 1989 movement marks a new era in modern Chinese history, a point of no return. As the Chinese saying goes, "Once you climb upon the tiger's back, it is difficult to get off." In the future, the events of 1989 will be remembered for the way they helped to achieve the goals for which Chinese have struggled for most of this century. When I spoke with the People's University graduate students, they acknowledged that their movement would take a long time. They saw what they were starting as the beginning of a slow educational process. But they were confident that in the end they would win, that they could then get off the tiger's back.

A NOTE ON SOURCES

In Chapter One, the information about the early examination candidate protests comes from Chow Tse-tsung, *The May Fourth Movement: Intellectual Revolution In Modern China* (Stanford, 1960), p. 12. The quotations from Chen Duxiu come from *Shian zizhuan* (Chen Duxiu's autobiography), pp. 23–47. This has been translated by Richard Kagan, *China Quarterly,* 50 (April–June 1972), 301–314. In this chapter I have also quoted: John Stuart Thompson, *China Revolutionized* (Indianapolis, 1913), p. 135; Guo Morou, *Xinhai chubanshe* (Shanghai, 1956), as extracted in *Chinese Education,* Vol. 3, Summer–Fall 1970, "The Spring and Autumn of Revolution," p. 119; Chiang Monlin, *Tides from the West* (New Haven, 1947), p. 48; "Xianfa yu kongjiao" (The Constitution and Confucius), *Xin qingnian* (New Youth) 2:3 (Nov. 1, 1916); Cyrus H. Peake, *Nationalism and Education in Modern China* (New York, 1932), pp. 84–85; and Edgar Snow, *Red Star over China* (New York, 1961), p. 141.

For more information about the study societies and revolutionary organizations favored by early Chinese students see Mao Zedong's article "The Great Union of the Popular Masses," in Stuart Schram, *The Political Thought of Mao Tse-tung* (New York, 1969); also Ku Chieh-kang, *Autobiography of a Chinese Historian*

(Leyden, 1931), pp. 26–30; and Hsü Kai-yu, *China's Grey Eminence* (New York, 1969), p. 13.

In Chapter Two, the first three quotes from Mao Zedong come from Stuart Schram's translations in *The Political Thought of Mao Tse-tung,* pp. 354–355; p. 353; and p. 356. In much of the rest of the chapter I have used the Red Guard diary of Liu Guokai which was edited by Anita Chan and has been titled *A Brief Analysis of the Cultural Revolution* (New York, 1987). I have quoted from pp. 18, 26, 27–28, 45–47, and 116–117 of this work. I have also quoted from Lowell Dittmer, *Liu Shao-ch'i and the Chinese Cultural Revolution: The Politics of Mass Criticism* (Berkeley, 1974), pp. 86–87; David Milton and Nancy Dall Milton, *The Wind Will Not Subside: Years in Revolutionary China, 1964–1969* (New York, 1976), p. 151; and Maurice Meisner, *Mao's China and After* (New York, 1988), pp. 349, 91–92, and 361. I have also relied on Tang Tsou's work *The Cultural Revolution and Post-Mao Reforms: A Historical Perspective* (Chicago, 1986).

In Chapter Four I have cited Hong Yung Lee, *The Politics of the Chinese Cultural Revolution* (Berkeley, 1968), pp. 343–344; Roger Garside, *Coming Alive: China After Mao* (New York, 1981), pp. 132, 254; Robert Delfs, "Purging the Future," *Far Eastern Economic Review,* July 6, 1989, p. 11; Meisner, *Mao's China,* p. 452; Wang Xizhe, *Mao Zedong and the Cultural Revolution,* as translated in Joe Morrison and Jonathan Unger, ed., *Chinese Law and Government,* Summer 1985, pp. 67–68; Tang Tsou, "The Historic Change in Direction and Continuity with the Past," *China Quarterly,* No. 98 (June 1984), pp. 320–347; John P. Burns, "Contemporary China's Nomenklatura System," *Chinese Law and Government,* Winter 1987–1988, p. 3; Lawrence R. Sullivan, "Assault on the Reforms: Conservative Criticism of Political and Economic Liberalization in China, 1985–86," *China Quarterly,* June 1988, pp. 201, 208; Robert Delfs and Robert Cottrell, "Enough Is Enough," *Far Eastern Economic Review,* January 1, 1987, pp. 12–14; "Deng Xiaoping guanyu dangqian xuesheng naoshi wenti jianghua yaodian" (Main Points of Deng Xiaoping's Speech on the Current Problem of Student Disturbance), as translated in *Chinese Law and Government,* Spring 1988, James Tong, ed.; and "The Past Week," *Ta Kung Pao,* Jan 1–7, p. 2, as reprinted in Foreign Broadcast Information

Service Daily Report—China (Washington, D.C.—hereafter F.B.I.S.), January 2, 1987, p. K3.

In this chapter I have also relied on Andrew Nathan, *Chinese Democracy* (Berkeley, 1985) and David Bachman, "Differing Visions of China's Post-Mao Economy: The Ideas of Chen Yu, Deng Xiaoping, and Zhao Ziyang," *Asian Survey,* Vol. 26, No. 3 (March 1986), pp. 292–322. And I also used Lev P. Deliusin, "Reforms in China," *Asian Survey,* Vol. 28, No. 11 (November 1988), p. 1103; Andrew G. Walder, "Factory and Manager in an Era of Reform," *China Quarterly,* 118 (June 1989), pp. 242–265; Fang Lizhi, "The Social Responsibilities of Young Intellectuals Today," *Chinese Law and Government,* Summer 1988, pp. 68, 106; and Robert Delfs, "Tighten Your Belts," *Far Eastern Economic Review,* March 30, 1989, pp. 10–11.

The best chronology for the events discussed in Chapter Five is available in Xiao Dan, "The Signature Campaigns for the Release of Political Prisoners in China and Related Incidents," *Shiyue pinglun* (October Magazine), 1989, Vol. 16, Issue 3, pp. 89–92. I have also relied on "Chinese Debate Scholar Status," Associated Press, as printed in *Electronic Newsletter for Chinese Students,* No. 38, February 25, 1989; Robert Delfs, "Students Seek Recognition," *Far Eastern Economic Review,* April 21, 1988; Robert Delfs, "Avoiding the Issues," *Far Eastern Economic Review,* April 6, 1989, p. 13; Marlowe Hood, *South China Morning Post,* February 23, 1989, as reported in F.B.I.S. (February 23, 1989). A summary of the debate on the new authoritarianism is available in Robert Delfs, "Little Dragon Model," *Far Eastern Economic Review,* March 9, 1989, p. 12.

The information in Chapters Six through Ten is derived principally from firsthand observations or interviews. Where I could not personally confirm facts, I have used them only if they are derived from more than one source. In cases where I could not do this kind of checking, I have stated that the knowledge is based on rumor or hearsay. I was able to use two eyewitness analyses of the protest movement sent to me from Amsterdam by Tony Saich and Frank Pieke. Their journal, *China Information,* has already begun to publish interesting articles on the student protests. See especially articles by Stefan R. Landsberger, Flemming Christiansen, and W. L.

Chong. I should also mention *China Update* (Cambridge), a bulletin devoted solely to the movement.

The quote from Wuer Kaixi in Chapter Seven is from Orville Schell, "Children of Tiananmen," *Rolling Stone,* 1989 yearbook edition, p. 195. The ending of Chapter Eight is from Mao Zedong, "Talk to Leaders of the Centre," as translated in Stuart Schram, *Chairman Mao Talks to the People* (New York, 1974). The quote on Burma in Chapter Ten is from Stan Sesser, "A Reporter at Large," *New Yorker*, October 9, 1989.

One other source on which I have relied is the media. Although I have been critical in this book of some of the interpretations of events which appeared in the Western press, I believe that overall most journalists did a remarkable job, under considerable pressure, in covering events in China in the spring of 1989. One source of information from the various Chinese-language presses is the day-by-day account in *Bajiu zhongguo minyun jishi* (Daily Reports on the 1989 Movement for Democracy in China), Vol. 1 and 2 (New York, 1989). In addition to articles in the Chinese press, I have principally utilized the *New York Times*, the *Washington Post*, the *Chicago Tribune*, the *Wall Street Journal*, the *South China Morning Post*, the *Hong Kong Standard, Time, Newsweek, U.S. News and World Report*, and the Associated Press. I have also been grateful for the excellent articles in the *Far Eastern Economic Review.* Among Hong Kong sources, *Ming Pao, October Review, The Eighties, Ching Pao,* and *Cheng Ming* have provided excellent insights into aspects of the demonstrations and have assembled a number of sources. I have also used the translations in *Foreign Broadcast Information Service Daily Report—China.* In checking through these newspapers and magazines, I have followed the rule of not using any source unless it could also be confirmed independently.

Just as I was completing this book, a number of good narratives of the demonstrations began appearing. Those I have seen are Michael Fathers and Andrew Higgins, *Tiananmen: The Rape of Peking* (London, 1989); Scott Simmie and Bob Nixon, *Tiananmen Square* (Vancouver, 1989); and Zi Jin and Qin Zhou, translators, *June Four: A Chronicle of the Chinese Democratic Uprising.*

INDEX

A NOTE ON THE AUTHOR

Lee Feigon is Associate Professor of History and director of the East Asian Studies Program at Colby College in Waterville, Maine. Born in Chicago, he studied at the University of California, Berkeley, the University of Chicago, and the University of Wisconsin, Madison. His research, which has taken him frequently to Taiwan, Japan, Hong Kong, and especially to the People's Republic of China, has been supported by grants from the Ford Foundation, the Mellon Foundation, and Fulbright-Hays, among others. Mr. Feigon has written extensively on Chinese history and politics, including the book *Chen Duxiu: Founder of the Chinese Communist Party*, and articles in the *Atlantic*, the *Wall Street Journal*, the *Nation*, *Barron's*, and the *Chicago Tribune*, as well as in the *Journal of Asian Studies* and the *American Historical Review*. He lives in China, Maine, with his wife and three daughters.